6000 years of the Bible

6000 years
of the Bible

G. S. WEGENER

223 illustrations

HARPER & ROW · PUBLISHERS

New York and Evanston

6000 YEARS OF THE BIBLE
Translated by Margaret Shenfield from
6000 Jahre und ein Buch © 1958 J. G. Oncken Verlag Kassel
This edition copyright © 1963 by Thames and Hudson Ltd London
Designed by Ruth Rosenberg

Library of Congress Catalog Card Number: 63-16406

CONTENTS

PART III

'What need we any further witness?'

This is not a work of theology. It is simply the story of the birth and existence of a unique book—the Bible. In that book the believing Christian finds the Word of God. But the doubter too, even the unbeliever, must acknowledge that the Bible has left its mark on the history of mankind as no other book has done, and has exercised a decisive influence on the Western world. Its story is part of the fabric of our civilization; its importance transcends the boundaries of sect and schism. It is not a college textbook, required reading for students of divinity: it is a messenger bringing news of vital concern to men and women of every creed, colour, and condition.

That is why I have written, as you can see, about the Bible not as an object of learned study but as a book for everyone.

I wanted to show the thread running through the centuries, so I had to begin by sketching the civilizations of the ancient world, and particularly of the Israelites. For theirs is the soil that nourished the traditions, the stories, and the songs, which eventually became Holy Writ.

Obviously, such a brief summary of the centuries must mean a certain degree of simplification, which some will object to; but it does not, I think, lead to falsification. I chose this method deliberately, so that my story could follow a single broad, consistent line—a line that stretches unbroken from the age of Moses to our own day.

G. S. W.

Prologue

'The flood of waters was upon the earth'

MYTH OR HISTORY

'And it came to pass after seven days, that the waters of the flood were upon the earth . . . And the waters prevailed exceedingly upon the earth; and all the high hills, that were under the whole heaven, were covered . . .'

So says the First Book of Moses called Genesis. But is it true? Did the catastrophe, which the Bible describes with so much detail, really take place? And if it did, then where and when?

Less than a century ago scientists would have scoffed at such questions and historians would have given, at best, a pained shrug. The story of the Flood had no place among matters of fact; it was considered to be nothing more than an ancient legend. In their prevailing mood of detached scepticism, particularly where religious beliefs were concerned, scholars at that time never regarded the Bible as history. They suspected its stories to be as 'untrue' as those of Homer, and serious historical research, which insisted on verifiable evidence, could not be bothered with such fables.

The story was not exclusive to the Bible. This tale of a deluge which in remote times had devastated the earth was known even then to belong to a widespread tradition. There were many versions of it. The account given in the Old Testament was the one best known in the West; but there was also a Phrygian story, an Indian deluge legend, a Zoroastrian myth, and it was also found in the folklore of Tibet, Australia, Polynesia, and the Americas. All these stories were similar, yet it was not supposed they could all refer to the same event; they seemed to belong to a worldwide network of legends, impossible to pin down to a particular happening.

All the same, legends do not appear from nowhere; they too have their beginning in time and space; so scholars offered various hypotheses for the origin of these diverse stories. It was suggested that they might be a nature myth portraying the departure of winter, the rainy season, and the return of spring. Or they might be a variant of the creation myth, representing not the devastation of the earth but its first emergence out of the waters. Or again they might simply perpetuate the tradition of some local disaster, hugely magnified as it was handed down through the ages.

A local disaster, or rather a number of disasters, which had taken place at different times in various parts of the world—this explanation seemed the most probable. But it still left the Biblical flood a legend with nothing to indicate where and when this particular local disaster might have occurred. The sequence of verifiable facts, dates, and events which we call history began with the Greece of classical antiquity; what lay beyond was mythology, and to mythology, it seemed, the Flood must belong.

It was archaeology, making as great progress as the other branches of science during the second half of the last century, which finally upset these assumptions. A remarkable series of discoveries kept pushing the frontiers of verifiable history further and further into the remote past, and showed one 'myth' after another to have its roots planted in reality. Heinrich Schliemann searched for Homer's city of Troy—and found it. Paul Emile Botta dug up Khorsabad, the four-thousand-year-old capital of Assyria, and produced proof that its famous King Sargon, mentioned in the Bible, had indeed lived. Austen Henry Layard discovered Nimrud, the Biblical city of Calah. And soon afterwards Henry Creswicke Rawlinson unearthed the Babylonian town of Nineveh complete with King Ashurbanipal's palace and library.

Rawlinson's discovery took the story an important step further. In the ruins of the Nineveh library he found, inscribed on twelve large clay tablets, the great Babylonian epic of Gilgamesh; and of these tablets the eleventh gave yet another, hitherto unknown, account of a flood disaster. Still more significantly, this Babylonian version, dating from about 1700 BC, so closely resembled the Biblical account in almost every detail that the coincidence could scarcely be accidental. But whether or not these two accounts referred to the same event, one thing seemed certain: the description in the Gilga-mesh version could have come only from someone who had seen

The Babylonian version *of the Flood story,
found on this tablet in the royal library at
Nineveh, coincides in almost every detail with
the Biblical story of Noah.*

the deluge himself and had survived it. There could be no doubt that this particular 'local disaster' had historic viability. For who but someone who had witnessed it would report: 'And all mankind had turned to clay . . .'?

THE CLAY OF TELL MUQAYYAR

But still the question remained: where and when? So long as there was no answer to this, the Flood must remain an 'unhistoric' myth. The answer came thirty years after the cuneiform writing on the Gilgamesh tablets had been deciphered. This writing had shown that the original authors of the epic were not Babylonians, but Sumerians, a far older people whose capital had been Abraham's city of Ur. And it was from Ur in Mesopotamia that Leonard Woolley, the British archaeologist, in the summer of 1929 electrified the civilized world with the message: 'We have found the Flood!'

They had indeed. Woolley had excavated a group of mounds or 'high hills' surrounding the staged tower known as Tell Muqayyar, near the Persian Gulf. This was believed to be the site of ancient Ur, which the Bible mentions as Ur of the Chaldees and the birthplace of Abraham. Woolley had found the fabulous city and in six years of painstaking labour had laid it bare in all its splendour. His most magnificent discovery in one of the mounds was the 'Royal Cemetery', a row of superimposed stone burial vaults filled with treasures. The lowest and last of these tombs took him down to about 2800 BC, but Woolley doubted whether this was the bottom. He removed the foundations of the tomb and, digging on, came to, not virgin soil, but rubble from ancient buildings, broken pottery, and clay tablets. These proved to be two or three hundred years older than the tombs. Woolley had found relics of the year 3000 BC. He continued to dig and more rubble and potsherds came up the shaft.

Suddenly it all ceased. There were no more traces of human settlement. But the diggers had not reached virgin soil either. Their spades had struck a layer of pure clean clay. Only water could have placed it there. But what water? It could not have been the river Euphrates because the layer was too high above ground, and besides it was too thick. Woolley went on digging and had gone through nearly ten feet of the bed before the clay ceased again as suddenly as it had begun. And beneath it he came once again not upon the expected virgin soil but upon new rubble, more fragments of pottery, fresh traces of human settlement. But these remnants below the clay were very different from those above it. There was a clear difference between the relics found in the two strata, the upper and the lower; and those in the lower belonged unmistakably to the Stone Age.

Traces of a catastrophic flood *are shown in this cross-section of Woolley's excavations at Ur. Relics of burials going back to 3000 BC give place to a deposit of clay ten feet thick. Below this are traces of Stone Age settlement. Only floodwaters can have deposited this enormous blanket of clay.*

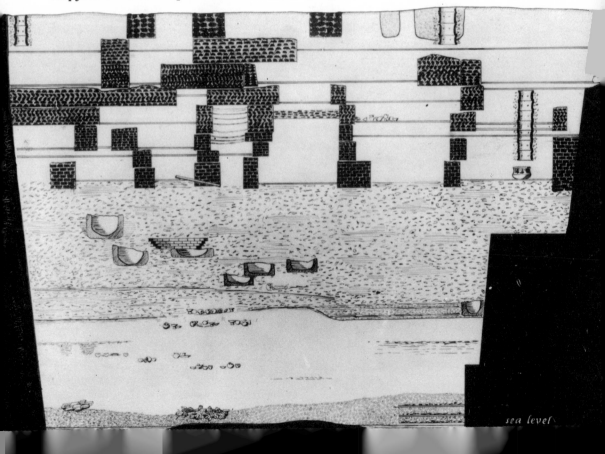

sea level

Clearly, some mighty event had caused the break in the cultural tradition of these two series of artifacts. Some natural catastrophe had overwhelmed the older civilization, covered it with ten feet of clay and thus, sealing it off, had killed it. After the catastrophe, the survivors had rebuilt their city on top of the clay. There could be little doubt that a vast flood had come over this land, swamping it and drowning all that had lived on it. The evidence was conclusive. Probing shafts in other mounds revealed similar layers of clay at the same level, whereas the natural, and not man-made, elevations of the ground contained none. And before long Stephen Langdon, excavating the ancient city of Kish near Babylon, came upon two similar layers, except that these were less thick.

The land where 'all mankind had turned to clay' had been found. The Flood of the Bible was a legend no longer. There was proof that it had happened. The place where it had occurred was known; and the time of the event could be established. Woolley's and Langdon's calculations agreed in dating it about 4000 BC. There was nothing mythical about it. It was established history.

Woolley's discovery was a landmark in archaeology. Sceptical science had come down on the side of simple belief and confirmed the Bible instead of discrediting it. But if the Bible and Woolley were right, some people drew false inferences from the new discoveries, notably the idea that the truth of statements made in the Bible could be proved by archaeology. Archaeology can furnish no such proof. Essentially the Bible is neither a historical nor a scientific textbook. It is an account of God's dealing with man, and in the final analysis, its truths spring from faith.

All the same, mankind is deeply indebted to archaeology and its achievements of the last decades. It has widened and clarified our knowledge of daily life in the ancient world, and this knowledge is an invaluable help towards our understanding and appreciation of the Bible. What archaeology can and does contribute to this appreciation is not proof or support of the Biblical word but its illustration and indeed illumination. It provides us with a multitude of pictures

The scale of operations *is shown in this picture of Woolley's workmen grouped about the excavation at Ur. The flood clay starts about halfway down the flight of steps.*

fashioned from stone, clay, loam, iron, bronze, silver, and gold which, taken together and seen as a whole, form the vivid background against which the story of the Bible unfolds.

The most ancient of these pictures is the one we have been looking at, the picture of the Flood, and it is the first in the Bible. The Flood is the point from which any account of the lifestory of the Bible must begin. To understand how the Bible came to be written, we must know the men who wrote it, the world in which they lived, and the times and events mirrored in their writings. We must go back six thousand years, back to 4000 BC, the era of the Flood.

I

'Speak unto the children of Israel, that they bring me an offering'

THE CRADLE OF HISTORY

PYRAMIDS AND THE GOD OF THE SUN

It was during the fourth millennium before Christ that men took their first steps towards civilization.

In Europe the Ice Age was over. The great glaciers under which the entire continent had formerly been buried had melted and receded, and the European tundra was beginning to appear. The huge sea of ice which had covered the north of the continent far into Russia was gradually shrinking to the size of the present-day Baltic Sea. Trees were raising themselves and growing into forests which became steadily larger and more impenetrable.

The men of this time were hunters and gatherers without fixed settlements. They lived off their quarry and wild berries, nuts, roots, and herbs. They had not yet learned to till the soil or to breed live-stock, and they did not know how to use metal. Their roughly fashioned tools and weapons, made of bone and stone, have given the period its name: the Stone Age.

But while the Stone Age hunters were still roaming in sprawling, nomadic hordes across the steppes and forests of Europe, the first great civilizations were already growing up in the land-mass to the south. Three distinct settlement areas emerged at this time: the fertile valley of the Nile; the equally rich plains of the twin rivers Euphrates and Tigris; and the rugged country of Canaan. These were the nurseries of what we mean by civilization; and together they are the ground on which Biblical history took place. We must look at these three areas in turn, briefly at the first two, more closely at the third.

The history of the Ancient Egyptians gives the same impression of measured earnestness and dignified straightness as does the formal and stiff style of their murals and sculpture.

Egypt's verifiable history begins with King Menes who in about 3000 BC unified the country and founded the long line of Pharaohs which, running through thirty dynasties, was to reign until 525 BC. Towards the middle of the third millennium, at the time of the fourth and fifth dynasties, Egypt reached the first peak in its history, and its civilization was by then highly developed. It was the Pharaohs of that time, Cheops and Chefren, who built those mighty tombs, the pyramids, on the banks of the Nile.

These Pharaohs, gods as well as kings and consequently wielding almost unlimited power, made an important discovery: the delega-tion of power and authority. They 'invented' administration and so brought bureaucracy into the Western world. They had reason for doing so. The country was large, stretching as far as Nubia and almost to the sources of the Nile, and so the Pharaoh needed a class of conscientious men on whom he could rely to represent his power in the furthermost provinces of his realm. Inevitably there was spun a vast web of administrators and officials, who formed a separate and distinct class, a permanent Civil Service.

But what was originally conceived as a servant to the Crown eventually became its master and destroyer. Bureaucracy, at one time a solemn and dignified creation, degenerated into an elephan-tine system of exploitation. The officials who at first had exercised power in the name of the Pharaoh came more and more to use it on their own behalf; they levied their own taxes, proclaimed their offices to be hereditary, styled themselves 'princes', and finally laid hands on the Crown itself. The Pharaohs of the eleventh and part of the twelfth dynasty came from the provinces and were formerly civil servants.

This was the condition of Egypt around 1680 BC. Centralized authority had virtually broken down when suddenly, like a hurri-cane, strangers rushed upon the country from the east and com-

Gods as well as
kings, *the Pharaohs
wielded unlimited
power, symbolized
by the mighty pyramids
they built for their
tombs. Chefren (above)
reigned from
about 2625 to 2600 BC.
His pyramid, one of the
largest of the Giza
group, is the centre one.*

pletely disrupted its accustomed pattern of life. They came from somewhere in the hinterland of Asia—fierce warriors who brought with them bows and arrows, horses and chariots. They overran the Egyptian frontier forts and swept through the country, killing the inhabitants, burning the temples and palaces, sacking and pillaging as they went. They were superior fighters, bold, swift and agile, and the Egyptians offered little resistance. Eventually the invaders occupied all Egypt and made themselves masters in the

The horse and chariot, *introduced by the Hyksos, revolutionized warfare but by David's time they were no longer invincible. This relief from Gozan shows Aramaean charioteers.*

ancient Nile kingdom. They were called the Hyksos—the 'Shep-herd Kings' or 'Lords from the East'.

Although their reign began in murder and destruction, the Hyksos brought the country the priceless gift of the horse, a beast hitherto unknown to civilization. Until then, camels and donkeys had served for riding, working, and carrying loads. The new animal immediately captivated the men of the Middle East; even now it is still the Arab's pride and is rarely degraded into serving

as a beast of burden. The Hyksos harnessed the horse to their armoured chariots and this novel and fearful combination not only contributed largely to their own military success but revolutionized the traditional methods of warfare elsewhere.

The conquerors established themselves on the throne of the Pharaohs, and from it they ruled not only Egypt but also parts of Canaan as far east as Mesopotamia. This opened a new era for Egypt. For almost fifteen hundred years Egyptians had lived in proud and splendid isolation. Now a brisk cultural exchange with the centres of civilization on the Tigris and Euphrates began.

But the reign of the Hyksos was only an interlude. After little more than one hundred years they were defeated by Kames, a local dynast from Upper Egypt who drove them out of the country and gave Egypt back to the Egyptians. With Kames began a new Golden Age, the so-called New Kingdom, which culminated in the reign of Rameses II who died in 1232 BC. During this period Egypt gradually transformed itself from a bureaucracy into a military state, powerful enough to engage in wars of conquest and extending its frontiers far into the east. And strangely, as the might of the soldiers grew, so did the power of the priests. The military state developed into a theocracy. Herihor, who founded the twenty-first dynasty in 1085 BC, was a high priest of the sun-god Amun-Ra.

From then onwards, over the next five hundred years, Egypt steadily decayed and disintegrated. The throne was occupied by a succession of feeble and self-indulgent Pharaohs, among them commanders of mercenary troops, Nubians, Libyans, and other foreigners. When finally, in 525 BC, the Persians under their King Cambyses invaded the country, the national morale was so rotten that Egypt succumbed without a fight. The Persians annexed the country, and all the glory and splendour of its Empire was swept away. The supremacy of a people who for 2,500 years had preserved its military power, maintained its political domain, and kept alive its superior civilization with a consistency unique in history, had finally been overthrown.

The sun-god *Amun-ra: a gold-plated silver statuette.*

The history of Mesopotamia, the second of the three great settlement areas of antiquity, followed a course very different from that of Egypt.

The two countries had only one thing in common. Both depended for their existence on the waters of their great rivers which once a year overflowed their banks and made the land fertile. As the Nile shaped the face of Egypt, so the Euphrates and the Tigris determined the rhythm of life in Mesopotamia; and the rituals of the two nations, in so far as these derived from the seasonal rise and fall of their rivers, bore a distinct resemblance to one another.

The twin rivers, *Euphrates and Tigris, are symbolized in the brick façade of a temple at Uruk in S. Mesopotamia.*

But the resemblance ends there. Mesopotamia was a far more fertile land than Egypt; and it possessed none of the natural barriers which enabled Egypt to dwell in security and seclusion. Rich and unprotected, it was bound to attract invaders, despoilers, conquerors, and settlers in constant succession, and it is no wonder that its history is dramatic and diverse.

The first inhabitants of the twin-river country of whom we have definite knowledge were the people who can claim to have been the founders of the world's oldest known civilization—the Sumerians. Their home was in the southern part of the country, on the lower reaches of the Euphrates, down to the Persian Gulf. At the time when the Stone Age hunters in Europe were still killing the aurochs with their clubs, the Sumerians were already building Ur and Erech, their first cities.

They fashioned bricks from clay and dried them in the sun; they erected walls; they built temples, palaces, and ordinary dwelling-houses; and they decorated these with paintings and elaborate mosaics. They made weapons from bronze, and jewellery and ornaments from gold and silver. They invented the cart, the spinning wheel—and the art of writing. Their cities were protective fortresses as well as centres of political and cultural power; and the 'mayors' of these city-states, who ruled over the surrounding countryside, proudly called themselves kings.

The Sumerians had a passion for order; disorderliness, in whatever sphere, offended their nature. No sooner had they established themselves in their cities than they set about creating order. They divided the year into twelve months, the day into twelve hours, and the hour into sixty minutes. They split up the circle into 360 degrees, laid down rules for measurement and weight, and plotted the course of the stars. It was good calculation, and it is still valid after five thousand years.

Nor was this all. In their thoroughness, they tidied up the supernatural as well as the natural world and arranged their many gods in a well-planned system. There were Anu and Enlil, Ea and

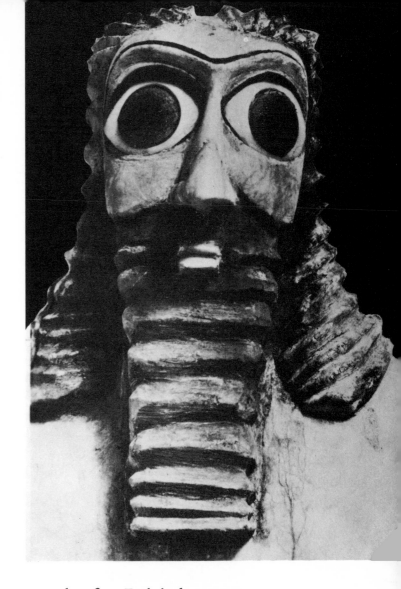

Anu, the ruler of heaven, *may be the god represented by the so-called 'worshipper statue' from Tell Asmar, Mesopotamia. This close-up of the head emphasizes the strange staring eyes and the formal treatment of beard and hair.*

Inana, the great mother, to name only a few. Each had a separate sphere of authority. Anu ruled over the heavens; Enlil over the earth; Ea over the water; and so on. Jointly the gods owned all land, and the king or high priest merely leased it to the peasants on their behalf. Like the Egyptians they practised the death-cult, though on a smaller scale than the Pharaohs had done. All the same, their 'royal tombs', unearthed by Woolley in 1927–29, revealed magnificent treasures; and elsewhere even the poorest citizens were given

'Lord of the Four Heavens': *life-size bronze head of an Akkadian king from Nineveh. About 2300 BC the Sumerians of Mesopotamia came under the dominance of the more dynamic Akkadians.*

some small gift to take with them on the long journey to the realm of the dead. As a people the Sumerians were superstitious and took precautions against demons and evil spirits.

It may well have been their devotion to orderliness which eventually brought about the downfall of the Sumerians. Order needs peace, and being essentially a peaceful people they lacked fighting spirit. They never acquired military prowess. Thus, when in 2300 BC their northern neighbours, the Akkadians, under their King Sargon I, overran their country, the Sumerians were quickly conquered and subjugated.

The four corners *of the Babylonian world. This early map* (c. 2300 BC) *shows a circular world surrounded by ocean, and with Babylon on the Euphrates at its centre.*

Unlike the Sumerians, the Akkadians were Semites; originally a nomadic people, they had gradually become settled and had assimilated Sumerian civilization. Their king was also their god and his rule was severe. Sargon I, for instance, who called himself 'King of Sumer and Akkad' or 'Lord of the Four Heavens', declared it was his aim to set up a 'universal' empire. But their rule lasted for only three hundred years; it was brought to an end by the Guti people who burst in from Iran, only to be deposed after a mere one hundred years. Once again the Sumerians rose to power and splendour, this time together with the Akkadians.

31

In this late Sumerian era architecture and the arts flourished as never before. A multitude of superbly sumptuous buildings arose, among them the magnificent temples at Ur and Lagash; and Sumerian classical literature with its hymns, legends, and epics lived through its golden age. The number of gods multiplied almost beyond reckoning; there were now between two and three thousand of them, but they were still just as carefully ordered as was the structure and administration of the State. A powerful bureaucracy grew up whose primary aim seems to have been to fill its files, and the golden rule of the civil service was formulated for the first time: *Quod non est in actis, non est in mundo* (What is not recorded does not exist).

But after the year 2000 BC this Sumerian-Akkadian state ceased to enjoy peace and orderliness. There were constant disturbances. Again and again Semitic bedouins from eastern Canaan broke into the wealthy and prosperous country, and in 1955 BC the invader Ishbi-Eyra destroyed the ancient city of Ur. Although Sumerian civilization was to have another period of late flowering, the

Sumerians and their state never regained any power or influence. A new city had suddenly acquired predominance in the twin-river country: Babylon.

Under their famous ruler Hammurabi, the Babylonians conquered all Mesopotamia. Hammurabi was the great law-giver of the ancient world. He laid down a comprehensive code of civil, criminal, and commercial law and had large portions of it carved on stone pillars for all to see. The basic principle of Hammurabi's law was 'an eye for an eye, a tooth for a tooth', and it relied heavily on the death penalty. Against this, it was the first in the history of mankind to grant considerable rights to women. It stated, for instance, that a divorce could only be granted if proof of adultery were shown.

For a while one small state in the middle Euphrates country was able to maintain its independence beside Babylon. This was Mari, probably the Haran of the Bible, where Abraham lived with his family after he had left Ur. Here, in Abraham's day, the first law for the levying of taxes was framed, and so neatly was it worked out

he multiplicity of gods in the late Sumerian period as reflected in the thousands of cylinder seals that have en found. On the left is the goddess Ishtar; centre and ght, probably Marduk, the chief Babylonian deity.

Hammurabi the law-giver *stands before the seated sun-god, giver of justice, at the head of a stone pillar inscribed with his code of laws—the first comprehensive legal code in history. Similar inscribed pillars were set up in many places so that the people might be familiar with the laws.*

that its principles hold good to this day. But in the end Mari, too, fell before Hammurabi, and Babylon became the sole power in the territory between the two rivers. Its religion, which frequently expressed itself in debauchery, ousted all other cults; and its temples, built in the shape of soaring towers which dominated the country-side, were an ever-present reminder of its supremacy.

But although Hammurabi's empire represented an enormous concentration of power, it did not survive for long. First the Hittites invaded Babylon from the region of the Black Sea, in the far north, and shortly afterwards the Kassites and Hurrians swept across from Iran. The Hyksos, operating from Egypt, occupied parts of the country adjoining their own, and after their expulsion from the Nile the pursuing Egyptians themselves invaded Meso-potamian territory. And all the time the Aramaeans, tribes of Semitic bedouins who came raiding across the border, were a con-stant threat.

It was the natural course of Mesopotamian history: a perpetual up and down of fortune, an unending confusion and tangle of peoples and tribes. Conquerors came and went; civilizations were born and died; cities and empires were built and crashed again. It was not until 1100 BC that another single and all-embracing state arose again in the land of the Tigris and the Euphrates. This was the empire of the Assyrians.

The Assyrians were born warriors, men who are pictured with tall and muscular build, favouring an imperious style of dressing their hair and beards. Their homeland was the upper Tigris where they had learned much from the Akkadians, taken over their civilization and, above all, adopted their ambition of world domination. Under their kings Ashurbanipal and Shalmanazer they conquered all Mesopotamia, Syria, and Canaan; they dominated a large part of Asia Minor; and they even penetrated as far as Egypt.

Their rulers felt no scruples in their choice of political expedients. They uprooted whole races and transplanted them in alien lands. They eliminated their opponents and ruthlessly exterminated every-

Dominating the countryside, *ziggurats, temples of the Babylonian religion, were an ever-prese. reminder of the supremacy of the gods. Opposite: the wind-worn ruins of Aqarquf* (14th–13th century BC

The warlike Assyrians *from the upper Tigris dominated Mesopotamia from the 11th to the 7th century* B

Ashur, *god of the Assyrians, from a relief at Khorsabad.*

body and everything that would not bend to their will. Their god Ashur, from whom they derived their name, was forced upon the conquered peoples. Their empire reached its peak under King Ashurbanipal between 669 and 626 BC. Thereafter, exhausted by its ceaseless wars, it crumbled and fell.

Once again, for a short spell, the star of Babylon rose. Nebuchadnezzar, its ill-famed king, unified the country and was responsible for the first complete destruction of Jerusalem. Then Persia, the all-powerful, engulfed Mesopotamia as it had Egypt, and the long and stormy history of two and a half thousand years was brought to a final close. The Persians were followed by the Greeks, the Greeks by the Romans, and the centre of political, spiritual,

Their power reached its peak under Ashurbanipal, whose campaigns were recorded in a series of bas-reliefs.

and cultural power gradually shifted away from the east and moved north towards Central Europe.

The countries of the Nile and of Tigris and Euphrates sank back into oblivion. The great empires in which our civilization was cradled, and in which were created the order and the law that are the foundation of our own, were forgotten; and but for archaeology we would not know that they had ever existed.

'THE DESERT SHALL REJOICE'

Of the three great settlement areas of the ancient world only the third, Canaan, called in turn Palestine, the Holy Land, and Israel, was able to hand down its cultural heritage alive through the ages.

The name of Israel *appears once, and once only, in Egyptian writing—on the stela of Merenptah at Thebes. Dated to about 1230 BC, this is Israel's first appearance in recorded history.*

The countryside was infinitely poorer, less fertile, harder to defend than either Egypt or Mesopotamia. Canaan never became a great world power. No pyramids were built there, and it brought forth no dominant civilization. And yet its people achieved one tremendous creation that never died. All that Canaan gave to the world was a book. But this book, the Bible, permanently changed the course of history.

The name Canaan was probably derived from 'kinahu', a Hurrian word meaning 'reddish purple'—a most precious and famous dye. Purple dye was extracted from a shellfish, *Murex brandaris*, commonly found along the east coast of the Mediterranean, and was a highly prized product.

Geographically, Canaan was unimpressive. Bounded by the mountains of Lebanon in the north, the Arabian desert in the east,

38

the Negev desert in the south, and the Mediterranean in the west, it was cleft from north to south by a huge rift, the valley of the river Jordan, which divided all Canaan into two long, narrow strips. West of the Jordan the land was varied enough; wooded hills and fertile valleys, rich pastures and flowering oases alternated with jagged rocks, steep precipices, sandy plains, and deserts. But to the east of the river, the land was waterless and almost useless for cultivation. The west wind, blowing from the Mediterranean, brought annual rainfalls, but the east wind, which blew from the desert, rarely brought anything but scorching heat.

As varied as the face of the land was its animal life. Wolves, bears, lions, and hyenas preyed on the meagre herds of livestock that the inhabitants managed to raise; and the locust, the greatest scourge of all, would periodically descend on the fields in huge

swarms, devour the crops, and destroy in minutes the work of months and even years, to bring famine in its train.

Little is known about the first people who lived here. That there were earlier inhabitants than the Edomites, Moabites, Ammonites, Aramaeans, and Phoenicians is certain; but who they were and where they came from is still a mystery. A few ruins tell us that people lived here thousands of years ago; and one of their cities, Jericho—the oldest known city in the world—is believed to date from a period well before the Flood and to belong to a civilization contemporary with the Ice Age in Europe. Canaan was certainly inhabited as early as were Egypt and Mesopotamia, and though we know next to nothing of its early civilization this is simply because the poorer quality of its bricks led to its buildings perishing.

Like Egypt and Mesopotamia, the country was dominated by a number of city-states such as Jericho, Ugarit, Sidon, Byblos, Askelon, Gaza, and Gath. These cities lay widely scattered and in between them grazed the herds of the nomadic tribes. In the Sinai desert lived the Malachites, in the east the Midianites, Ishmaelites, and Arabs—proud nomads these, who would burst upon the countryside, riding their camels, pillage the fields, and disappear in a whirl of sand.

Towards the middle of the second millennium BC the Hyksos, driven out of Egypt, penetrated into Canaan, conquered some of its independent cities, and established themselves there. They were followed by the Egyptians, and after them the Hittites and the Assyrians took control of the country. But none of these people, neither its original inhabitants nor their conquerors, succeeded in making Canaan a political power. The country was too vulnerable, too sprawling, too divided to concentrate and unify its strength. Consequently it remained outside the main stream of world history, off the highway of bloody conquests, and remote from the splendour of past civilizations.

Canaan had to wait a long time for its hour of destiny. It came about 1200 BC with the arrival of the Israelites.

A Semitic captive of the Pharaoh (c. 1150 BC), portrayed on a blue faience tile, indicates penetration of Canaan by the Egyptians.

2

CHILDREN OF ISRAEL

The Israelites, yet another Semitic people, drifted into Canaan from the desert and brought with them their chieftains, families, and servants, and their herds of cattle, sheep, and goats. They lived in black tents, and they sought grazing for their animals on the meagre land on either side of the route along which they travelled. They were migrants, not invading conquerors, and they came to Canaan because they had nowhere else to go. All they wanted was a resting-place where they could set up their tents without displacing other people or involving themselves in fighting. When they found what they were looking for they settled down side by side with the people who already occupied the country. Now and then small troubles arose and fighting broke out, but there was no full-scale war. The Israelites, who fought on foot, found the Canaanite cavalry and war-chariots terrifying, and preferred to keep out of their way and avoid trouble. The Canaanites, for their part, were not unduly jealous of the Israelites. There was still plenty of land left in Canaan if the newcomers occupied the out-of-the-way mountains and forests. So, undisturbed, the Israelites grazed their herds on the barren fields and built their primitive villages, and the country was to them what God had promised.

These people—Israelites, Hebrews, Jews—were made up of several tribes, but the Bible symbolically condenses them all into one and calls it the tribe of Abraham. Abraham was born about 1900 BC in Ur in the country of the Sumerians. Obedient to God's commands—'Now the Lord had said unto Abraham, Get thee out of thy country, and from thy kindred, and from thy father's house, unto a land which I will show thee . . .'—he left Ur, first for Mari, on the middle Euphrates, and later for Egypt. The Bible says that the tribe migrated to Egypt because there was famine where they were living. Egypt was fertile, a land where the supply and storing of provisions was highly organized, and many nomadic tribes wandered over its borders in search of the food which was so hard to come by elsewhere.

The Pharaoh of that time accepted Abraham and his tribesmen, fugitives from hunger and thirst. But when this Pharaoh died he was succeeded by another who was less tolerant. He used the Hebrew settlers as a source of unpaid labour and transformed them into second-class citizens with limited rights; in effect, into slaves. An Egyptian document of the time of Rameses II lays it down that the Hebrews must 'carry stones for the great citadel of the city of Rameses, the beloved of Ammon', and that they must 'hew stones for the god Re, even the Re of Rameses, the beloved of Ammon, in the south part of Memphis'. There are various accounts of Hebrews being forced to work in the quarries of Wadi Hammumat, east of Thebes, and the Bible speaks of those who were set to build the towns of Pithom and Rameses in the eastern Nile delta.

At last a man emerged from this oppressed class who was to lead it to freedom. This man was Moses. He united the Israelite slaves, secretly prepared an itinerary for them, and finally led them out of Egypt one night. The Pharaoh sent a troop of cavalry after the fugitives, but it lost its way and was drowned in the Red Sea with its horses and chariots. 'The Lord overthrew the Egyptians in the midst of the sea.' The Israelites were free.

But they had to buy their freedom at a price. They did not know where to find a new homeland and had no choice but to embark on a tortuous journey across the desert. The Bible records that this journey lasted forty years. But here we must be on our guard. The Biblical writers use the number 40 when they wish to indicate a time of crisis. Thus, Elijah travelled for 'forty' days before he came to

Moses leading the Israelites *across the Red Sea: a 3rd-century* AD *wall painting in the ancient synagogue of Dura Europos on the Euphrates.*

the mountain of God, Jesus fasted for 'forty' days in solitude before his baptism, and 'forty' days elapsed before the Ascension. What is certain is that after 'forty' years of wandering in the desert the Israelites had at last been welded into a nation.

Moses led his people towards the south, along the coast of the Gulf of Suez, near the edge of the desert. Plagued by drought, in constant danger from marauders and wild animals, the wanderers passed by Mara and Elim, Dophka and Raphidim. The mountains of Sinai rose before them; doggedly the Israelites climbed through the steep passes.

43

It was on Mount Sinai that Moses received the Ten Commandments direct from God. 'Moses spake, and God answered him by a
voice.' This event was the foundation on which everything else in
Jewish history was built. From the Ten Commandments derives
the whole structure of Jewish law, the greater part of Jewish social
life, and all of Jewish religion, as well as those many important
elements in Christianity which can be traced back either to the
ecstatic trance of a Jewish megalomaniac standing, feverish with
hunger and exhaustion, on a mountain top; or to Moses talking to
God—whichever way one cares to look at it. The palaces and
temples of the Egyptians, Sumerians, Akkadians, and Assyrians
long ago crumbled to dust and were forgotten. The once powerful
Re and Ammon have faded to myths and legends. But the Ten
Commandments are still revered by Jews, Christians, and Moslems.

Moses built a throne for God, the Ark of the Covenant. This
became the most sacred possession of the Israelites, the focal point of
all the inhabitants of Canaan; for in time all the Semitic people
living in the country voluntarily submitted to Jehovah, the God of
Israel, not under duress as the peoples conquered by the Assyrians
had been forced to accept Ashur, but of their own free will, recog-
nizing him as the Lord who had led Abraham's people out of
Egypt, protected them, guided them, and ruled over them.

After Sinai the journey of the Israelites turned northwards. Past
Hazeroth and Ezion-Geber on the Gulf of Akaba the tribes
followed a straight course into the wilderness. Once again hunger
and thirst, privation and hardship for months and years . . .

At last came the moment when Moses' gaze lighted on the final
goal, the promised land of Canaan. He was not himself destined to
set foot on it, but for him it was enough to have seen it before he
died. 'The Lord said unto him . . . I have caused thee to see it with
thine eyes, but thou shalt not go over thither.' His successor, Joshua,
finished the work he had begun, and the entry of the Israelites into
Israel was accomplished somewhere about 1200 BC.

The wanderings in the wilderness had fused the tribes into one people, one nation. Politically, however, the state they set up was extremely loosely organized. There was no central government and no ruler. Each tribe defended itself against attack. As attacks were frequent, temporary alliances were formed between one tribe and another to repel the common enemy. But when the danger was past, each tribe returned to its independence and isolation. Nevertheless the tribes shared something which was more important to them than treaties and political agreements. This was their one God, common to them all. The Ark, God's throne, was the focal point of Judaism and thus the centre of the nation. Religion and politics were one and the same thing, an indivisible whole.

The Ark of the Covenant, throne of God, was the Israelites' most precious possession and the symbol of a faith kept pure through 'forty years in the wilderness'. This relief on the frieze of the Capernaum synagogue represents the Ark as a temple mounted on wheels, as it would have been for its long journey over the desert.

The twelve tribes *are represented in this wall painting from Dura Europos. Moses, their spiritual leader, distributes water to each of the twelve, and in the centre stands the Menorah, the seven-branched candelabrum.*

The Ark had no permanent resting-place, but moved from one town to another as occasion required. For a while it was at Shechem, then at Bethel, then Gilgal, and finally Shiloh. Every month it was watched over by a priest from a different tribe. Twelve was an important number to the Jews; twelve months demanded twelve tribes. When the tribe of Levi died out, for instance, that of Joseph was speedily divided into two to supply the deficiency.

Although, ethnologically speaking, they were all of one family, the different tribes preserved their different identities. Some remained small and insignificant, and went through bitter struggles with the Canaanites and the Aramaic nomads who periodically attacked them; others rose to a position of leadership and authority and were able to live on their own terms. Each stayed rooted to its particular locality: Issachar, Naphtali, Zebulun, and Asher in the north; Joseph, with its branches Ephraim and Manasseh in the centre; and Dan, Benjamin, Gad, Reuben, Simeon, and Judah (also Levi during its short existence) in the south.

46

As soon as they became used to a settled life, the Israelites began to build. The towns were small and rarely contained more than a thousand people, and often fewer than a hundred. Jerusalem, the capital, measured only about 400 yards by 100 yards during its first decades—an area no larger than that of a modern factory. There were no streets as such. Each man built as he fancied, and the result was a complicated tangle of narrow alleyways and winding lanes.

There was only one spot in these towns where people could foregather without being over-cramped—the town-gate. This was so arranged that a large covered recess was created in the town-wall. Here business was transacted, councils were held, and law was administered.

And so the daily life of Israel went on. The women ground flour, spun wool, and baked their flat loaves; the men went out to work in the fields and vineyards or tended their flocks. At this time, seven qualities were required of the complete man: he had to be musical, sociable, truthful, eloquent, thrifty, handsome, and godly. The main social gathering of the day took place in the evening. The men of the town would congregate in the open air, under a tree, by a spring, or in the town-gate and tell stories and jokes, sing and dance. Above all, this was the time when the old figures of their history were conjured up and Israel's traditions were kept alive. It was at this evening gathering that each generation in turn learned of the Creation, the Patriarchs, the Flood, the sufferings of their people under Egyptian bondage, and the message of Jehovah, the one God.

Once a year the elders of the twelve tribes met before the Holy Ark. This occasion was a kind of pilgrimage to the centre of religion, the rallying point of all the tribes. Every male Israelite had to undertake the journey at least once during his lifetime. The festival began with sacrifices at the altar and the renewal of religious vows. Every year the tribesmen repeated their allegiance to God, committed themselves to his care, abjured idolatry, and promised to be obedient and faithful to the divine commands.

47

The space in front of the Ark was also the central law court; religious and civil law meant one and the same thing to this dedicated people. It was here that judgment was given in disputes that threatened to disrupt national unity. Once, the tribe of Benjamin fell into sin. A Levite had journeyed to Gibea, the home of the tribe of Benjamin, and rested there overnight with his wife. While he was asleep, some men attacked the wife and raped her so violently that she died the same night. Her husband returned to his tribe, and the Levites bitterly demanded the exposure of the culprits. The Benjamites hesitated; the case was brought before the highest court of all, the yearly meeting of the tribes before the Ark; and the whole tribe was unanimously condemned and punished. Thus order was re-established; the crime was atoned for, and the disgrace was wiped out.

Social order was sacrosanct and it was embodied principally in one man, the Judge. This term, 'Judge', is the traditional translation of a Hebrew word but it is not altogether accurate. The judges of Israel were a combination of president and high-priest and they administered the law, which was based on God's testimony to Moses. They led their people to wars upon whose outcome the existence of the state depended. They gave the final verdict in inter-tribal quarrels and decided all religious disputes. They were politicians and priests, generals and philosophers. It was they who, in the last resort, interpreted anything in the Holy Scriptures that might be called in question. This interpretation was given at the yearly pilgrimage. Thus, the first Holy Scriptures were probably already in existence at the time of the Judges; moreover, they may already have been ancient documents, sacred words which had been handed down from generation to generation. It is possible that the first writings of Israel belong to a period before the settlement in Canaan, to the time, indeed, when Moses was leading his people through the desert.

The so-called 'five books of Moses' cannot have been written from beginning to end by Moses himself—the description of his death in the last chapter, if nothing else, shows that this is an impossibility. They are, rather, a careful collection of work by many hands, of ancient laws, traditions, and stories which had been told for centuries in the tents of the nomads, in Egypt, during the Exodus in the wilderness, and in the newly built towns and villages.

'And the Lord said unto Moses, Write this for a memorial in a book...' These words come from the seventeenth chapter of Exodus and are the first mention of writing in the Bible. With these early writings began the book which was to dominate the whole of the western world and to constitute Israel's true empire—an empire greater and more lasting than any which military or political power could ever produce.

Emblems of Jewry on a gold glass found in Rome: the Ark, flanked by lions, and (below) seven-branched candlesticks, rams' horns, a palm branch and an oil jar.

3

THE BIRTH OF READING AND WRITING

The art of writing was not contrived at a stroke by one great genius of the human race. It was a slow creation which passed through innumerable stages before it reached full growth.

It began as a simple matter of convenience. Once men had acquired the habit of living together they found that they needed to be able to identify their own tools as insurance against thieves and casual borrowers. So each man invented a 'trademark' for himself which he carved on all his axes, daggers, knives, and scrapers; this marked them as his property and his alone. With the growth of towns, trade sprang up. Although the farmer in the village was able to provide for himself, the townsman had to get his food, wool, and linen from others. A class of men was formed who lived by buying from one party and selling to another. The simplicity of primitive life fast disappeared; the tradesmen had to be able to send messages to their business associates in other towns; they had to keep accounts, and make some kind of record of transactions they had completed. A merchant of Ur one day sold a bale of linen for four oxen to a fellow-merchant in Erech. He lacked confidence in his messenger's intelligence, and so he scratched a picture of four oxen on a clay tablet and sent it along with the consignment. All over the East businessmen were having the same idea. So began the first rudimentary picture-writing.

One can easily imagine how this practice developed. At first, people merely drew simple pictures of the objects they wished to describe, but gradually these drawings became the normal means

The scribe was a professional man in ancient Egypt, of high standing and in great demand

of communication when speech was impossible. Such pictures evolved into certain uniform, generally understood 'abbreviations'. They also increased in number. After a time a way was found of designating not only objects, such as a sheep, an axe, or a bow, but also actions, such as walking, eating, and shaving. By means of grouping individual drawings together, the eager penman found he could express abstract concepts, including love, hate, and revenge. And eventually he even devised methods of writing proper names and such apparently ungraphic ideas as 'I' and 'you'.

Writing became more and more complex as it became more flexible. Presently the merchant considered it beneath his dignity to write his own letters, and a new occupation, that of the scribe, emerged. The scribe class grew up under the Egyptians and Sumerians and resembled a caste in that its skills were handed down from father to son. Scribes generally belonged to the upper classes; often they were officials, sometimes priests. They were in great

52

demand in every sphere of life and for every purpose—to prepare written business instructions, to write personal letters, to compile the royal chronicles, and, of course, to read what others had written. In time their profession also acquired its tools, and dictionaries and lexicons came into being. Writing, however, was still a most laborious task. Since every word had its own picture, the number of pictures rapidly exceeded all reasonable limits. Condensation became necessary and syllable-writing was invented.

Syllable-writing differed from picture-writing by representing not objects, actions, and concepts but the *sounds* of words. The process somewhat resembles the joke-translations with which schoolboys amuse their classmates. In every school-generation some bright fourth-former will translate *Caesar parvus equus erat* as 'Caesar was a little hoarse'. The same kind of transliteration, by sound rather than by sense, is at the bottom of all phonetic-writing.

The language of the Aztecs has given a clear demonstration of how this process evolves. These Central American people were still using a primitive picture-language in the sixteenth century at the time of the Spanish and Portuguese invasions. The invaders brought with them priests who wished to teach the new-found society their religion; at the same time the more scholarly of the Aztecs were anxious to take down and preserve what they were taught. But how could the missionaries express the Lord's Prayer, let alone the more difficult precepts of Christianity, in picture-writing? They did it by equating Latin sounds with pictures which stood for words with similar sounds in Aztec. The first words of the Lord's Prayer in Latin, for instance, were indicated by a flag, a stone, a thistle, and then another stone. The Aztec words for these objects were, respectively, '*pantl*', '*tetl*', and '*nostli*'; their first syllables, if strung together, give something resembling the Latin: 'Pate(r). noste(r)'. The loss of the 'r' did not matter because the Aztecs were unable to pronounce it. In this way, each picture gradually lost its direct significance and came to represent only a sound. Exactly the same process went on in the Middle East about 2000 BC. Eventually it led to the most influential development in the history of language, perhaps in the history of man generally. Letters were invented and it was no longer necessary to have a different sign for every object or even for every possible syllable: everything, even the most abstract idea, could now be expressed in writing by means of a mere twenty or so characters. Reading ceased to be the sort of teasing puzzle it had been when hieroglyphs were used, and became, instead, a precise science.

With the alphabet there came a more uniform system of line arrangement. Previously, words had been arranged as the writer thought fit, sometimes from left to right, sometimes from top to bottom, sometimes even in a circle. Rules were now laid down, although these varied from language to language. Hebrew, for instance, was written from right to left, while Ancient Syrian ran from left to right.

A LANGUAGE WITHOUT VOWELS

The languages of this period had no vowels, only consonants. When a language was in current use the lack of vowels was scarcely felt, since the complete word could usually be understood from its context; but to present-day scholars, who are dealing with a language long dead, the absence of vowels presents a serious problem. For instance, if the English words 'the ten huts' were written without vowels—'th tn hts'—these could equally well be read as 'the tin hats', 'thy tan hurts', 'the tun hits', or some other combination of words. Generally, of course, the context gives the meaning; the difficulty comes with proper names. To this day it is not known whether King Nebuchadnezzar, who held the Israelites in captivity in Babylon, was really Nebuchadnezzar or Nabuko-donosor. Both theories have their adherents, and since the name was written 'nbkdnsr' there is no way of deciding which is right. Similarly there is no way of knowing what was the true name of the small country which existed on the coast of the Mediterranean when the Hebrews took over Canaan. It was written 'tkr' and could be

Tukur, Taker, or one of several other combinations of vowels with the given consonants.

Even more names would no doubt have been lost if it had not been for the early Greek translations of Hebrew texts. The Greek alphabet contained vowels, so all names had to be written out in full, and fortunately scholars who worked on these translations were sufficiently acquainted with vocalized Hebrew to be able to give accurate renderings.

There is a curious family relationship between the early alphabets and the picture-scripts which preceded them. The ancestor of our letter H, for example, was the Egyptian hieroglyph *chet*, which was pronounced rather like the ch in the Scots word 'loch.' (Antiquity had no aspirates as such.) *Chet* as a word, meant 'an empty space' or 'womb', also 'a pond' and 'a ditch'. Incidentally this shows how ambiguous and confusing picture-writing could be. The sign for *chet* was a square enclosing one or more curved lines, a stylized picture of a pond. In time this picture became more and more stereotyped until it was, first, a square with one line in it, and then a ladder-shaped sign, with both uprights extending beyond the central square. The Greeks adopted the sign, practically unchanged, for their *eta*, and it was passed on to the Etruscans, the first known inhabitants of Italy. The Romans, by leaving the top and bottom of the square entirely open, created the H that is used today.

HIEROGLYPH	OLD PHOENICIAN	OLD HEBREW	HEBREW QUADRATIC
▭	⊟	Ħ	Н
॒	⊟	⊟	H
HEBREW CURSIVE	OLD GREEK	ETRUSCAN	OLD ROMAN

From hieroglyphs to modern times: *evolution of the letter H.*

Well over five thousand years ago *writin[g] of a sort was in use. The limestone table[t] (left), of about 3300 BC, bears obviou[s] pictographic signs ('foot', 'hand', numeral[s], etc.), but their meaning is as yet unread. Th[e] clay tablets opposite (from Nuzi, N. Ira[q] c. 1400 BC) were impressed with cuneiform (wedge-shaped) marks, and then baked dry.*

The scripts of antiquity were as varied and numerous as their languages and peoples. The first to develop were the picture-writings of the Egyptians and Sumerians. There is something about this mysterious, symbolical puzzle-language which has fascinated scholars throughout the ages; as late as the sixteenth century, Leonardo da Vinci tried to compose a picture-script of his own from drawings and symbols. While picture-writing was still holding its own in Egypt, it was being replaced in Mesopotamia by cunei-form script, which was invented and perfected by the Babylonians. Finally, the Phoenicians in Byblos created the first phonetic script, out of which grew all the many alphabets of antiquity and their descendants.

Although the different scripts ran into thousands, the methods of reproducing them were comparatively limited. The first writing materials were stone and chisel; it was the merchant who, requiring something more portable and economical, devised the method of engraving on small clay tablets. This process came in time to be used by kings and priests for recording their laws, historical documents,

chronicles, and religious writings. Extensive libraries of tablets were collected by monarchs with a taste for learning, such as Ashur banipal who had 20,000, and the King of Mari of Abraham's time who had 23,000. When archaeologists dug up these libraries, the contents had to be transported in lorries and a generation of scholars was occupied in translating the writing on the tablets.

The clay of which these tablets were made probably had a strong influence on the shape of the cuneiform scripts used by the Sumerians and Babylonians. Their method was to make impressions on the wet clay with a small stick or ivory stylus, about as long as a foun tain pen and perhaps three quarters of an inch wide by a quarter of an inch thick. This impression would, of course, be slightly deeper at one end than at the other, according to the pressure applied, and a system of word notation was evolved from these wedge shaped marks. Occasionally a black ink, made from soot, was used for writing on the clay. The size of the tablets became standardized; they were generally about 4 inches by 9, or 9 inches by 15, although hexagonal and octagonal shaped tablets also were used.

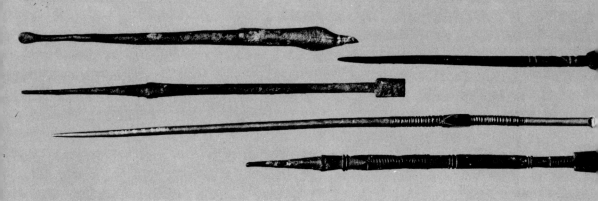

From the earliest days of writing *to comparatively modern times, the implements changed very little. The pens above and the inkpot below are from the Roman Empire. Very similar equipment served Egyptian scribes for writing on papyrus.*

The leaves of the papyrus reed *made a writing surface equal to the best hand-made paper. The papyrus scroll opposite (above) shows how durable this material can be. The painting of Moses from Dura Europos shows the way to hold a scroll for reading.*

PAPYRUS, PARCHMENT AND CLAY

Another, more expensive, method of writing was with a pen and ink on papyrus. Papyrus was the discovery and monopoly of Egypt. Papyrus reeds, which grew in thickets on the banks of the Nile, were manufactured into a writing material by cutting the leaves into long thin strips, laying these pieces criss-cross upon each other and saturating them with a calcium solution. The product was the equivalent of the best handmade paper, and was so durable that some of it has lasted in the dry Egyptian climate until the present day.

After the clay tablet, papyrus was the most widely used writing material of antiquity, though it was a luxury which only the wealthy could afford, because Egypt cornered the market and charged dearly for the papyrus she exported. Not unnaturally, people cast around

for a cheaper substitute and they found it in parchment, the tanned animal hide which is still sometimes used by ornamental calli-graphers. Parchment was the discovery of the Greek town of Pergamon from which it derives its name (by way of the Latin *pergamentum*). Like papyrus, it was written on with ink. It was so tough that its writing could be erased and the sheet used over and over again. This was a frequent practice in the Middle Ages. The monks, who were not interested in the treasures of this world, made a habit of erasing old manuscripts and re-using the parchment. The fact that they were destroying a probably irreplaceable document to find room for their household accounts did not worry them. Why should it? They had no idea of the value of these old scribblings. It is only recently that science has discovered how to read the traces of the original writing by means of infra-red photography. These twice-used parchments (*palimpsests*, as specialists call them), are a subject of much study today.

As an alternative to parchment, the writers of antiquity some-times used coarse leather, and one of the Dead Sea Scrolls was made of rolled copper, because it was a particularly precious document (being a list of buried treasures). But paper was still unknown.

The book, as we know it, is a relatively late-comer. Its forerunner was the scroll. Papyrus was too brittle to be folded, and so it was rolled to form a scroll. Sometimes a scroll was forty yards in length and was made of separate papyrus leaves which were stuck together and written on in columns. The reader held the scroll in both hands and gradually rolled up what he had read while he unrolled a new portion. The scroll was mainly a possession of the wealthy, and it held the field until the first centuries after Christ when the book, or rather the codex, made of folded, bound sheets, came into use. The first Christians were not wealthy and could not afford costly scrolls, sometimes encased in ivory, silver, or gold. Their only means of writing the Christian message was on any strips of parchment they could obtain. These strips were then sewn together and formed a codex, which was read by turning the pages.

Half-hidden under lines of later Syriac writing, the Gospel of St Luke in Greek appears on these twice-used leaves of parchment. The Greek manuscript runs up the page; the later scribe partly erased them and wrote across.

Five thousand years have passed since the first written records were made. The history of writing is mysterious and wonderful, and yet the greatest wonder lies elsewhere. It is neither the invention of the alphabet nor the discovery of papyrus, but the preservation of the thoughts, the mighty words, these made possible. And thoughts will always be the greatest wonder of mankind, whether they are reproduced by a stylus on clay or by a rotary press on newsprint.

4

THE KINGS OF ISRAEL

INTO THE HANDS OF THE PHILISTINES

By 1022 BC the Hebrews had settled in Canaan and built their villages and towns. They lived a simple, mainly agricultural life, grazing their flocks in the fertile valley of the Jordan, and harvesting sufficient crops for their own needs. They made obeisance to one sacred emblem alone, the Ark, which was the throne of Jehovah, the one true God who was their God; and they already had their first Holy Scriptures to consult, study, and treasure.

This idyllic life was suddenly disrupted by a terrible enemy who attacked the western borders of Canaan.

This enemy—the Philistines—had come down from the north, crossed the sea, and followed the coastline southwards. The invaders were tall blond men who were dedicated to war. Nobody knows where they came from, although many theories have been advanced, one of which makes Atlantis their country of origin. But this involves us in yet another mystery. Where was Atlantis? At least two thousand books have been written in attempts to answer this question, but a satisfactory solution seems to be as far off as ever. Some scholars identify the island with Crete; others with the Spanish trading centre of Tartessos; and there is one school which places it in the Sahara Desert. There are those who hold that Atlantis was one of the Azores which sank into the sea. The only possible verdict in each instance is 'not proven'.

Whatever their origin may have been, the Philistines swept over the ancient cities like a fire driven by the wind. Different races called them by different names, most of which have been lost; the Egyp-

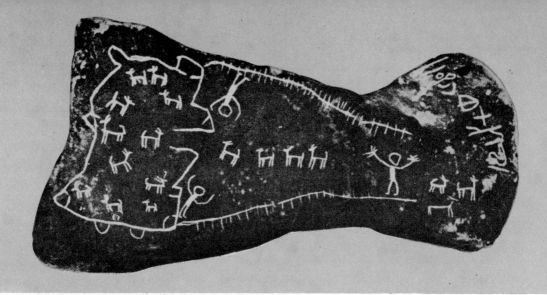

The Israelites grazed their flocks *in Canaan—a land 'flowing with milk and honey' but still one where the new settlers needed to be vigilant against attack. A rock drawing from Amman of the first millennium* AD *shows the kind of fortified sheepfold they would have used, with a narrow entrance guarded by extended walls.*

tians, for instance, spelled the name they gave them *prst*, but it is impossible to say how they pronounced it. The Hebrews called them the Philistines.

The word was dreaded by the whole of the Near East. The Philistines had conquered all the ports and were turning their eyes towards the interior, looking greedily towards Canaan where they hoped to find a place to settle. The small, uncoordinated state of Israel could hold few terrors for these warriors with their extensive armoury and long battle experience. There had, indeed, been times when the Israelites had united to fight back invaders—under the heroic Judge, Samson, for instance—but such contests had been little more than skirmishes. Before the Israelites had time to plan a strategy to meet the new situation, the full army of the Philistines was confronting them on their own ground. The Israelites did the only wise thing they could do in such circumstances: they banded together and chose a king. 'And all the people went to Gilgal, and there they made Saul king before the Lord.' It was a historic moment. For the first time, the Israelites were acting not as individual tribes but as one nation, one state.

Saul moved quickly. He gathered an army and attacked the Philistines' military posts in Gibea which, taken by surprise, surrendered. Encouraged by this success, Saul next destroyed some more outposts and the Israelites began to feel secure again. But they were only deluding themselves. The Philistines were not going to give up the prospect of capturing a country because they had lost a few military outposts. A counter-attack was prepared. The Philistines assembled their troops in Aphek from where they marched, in full battle-order, on to the Jezreel plain to meet Saul's army. But the battle was decided before it was begun. The forces of the Philistines, superior in arms, training, and numbers, determined the outcome from the start. Saul's courage failed. The Bible tells how, in his doubt and fear, he went by night to consult a witch. Her words were unequivocal: 'The Lord shall deliver the host of Israel into the hand of the Philistines.' The next day the armies met again, and the Hebrews were annihilated. All except one of Saul's sons were killed and the king himself committed suicide. Israel was in greater peril than ever before.

DAVID: REBEL, KING AND POET

At this moment a man appeared who was to become one of the greatest leaders of Israel. This man, David, made Israel into a great power, feared for the first and only time in its history.

The story of David's life has the pattern of a romantic novel. He was born, a shepherd's son, in Bethlehem, the chief city of the tribe of Judah. He joined Saul's army, distinguished himself by his courage, won the king's confidence, and eventually became Saul's personal armour-bearer. A candid, handsome, charming young man, he was popular with everyone, and this was his undoing. In his last years, Saul became more and more suspicious of those around him. The popularity of any other man aroused his envy, bringing with it the certainty of death. 'They have ascribed unto David ten thousands, and to me they have ascribed but thousands: and what can he have more but the kingdom? And Saul eyed David from that day and forward.' David recognized his danger and fled to the southern tip of the mountains west of the Jordan. In this stronghold he gathered round him a band of commandos with whom he raided the surrounding countryside. Saul raged, but he was powerless against his former servant. David was more than a petty rebel; although his followers were only adventurers, they swiftly increased in numbers. He nursed his growing strength carefully, established links between himself and various tribes, and showed himself to be a man who acted from clear and deliberate political ambition.

One day he went to the Philistines and offered them an alliance. The offer was not presumptuous; if accepted, the Philistines would gain both a troop of bold, well-trained men and good relations with several of the southern tribes. The Philistines accepted David's offer and made him leader of the mercenaries. They allowed him to set up his headquarters in Ziklag. He was now fully established in the Philistines' confidence, but he continued to go his own way and carry out his own plans. Although he did not give up his raids, he regularly sent presents from his booty to the elders of the southern tribes. He was single-minded, patient.

At last the deciding battle in the Israel-Philistine war took place, the one in Jezreel already referred to. The Philistines had sense enough to exclude David from this particular fight, for they feared that the man who had once been Saul's subject would defect. After Israel's defeat and the king's death, David knew that his opportunity had come. But he showed, not for the first time, his statesmanship, and waited. Instead of risking everything in an attempt to seize the throne, he began to carry out, step by step, his plan of campaign.

The disaster at Jezreel had scattered and divided the remnants of the tribes. Some of them, including Judah and Simeon, had gathered for consultation in the southern part of the country. David joined them and his sudden appearance made him seem a saviour from heaven to the unhappy elders. With his disciplined warriors, he represented strength. He was experienced both in warfare and diplomacy; through his first wife he was linked to the Kenites; his presents had conciliated the southern communities; and above all he was on friendly terms with the Philistines. He was unanimously elected ruler of this little group of tribes. And so at last David was a king—the King of Judah.

The other tribes acted in much the same way. They withdrew into the north and also chose a king, who, since he saw himself as ruler over the whole country, called himself the King of Israel. The Hebrew nation was thus split into two, and this division was to last until the end of their tribal organization as a people. The name 'Israel' took on two meanings: it described both the Hebrews as a whole and the northern tribes in particular, as distinct from the southern tribes who had gathered in the kingdom of Judah. But these Israelites of the north had no David. Their king, a weak incompetent man, was murdered shortly after his accession—an opportune event for David although it brought him embarrassment. The assassins came to him, showed him the King of Israel's head, and asked for a reward. Did David, in fact, have anything to do with the murder? We do not know; but he made, as always, the best of an awkward situation. He ordered the murderers to be put to death. Ethically this decision may be doubtful, but politically it could be justified.

Meanwhile, David had married one of Saul's daughters and so consolidated his position. He held the kingship of all Canaan in his hand, and before long he was appointed King of Israel and Judah in front of the Ark of Jehovah. 'And David perceived that the Lord had established him king over Israel, and that he had exalted his kingdom for his people Israel's sake.'

Up to now, the Philistines had merely looked on, but the march of events forced them to intervene. David had deprived them of the fruits of their victory, reunited the tribes, raised forces as strong as those of Saul in his heyday, and generally re-established the Hebrews as a nation. The Philistines mobilized their army again and marched to the Plain of Rephaim, 'to seek David'.

The king was fully aware that everything depended on the issue of the battle. If he was defeated, his dream of ruling Israel would be over and the subjugation of his people would be complete. But he was not another Saul to succumb to the threat of danger. He had known the hard life of a mercenary soldier, had fought in a hundred battles, and, above all, he had worked with the Philistines and knew their methods and their weaknesses. He achieved the seemingly impossible by scattering the enemy before they had drawn up their army in its accustomed battle-order. Although they rallied and gave battle a second time, David again beat them and drove them into the west, and he harried them until the last foreigner had left his country. From then on, the power of the Philistines, once the greatest power west of the Jordan, waned and became insignificant. Strength was represented by Israel, the kingdom of David.

As soon as the king was rid of the enemy, he set about reorganizing his own country. The widely separated city-states were joined to form a centralized system and were given a capital, Jerusalem. This city was chosen because it lay on neutral territory between Israel and Judah, and it became the heart of the nation. The Ark found its resting-place on Mount Zion in the centre of the city, and around it were built palaces and forts, houses and official buildings. As the seat of the government of the whole country, Jerusalem was occupied mainly by officials, soldiers, and priests.

From the first, David knew that to rest content with what he had accomplished would be fatal. He began systematically to annex the adjoining states with their peoples—the Moabites, the Aramaeans, the Ammonites. He laid siege to the Edomites and the province of Aram. He established diplomatic relations with the Phoenician towns on the coast, particularly with King Hiram of Tyre. David's sphere of influence extended far beyond the borders of Canaan. Israel was the principal power at this time and the only great state ever to exist in the Jordan basin. In a few years it was changed from a collection of weak, disunited, exhausted tribes into an invincible nation, single-minded, firm, ordered, and thrustful. 'And David

The power of the Philistines receded *when David came to the throne of Israel. An Egyptian relief from Medinet Habu shows two Philistine prisoners led by an Egyptian officer.*

ruled over all Israel; and David executed judgement and justice unto all his people.'

David made only one mistake throughout his career, but it was a mistake which was later to affect his people disastrously. Like many another great man he did not bequeath his qualities to any of his sons who, even in his lifetime, looked enviously at the crown. One of them, Absalom, organized a rebellion and marched upon his father's capital. But at this point David's patience gave way. The old lion showed he had not lost his claws, and Absalom and his rebellion were ruthlessly destroyed.

69

But David had still not chosen a successor, and when in the end he made up his mind and named his son, Solomon, it was too late. The authority of the king was not to be disobeyed, but all the same Solomon was not the right man to administer such an immense inheritance. In fact, the beginning of Israel's decline dates from David's death in 963 BC. Although Israel was at the height of glory when Solomon came to power, it was a glory which could continue only through increase, through continuous effort and care—it required to be nursed and not merely accepted. And Solomon was incapable of this.

As a king he had, and still has, a reputation for extraordinary wisdom and especially for psychological insight. There are many stories and anecdotes about his perspicacity. At the same time, he has also become a byword for luxury and extravagance.

He waged no wars, but nevertheless maintained an imposing army and armoury, and built an entire town expressly to house his horses and chariots. Building was, indeed, his ruling interest. He transformed Jerusalem from a garrison and governmental town into the cultural centre of Israel. His palace alone, which was separated by a wall from the rest of the city, was as large as the Jerusalem of his father's time. The Temple stood in the middle of the palace area and was the noblest house of God ever to be erected in Canaan. Solomon also built enormous warehouses, granaries, and silos which housed huge stores mainly for the court's use. And he surrounded himself with a lavish harem, whose principal attraction was an Egyptian princess. These undertakings naturally cost exorbitant sums of money. They were financed by dividing the country into separate tax-regions and setting over each a tax-collector whose sole duty was to wring regular contributions in money, and manpower for the building projects, from the region. The chief of the tax-collectors was also called 'Head of Forced Labour', which gives a clue to the methods of recruitment practised under Solomon's rule.

The noblest house of God *ever to be erected in Canaan was the great Temple built by Solomon. A 3rd-century* AD *wall painting in the synagogue of Dura Europos.*

The political growth of Israel was accompanied by a growth in the arts and learning. Culture no longer found its centre in the evening assembly at the town gate; it moved to the city and especially to the capital. Education became an end in itself, and the importance of the arts can be seen in the literature of that time.

Until then the writings of the Jews had been sparse and functional. There had been the ancient stories of the Patriarchs in the days before Israel had possessed a country of her own; a few old songs like the Song of Lamech (Genesis 4, 23–24), the Songs of Miriam (Exodus 15, 21) the Well (Numbers 21, 17–18), and Heshbon (Numbers 21, 27–29). During the occupation of Canaan there had been the genealogies of the Judges (Judges 10, 1–5; 12, 7–15), and the stories of their achievements which fill the greater part of the Book of Judges. The supreme literary work, which was also the legal code and, almost, the *raison d'être* of Israel, the Ten Commandments (Exodus 20, 1–17), must have been written in the time of the Judges. Under David, literature took on a new lease of life and comprehensive accounts of the wars were written, together with all the names and deeds of David's followers, the story of the Ark, and the life of Saul. These fill the two Books of Samuel.

The first lyrical writings were the Psalms of David. It is astonishing, in these days of specialization, that a soldier-diplomat could have written these poems, which rank among the finest ever to be offered to the glory of God. A large number of them may have been composed by David himself, and they may all have been written down for posterity during his lifetime.

There is a vast difference between the ancient writings and those of David's time. The first are religious documents or pleasant entertainment; the second are serious history. The technique of historical writing, making an exact record of verified facts, came to full flower under Solomon. The king had first one, and then two scribes, and these were by no means merely private secretaries but the highest officials in the state. Their duty was to record the activities of the king and his house. Just as Tacitus later wrote the chronicles of the Roman emperors, so, with equal attention to detail and relish for scandal, Solomon's scribes noted down the events of his empire. Parts of their chronicles are to be found in Samuel I and II.

Various proverbs and short biographies also date from this time, and it was then too that several traditional stories, such as that of the Creation, were given a permanent record. Two different versions of the Creation stories were preserved—one under David and the other under his son. There are small differences between these, differences stemming from the varying styles, temperaments, and viewpoints of the two writers. But it is remarkable how trifling these variations are when it is remembered that the story had been passed on by oral tradition only.

King Solomon's scribes *were important officials of state, and by no means mere secretaries. T.* *must often have been the case in an age of royal illiteracy. The relief opposite shows the Hittite k.* *Bar-rakab, whose scribe stands before the throne, respectful, but clearly aware of his status and worth.*

Solomon died in 929 BC and the history of the Jews began to plunge towards catastrophe. The rot which had started under Solomon festered until it was an all-pervading infection. Once more, the nation divided into the two kingdoms of Israel and Judah.

Judah believed that the throne was reserved to the house of David, and crowned Solomon's son, Rehoboam, king after Solomon's death. Rehoboam considered himself king over all Israel, but the northern tribes thought otherwise: 'What portion have we in David? Have we inheritance in the son of Jesse?' they cried, and in their envy they rejected the one person who could have saved them. They gathered in Shechem and chose Jeroboam as their king, thus dividing the nation and annulling David's great achievement.

Unlike the kings of Judah, Jeroboam had no tradition of hereditary monarchy behind him, but he contrived to ensure the succession of his son, Nadab, who, however, had no sooner been
crowned than he was murdered by a pretender to the throne,
Baasha. In his turn, Baasha was murdered by a high official of state
who won possession of the throne for seven days. Then disorder
broke loose, there was a time of chaos, and, as is usual in such
situations, the most ruthless man rose to the top. This was Omri, of
whose early life little is known; his name sounds Hebraic, and so
does that of his son, Ahab. Order of a sort was established under
the harsh discipline of Omri's house, who held the throne for thirty
years. But they in their turn were deposed by Jehu, who dealt with
them brutally. And so it went on—murder and assassination,
intrigue and revolt became the customary methods of the rulers of
Israel or those who aspired to the crown. This state of affairs lasted
for 200 years, interrupted only now and then by a brief interval of
peace under a more capable king, such as Jeroboam II who reigned
from 783 to 743. Of the eighteen kings who reigned during those
disordered centuries, only two died a natural death; all the others
were murdered.

Israel's death-blow was now struck. Unregarded by the rest of
the world, the old Assyrian empire had been re-emerging from
obscurity. In 745 BC the crown was assumed by King Tiglath-
pileser III, a man of undeviating purpose and animal ferocity. He
raised a powerful army of warriors whom he trained in the old
Assyrian military ways, and then set out on a campaign of conquest. Canaan was only one stage on the road to world-mastery.

At first Israel bought Assyrian favour with a voluntary tribute,
the yearly payment of an enormous sum of money. This continued
under Shalmanazar V, but then King Hosea, irked by this financial
burden, discontinued payments. He formed a secret alliance with
Egypt and hoped with this help to dislodge the Assyrians' hold on

his country. He 'brought no present to the king of Assyria, as he had done year by year'. Shalmanazar immediately attacked, occupied Israel, and imprisoned Hosea. The town of Samaria alone kept up a bitter resistance for three years, and Shalmanazar never managed to break it down. He died in 723. His successor continued the campaign and eventually led his troops into Samaria. Israel was more or less annihilated. The upper classes, the educated stratum of the people, were deported to Mesopotamia and their place was taken by Babylonians and Syrians. Israel was conquered, and its people were ruled by foreigners. 'In the ninth year of Hosea the king of Assyria took Samaria, and carried Israel away into Assyria, and placed them in Halah and in Habor by the river of Gozan; and in the cities of the Medes.'

Judah lasted longer. It too paid a tribute to Tiglath-pileser, but it was prudent enough to take no part in Hosea's rebellion, and consequently it escaped the first onrush of the Assyrian lust for power.

The only picture of an Israelite king *is on an obelisk from Nimrud (841 BC). In it Jehu, king of Israel, is doing obeisance to his overlord and protector, Shalmanazar III of Assyria.*

In 669 Ashurbanipal ascended the throne. He was the last male heir of the Assyrian royal house, and his bent was for scholarship rather than for warfare. He was the man who had a library of 20,000 clay tablets, and he was also a devoted student of dead languages, history, science, and music. But these gentler arts did not help him to prevent decay in his own country. Babylon, which still belonged to the Assyrian empire, revolted. Ashurbanipal sent his general Nabopolazar with an army to quell the uprising, but Nabopolazar turned traitor and joined the rebels. He formed an alliance with the Medes and rapidly conquered all Assyria. Power passed into the hands of the Babylonians.

It was the newly formed Babylonian empire which finally over-came Judah when its king was Josiah, a clever and energetic man who saw his opportunity in Assyria's decline. He re-affirmed his own rulership, began social reforms, and, above all, tried to eliminate the heathen elements which had crept into the religion of the Jews. A new era seemed to be dawning for Judah, but it was a false dawn. In 609 there was a trial of strength at Megiddo between Josiah and the Egyptian king Necho. Josiah was killed early in the battle. From then on all hope was lost; Judah was conquered for a few years by the Egyptians and then passed into the hands of the Babylonians, the principal enemy. Nabopalazar's successor, Nebu-chadnezzar, had no intention of remaining a passive spectator of events in the west. In due course he entered Canaan at the head of a well-equipped army and swept the Egyptians out of Judah. Not that it made any difference to the Hebrews whether their conquerors were Egyptians or Babylonians. Their land no longer belonged to them.

Nebuchadnezzar set up Josiah's son, Joachim, as puppet-king over the conquered territory on condition that he paid a yearly tribute. Joachim was an unworthy successor to his father. He was cruel, greedy, and brutal, and concerned, above all, with his own comfort and the construction of his luxurious palace. Although he must have been fully aware of the extent to which he was under

Babylon's thumb, he eventually did the very thing that had led to Israel's downfall: he ceased to pay tribute to Babylon and tried to intrigue against her.

This was in 602 BC. Joachim imagined he had lulled Babylon into indifference and that he was in a fair way to achieve his objective. But when Nebuchadnezzar heard of the plot, Joachim was swiftly undeceived. In 598 a Babylonian army camped before Jerusalem and announced it had come 'to chastise Joachim'. The King of Judah escaped punishment because he was already dead. His 18-year-old son, Joachin, inherited only a beleaguered, condemned city. He ruled for three months before the Babylonian army burst into the town, the palace, and the Temple. Retribution, how-

A unique source of information on the Captivity is the Babylonian Chronicle, a set of clay tablets inscribed in cuneiform, much of which has only recently been published in translation. This piece itemizes rations allocated to prisoners, among whom the young ex-king Joachin is mentioned.

ever, was relatively mild. The Temple, of course, was ransacked, and the king and his highest officials were deported, according to ancient custom. 'He carried away all Jerusalem, and all the princes, and the mighty men of valour, even ten thousand captives, and all the craftsmen and smiths: none remained, save the poorest sort of the people of the land.' Nebuchadnezzar set Joachin's uncle, Zedekiah, on the throne. But Joachin himself was treated indulgently; he was allowed to live comfortably in Babylon, where he passed the remainder of his life. Zedekiah saw the final destruction of Jerusalem. He was foolish enough to plot a rebellion during the first years of his puppet-reign and to try to make another alliance with Egypt. This time Nebuchadnezzar showed no mercy.

In 587 he conquered Jerusalem once again and this time the destruction was total. The palace walls were pulled down, the houses demolished, the Temple dismantled and razed to the ground. Paralysed by fear, shame, and distress, the inhabitants seemed powerless—cowering before the judgment of God. Zedekiah was brought before Nebuchadnezzar and was forced to look on while his sons were executed. Then his eyes were put out and he was led, in chains, to Babylon. And this time the punishment fell not only on the ruling classes but on the whole of the people. Israel went into exile and was held in captivity by the Babylonians. Its history as an independent state was closed, not to be reopened until AD 1948 when the modern state was founded.

From Solomon's death until the destruction of Jerusalem, Canaan experienced little but fighting, political muddle, rebellion and disorder; but as a literary period these years of unrest were fruitful. The histories of Ahab, Jehu, and Micah (Kings I and II) were compiled, the various stories about Elijah and Elisha were collected, more psalms were composed, and old documents, literary sources from the reigns of David and Solomon, were studied and collated.

Most important of all, the Law was carefully edited during Josiah's reign. It was, and still is, the core of Hebrew thinking and teaching, and it contained the Ten Commandments, along with a mass of priestly and religious laws which had sprung up around them. Over the centuries it had been remoulded again and again, not only with the aim of extending its scope and explaining its obscurities, but also to purify it of all that was foreign to its original intention when it had been conceived in the Mosaic period. Under Josiah a particularly valuable version of this book was discovered in the Temple; scholars used this precious 'master copy' to remove later accretions from the Law. This was the last new version of the Law; since then its content has remained unchanged.

Consequently, this period was both an end and a beginning—the end of the independence and national status of a small Near Eastern people, and the beginning of a great task which was to occupy scholars through the ages right up to the present day: the task of communicating the Bible's message as exactly and faithfully as possible.

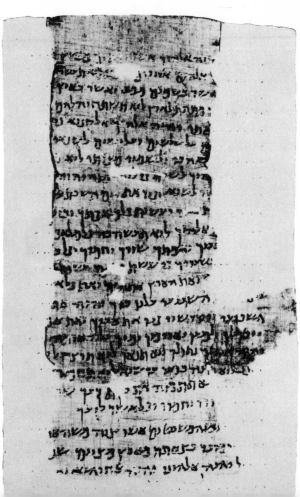

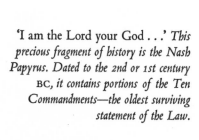

'I am the Lord your God . . .' *This precious fragment of history is the Nash Papyrus. Dated to the 2nd or 1st century* BC, *it contains portions of the Ten Commandments—the oldest surviving statement of the Law.*

5

THE LAW AND THE PROPHETS

The age of the kings was not only remarkable for political troubles: it also bred the Prophets, who made a new and important contribution to Jewish literature.

Who and what were the Prophets? It is important to grasp that they were not soothsayers, foretellers of the future, like the witch of Endor whom Saul had consulted before his last battle. Such people of course, had always existed, and have continued to exist, from the mysterious oracles of ancient Greece to the tea-leaf-readers, palmists, and astrologers of the present day. Man has always been obsessed by the desire to find out what will happen to him in the future, but the prophets of the Old Testament did not set out to gratify this desire. They were men who, impelled by the spirit of God within them, taught, advised, and admonished whoever would listen. Occasionally their sayings dealt with the future—as when Isaiah predicted the judgment of God and the fall of Jerusalem—but this was merely incidental to their prime purpose of opening the eyes of the people and making plain God's will.

There had been prophets of this kind in Israel ever since the settlement in Canaan. Deborah was a prophetess; Samuel, the man who anointed Israel's first king, later became a prophet; and, of course, Elijah and Elisha were also prophets of a kind. But the era of the 'classic' prophets, the *nevyim*, as they are called in Hebrew, began only with Israel's decline.

Amos was the first writer whose work was specifically called a 'prophetic book'. In spite of this, he did not look upon himself as a 'prophet', a man set apart from his people, but constantly emphasized his lowly, peasant origin. He was a shepherd and mulberry-grower whose only qualification for preaching was that he was driven to do so by an irresistible inner urge. He lived and worked under Jeroboam II, during a calm between two storms, a breathing-space when Israel's trade and industry were flourishing. Unfortunately extravagance, greed, trickery, and unrighteousness were flourishing also. These were Amos's targets: he preached goodwill, justice, social responsibility, and especially the doctrine that God is the God of all men, that His jurisdiction extends over all the world. 'For lo, I will command, and I will sift the house of Israel among all nations, like as corn is sifted in a sieve.'

Hosea, the one prophet who came from the north of the country, lived at about the same time as Amos, but otherwise there is little resemblance between the two men. Painful circumstances led to Hosea becoming a prophet. He had married a woman called Gomer who had proved to be a whore; from the pain and sorrow of this unhappy marriage he had won an insight which he was on fire to pass on to others. He preached the love of God—that all sins can be expiated through God's mercy. He was the first prophet to envisage not only a God of wrath and vengeance but also a loving and forgiving Father.

In 775 BC, at about the time when the first Olympic Games were being celebrated in Athens, the prophet Isaiah was born in Jerusalem. He was the first of the three great prophets—Isaiah, Jeremiah, and Ezekiel—whose words were to span the world and constitute the most profound message which had yet sprung from human

mouth. He was neither uneducated, like Amos, nor unhappy, like Hosea. On the contrary, he was a doctor, or perhaps a court-scribe, in the capital, an educated man who was widely esteemed for his wisdom. He attracted a circle of devoted pupils round him, rather like the Greek philosophers. But he lived in a dangerous age. The shadow of Assyria fell across Israel, and cruel rulers, such as Tiglath-pileser, Sargon, and Sennacherib, dominated its people's thoughts. Israel was demoralized, waiting only for the death-blow.

Isaiah preached divine retribution. 'A sinful nation, a people laden with iniquity, a seed of evildoers, children that are corruptors: they have forsaken the Lord, they have provoked the Holy One of Israel unto anger. . . .' Israel had brought punishment on herself by her evil ways, her idol-worship, her greed, and her pride. There was only one hope of salvation—reform and repentance, obedience to God and his commandments. Although he lived to be over seventy, Isaiah never ceased to rally his people, to warn them, rouse them, plead with them. Nevertheless he could not avert the dangers he foresaw; and the second great prophet, Jeremiah, was to experience them in person.

Jeremiah preached during some of Israel's unhappiest years. Like Isaiah, he stressed Israel's guilt, and he lived to see, what he had earlier predicted, the destruction of Jerusalem, the desecration of the Temple, and the taking of the Jews into captivity. After the mass deportation he wrote no more, and we know nothing of his later life and of his death. It is probable that he too was carried away to Babylon.

The conquests of Sennacherib *are set forth in the histories of his reign, such as the inscribed clay cylinder opposite, which tells of his campaigns against the Babylonians and the Medes. They are also glorified in the reliefs of Khorsabad, in one of which (right) two Assyrian scribes are reckoning enemy casualties.*

'The vision of Isaiah *the son of Amoz, which he saw concerning Judah and Jerusalem.' The oldest complete manuscript of any book of the Bible is this scroll of Isaiah, written in the 1st or 2nd century* BC *and*

discovered in 1947 in a cave near the Dead Sea. On the second line of the only fully visible column are the words 'The voice of him that crieth in the wilderness, Prepare ye the way of the Lord' (40: 3).

The third great prophet, Ezekiel, was born while the Hebrews were still in Israel. He first preached in Jerusalem where, like his contemporary, Jeremiah, he tried to warn and threaten his people into action before it was too late. But after the catastrophe his tone changed; he no longer threatened but comforted, and promised his compatriots, now homeless, oppressed, and deprived of all rights, that they would one day come into their own again, find a new home, and attain happiness. 'A new heart also will I give you, and a new spirit will I put within you.'

Ezekiel's is the most unified and well planned of the prophetic books. He was a born writer. Nevertheless, his writings are some-times thought to be among the most difficult in the Old Testament. When Rabbi Hanania later made a commentary on Ezekiel he is said to have burned three hundred jugs of midnight oil before com-pleting the work.

Parts of the prophetic books were not written down during the lifetime of the prophets concerned; they were passed on orally and later put together from surviving memories. The Jews in exile had no opportunity to continue their literature. They could record only small portions in secret and had to leave it to posterity to arrange these in correct order. Sometimes names were forgotten; Isaiah 40–55, for instance, is known to have been written by another prophet whose name has been lost. Scholars call him 'deutero-Isaiah', that is, the second Isaiah. An exile in Babylon, he openly predicted its fall, which took place in 539 BC. The Persian king, Cyrus, defeated the Babylonians and in so doing put an end both to the rule of Babylon and the captivity of the Jews. Their years of longing for home and for the holy city of Jerusalem, their weeping 'by the waters of Babylon', were over. Two years later they returned to their own country.

The last eleven chapters of Isaiah, which were probably written after the return to Jerusalem, are by yet a third hand, who may have been a disciple of deutero-Isaiah. Scholars call him 'trito-Isaiah' (the third Isaiah).

'By the waters of Babylon *we sat down and wept.' The picture opposite shows the ruins of* Ishtar Gate quarter of Babylon. In 539 BC the city surrendered without a fight to Cyrus, king of Persians, who ended the Captivity and returned the Jews to their homeland. The victory is recorded the Cylinder of Cyrus (below

Zerubbabel, the man whom Cyrus selected to be the new king of Israel, was ready to ascend the throne in Jerusalem, but he found nothing there except ruin and desolation. Everything had to be rebuilt. Luckily Cyrus, who looked on himself as the liberator of the Jews and wanted to compensate them for the wrongs they had suffered, agreed to act as patron of the reconstruction programme. He ordered the Temple to be rebuilt on Mount Zion and promised to finance the work.

The driving spirit behind the rebuilding of the Temple was another prophet, Haggai, who compiled an exact factual account of how the work was done. After Haggai there were others—Zechariah, Malachi, and many more whose names have been forgotten. But, like earlier prophets, such as Habakkuk, Zephaniah, Jonah, Obadiah, and Micah, they never measured up to Isaiah, Jeremiah, or Ezekiel. All the same, the records of their lives were, and still are, immensely important as documents of man's relationship with God. Two of them stand out above the rest—Nehemiah and Ezra.

Nehemiah came to Jerusalem in 445 BC, having been appointed governor of the whole province of Judah by the Persian king. That part of the country which had been Israel was now known as the Province of Samaria; it was small in comparison with the neighbouring province of Judah, which became the only real heir of the old Israelite traditions. Enmity grew up between the two provinces, and by the time Jesus was preaching it was considered a scandal in Judah that he should set foot on Samarian soil.

Nehemiah began the work of rebuilding Jerusalem and, under the protection of the King of Persia, made good progress. His governorship saw the city rebuilt, its walls laid out afresh, and its Temple reopened. He persuaded Cyrus to give back those treasures to the Temple that had been looted by the Babylonians. He organized transport for the return of his people from Babylon, and he began a programme of legal reform. Moreover, he kept an exact account of all his activities, and this has become the one completely reliable source of information we have about the life of the Jews after their return from captivity.

The Book of Nehemiah did not take on the form it has in the Bible until one hundred years later, in the middle of the fourth century BC, and its final editor is unknown. But Nehemiah's accounts are its core; the later author made merely a few additions and emendations.

While Nehemiah was reorganizing secular life, Ezra was revitalizing religion. It was he who gave the Jews their comprehensive legal code which still governs their daily life and ritual. He was the head of the religious community in Jerusalem, the chief priest, and the finest scholar. His official title defines his functions: 'Scribe and Guardian of the Law of the God of Heaven'. In modern terms he might be called 'Under-Secretary of State for Church Affairs in the Persian Government'.

The seat of Moses was the special seat set up in the synagogue for the principal teacher of the Law, such as Ezra was after the return from the Captivity. The one illustrated here was found in the ruins of a synagogue, probably of the 3rd century AD, near Capernaum.

Cyrus was the protector of the Jews even in religious matters. It is only fair to point out that although the Persians were nominally 'masters' of the Jews, they exercised their power with restraint and even benevolence. The Persians are perhaps the only example in history of a people who called themselves 'liberators' really being liberators and not oppressors. Until recently scholarship has been unjust to the Persians. Sympathy with the ancient Greeks and their civilization prompted many scholars to dismiss the Persians as 'barbarians'—rough, brutal, and uneducated. Yet the Jews suffered far less under the Persians than under the 'cultured' Greeks.

Like the Book of Nehemiah, Ezra's account of his actions was later re-edited. It is impossible to say how Nehemiah and Ezra actually wrote, because their editor translated their work into Aramaic, a language which gradually replaced Hebrew in Canaan. Another change took place at this time; Canaan began to be called Palestine. How and why this particular name came to be used is obscure, since the word means 'Land of the Philistines' and the Philistines were surely the last people to be identified with the country.

But the changes in language and name were both trivial beside the really radical change which overtook the Hebrews in the first century after the Exile. They ceased to be known as 'the Children of Israel' and became 'the Jews'.

It came about in this way. Ezra created the Law—not a new kind of law, since it still derived from God's commandments on Sinai, but a new conception of the traditional Law. The main stress was no longer on the precepts of the one merciful all-powerful God, but on the exact fulfilment of every clause, every word of the thousands of prescriptions and proscriptions. It is not surprising that in these circumstances the priests, who alone had a firm grasp of the legal code, became overweening. It was their task to see that every rule was carried out, that the Day of Rest was scrupulously kept, that prayers were offered when they ought to be, that the appointed festivals were celebrated in the exact form in which they were laid

As an everyday language, *Aramaic gradually replaced Hebrew in the centuries after the Exile, though Hebrew remained the language of the synagogue. These pot-handles are stamped with the word 'Hebron' in Aramaic.*

down. Above all, they had to make sure that the law forbidding mixed marriages was not broken. It was the beginning of theology, a difficult branch of learning confined to the educated few, as distinct from religion, the animating spirit of the common people.

Although there were synagogues in several towns, sacrifices were made only in Jerusalem, which was once more the religious centre of the country. And for the first time political and religious unity depended not on the common origins and blood-relationship of all the people, but on the fact of belonging to the Jewish community. For the first time, 'conversion' was possible; a man could become a Jew whether he was descended from the original tribes or not. The Jewish 'community' had taken the place of 'the *Children* of Israel'. Judaism, a religion as distinct from a racial description, had been born.

The positive side of the strict rule of the priests was that the holy scriptures were more carefully studied than ever before. In the centuries which followed the Exile, the new Books of Nehemiah and Ezra were written, more psalms were added to those already in existence, the two magnificent poems, the Book of Job and the Song of Solomon, were composed, and the history of David's reign was rewritten in the Book of Chronicles. In addition, more editing was done on the Pentateuch, or 'Torah' as it was now called—the five books of Moses which make up the Law. These were studied over and over again through the years. Generations of priests and scholars brooded over them, compared different manuscripts, interpreted them, and made commentaries on doubtful words. It was a monumental work, and present-day scholars are fully aware of the debt they owe these zealots who, many of them, devoted their whole lives to this one task.

About 330 BC the canon of the Pentateuch was completed. Almost a thousand years had passed since the first words of it had been scratched on clay tablets; now every synagogue possessed its own parchment scroll of the Law, the complete 'Torah'.

No sooner had this been achieved than the Persian Empire collapsed, defeated by Alexander the Great, who was at that time extending his conquests to Asia Minor, Egypt, Mesopotamia, and Palestine. Many soldiers have been called 'the greatest general of all time'; Alexander is one of the few men with a real claim to the title. Although he died when he was only thirty-three, he had already conquered half the world. After his death there were struggles for power among his successors, the Diadochi (captains). The Seleucids, a Syrian dynasty, won possession of the north and ruled from Antioch, 'Seleucia which is by the sea', a kingdom which extended from Thrace to the borders of India; the Ptolemies annexed the south and made Egypt their base. Once more the Jews had overlords.

The five books of Moses *reached their final, canonical form about 330 BC, almost a thousand years after their first words had been scratched on clay tablets. They were the Torah, the Law, which for ever after, written on parchment, has been the central possession of every synagogue. Here are parts of the fifth and sixth chapters of Leviticus, written in the 10th century* AD. *Opposite: a modern rabbi reads from the Torah—still devoutly preserved in its special container, and still, in an age of mass-production, written by hand on a parchment scroll.*

Alexander the Great (*left, on a Macedonian silver coin*) founded and gave his name to Alexandria, at the mouth of the Nile. This great city (*modern air view, below*) was planned as the cultural centre of the southern world, where all that was best in Greek learning would be preserved and fostered.

The Ptolemies ruled from Alexandria, the Egyptian town which had been founded by Alexander. Here lived 150,000 Greeks as well as Egyptians, Semites, Africans, and Parthians. From the beginning, Alexandria was planned as a capital and it became the cultural centre of the southern world, just as Athens and, later, Rome were to become the cultural centres of Europe. In it was founded the *Museion*, a sort of academy with a large library; in it worked great philosophers and scientists, mathematicians and writers—Apollonius and Eratosthenes, Euclid and Archimedes, Herophilus and Erasistratos, Theocritus and Zenodotus. In it poems were written and statues were sculpted. It became the home of the most brilliant Greek learning, the most elevated Greek thought, the most polished Greek wit. And, curiously enough, this monument to Hellenism

The Bible in Greek, *one of the most important steps in the spread of the scriptures through the world, first took shape in Alexandria. These shreds of papyrus contain part of Deuteronomy in Greek, written in the 2nd century* AD.

was to play a very important part in the dissemination of the Holy Scriptures of the Jews; for it was here that the first of all the many Bible translations, the Septuagint, was made.

Alexander, and after him Ptolemy, were both democratic rulers, allowing equal rights to every citizen. Both were favourably disposed towards the Jews, so that a large Jewish colony grew up in Alexandria. Its members tried to live strictly according to Ezra's code. They built a synagogue and celebrated all the festivals in their seasons. Nevertheless, the colony could not escape Greek influence altogether, and the first thing that they learned from it was the Greek language. After a time most Jews could no longer read the Torah in the original Hebrew, and so they determined to have it translated into Greek.

It is always impossible to be sure what would have happened if, at any given moment, history had taken a different course, but one thing is certain: if this translation of the Pentateuch had not been made, our Bible of today would have been full of omissions and errors. The importance which was attached to this translation even at that time can be seen from the fact that a book was written about the actual work of translating, by a man called Aristeas of Alexandria. Unfortunately his account is more striking than factual. He describes sensationally how Ptolemy II Philadelphus set the work afoot because without it his library would not be complete; how he ordered seventy-two Jewish scholars to be shut up in a monastery by the sea and to undertake the translation separately, each without reference to his neighbour; how, when all had finished, it was found that their translations tallied exactly, word for word.

The truth is probably that the few Alexandrian scholars who could still speak Hebrew undertook to translate the Torah for the community as a whole. Their work was certainly accurate to an unusual degree. As was mentioned earlier, the Hebrew script had only consonants; the Hebrew was obliged to supply the vowels according to the sense. In Greek, however, the words had to be written out in full, and this offered thousands of opportunities for error. It was fortunate that these first translators, on whom depended all future translations, were still expert in Hebrew.

It is from Aristeas's romantic story that the translation these scholars made derives its name. His contemporaries were so impressed with it that they called the new Greek Scriptures after his fictional seventy-two scholars—'The Seventy' or, in Latin, 'The Septuagint'. Nowadays this name is used in a wider sense, as the first Greek translation of the Old Testament—a work which was completed not long after the translation of the Pentateuch.

While the Law was being translated abroad, more original writings were appearing in Palestine—the Book of Esther, a lively and much embroidered account of an historical incident, and the older parts of the Book of Daniel, another memory of the horrors of Exile.

The Greek influence *on Jewish practice is seen in this silver coin of Bar-Kochba. Greek columns adorn the front of a synagogue, but within it the scrolls of the Law are still kept in the traditional tabernacle.*

Suddenly, history took a turn which was to have a profound influence on the Scriptures. In 198 BC the Seleucids swept down from Antioch in the north and seized Palestine from the Ptolemies. Ptolemy had always considered the Jews to have equal rights with his other subjects, and perhaps had known and esteemed their writings. All this changed under the Seleucids. At first, Antiochus the Great handled the Jews tactfully and tried to win their loyalty. But his son Seleucos was more oppressive, and Antiochus IV Epiphanes, brother and successor of Seleucos, brought events to a head. This emperor, described by contemporary writers as kindly and foolish, and by the historian Polybius re-named Epimanes, 'the mad', neither understood nor sympathized with the Jewish religion and way of life. In 170 BC he marched on Jerusalem, plundered the Temple treasury and installed a viceroy to complete the work of destruction. The religion of the Jews was to be completely rooted out, the holy writings burnt, and the worship of Jehovah declared illegal. It was decreed that the only god to be

worshipped in the holy place was to be the Greek god Zeus, to whom an altar was erected in the Temple. The first sacrifice to Zeus in the Temple of Jerusalem took place in December 168.

After that the impossible happened. The tiny Jewish nation, lacking freedom and power, political influence and a military machine, rose up against the all-powerful Greeks. The indignation of the Jews at the desecration of their holiest places, and the mocking at their faith and their Scriptures, drove them to an act that ought to have ended in mass suicide. But it did not. In 166 BC a rebellion broke out. This was at first led by a priest, Mattathias, and later by his son Judas Maccabaeus—'the hammer'. Against all expectations, the Jews held their own.

Judas Maccabaeus was idolized as the liberator of his people. Two years after the rebellion began, the religion of Jehovah was once again practised by the Jews, and Zeus was ejected from God's Temple. Fighting, however, still went on, even after Judas's death in 160 BC. His work was continued by his brothers, and the reign of the Maccabaean family, or Hasmonaeans as they were called in

The destruction of the Temple *in 170 BC at the orders of Antiochus the Mad ended the era of toleration which the Jews had enjoyed under the Ptolemies. The painting opposite, from the synagogue of Dura Europos, shows the treasures of the Temple lying scattered in the street, while the tabernacle on its wheeled carriage is removed to safety.* Right: *a 3rd-century BC bronze statue of Zeus, to whose worship the plundered Temple was converted. This final profanation sparked off the revolt of the Maccabees.*

Hebrew, began. This was to be the last time that the Jews governed themselves for two thousand years. Even then, the broad lines of destiny were laid down from outside in the north, in Greece and Rome. Eventually this small amount of power was taken out of their hands; Rome took Palestine in 63 BC, and in 37 BC the family of the Maccabaeans was exterminated by Antony's order, at the request of Herod. The last of this line of king-priests was called Mattathias, like the first one who had risen against the Greeks several generations earlier.

The time of the Maccabaeans was not only disturbed and disrupted from outside; rifts had begun to appear within the Jewish nation itself. A new sect, the Sadducees, had sprung up in opposition to the orthodox, strictly law-abiding, pedantic Pharisees. Among the Sadducees were many lawyers who had been strongly influenced by the Greeks and had introduced much essentially Hellenistic thought into their religious practice—it was, in fact, a liberal element within Judaism. And there were other sects too; the Essenes, for instance, who rejected both the hair-splitting of the Pharisees and the Hellenism of the Sadducees, and lived either as hermits or in withdrawn monasteries. Their influence was slight, but many of their writings survive.

The important documents of this period are first, the Book of Daniel, which gives an apocalyptic picture of the Maccabaean revolt; then there are the two Books of the Maccabees, which recount the struggle for freedom. These were among the last books of classical Jewish literature to be based on historical events, although other books were written at this time, such as 'The Story of Susanna', 'Bel and the Dragon', 'The Prayer of Manasses', and 'The Song of the Three Children'. None of these is included in the Protestant canon of the Bible, but they form part of a second book, the Apocrypha (from the Greek word *apokruphos*, originally meaning 'hidden' or 'concealed'). By AD 90 the Old Testament had taken the shape in which it is today known to Protestants (the Roman Catholic canon includes some of the Apocrypha). It contained

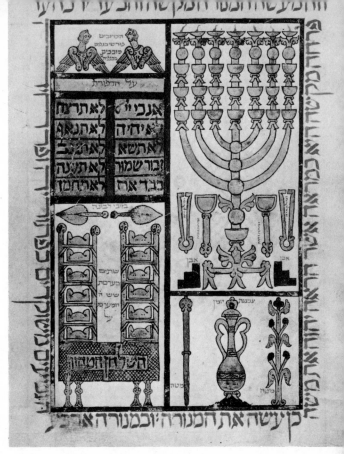

The outward signs of a faith founded on the Old Testament are seen on a Masoretic text of 1299: the seven-branched candlestick, the rod of Aaron, the Tables of the Law. These are symbols of Jewry today, as they were when the star shone over Bethlehem.

seventeen historical books, from Genesis to Esther, five teaching books, from Job to the Song of Songs, and sixteen prophetic books, from Isaiah to Malachi. The two Books of the Maccabees, the Wisdom of Solomon, and Ecclesiasticus were also included at this time, but have since been placed in the Apocrypha, a word now meaning 'spurious' or 'of less certain authenticity'.

The Old Testament is a monumental work, a book which was built up over a thousand years, written by hundreds of men, edited by thousands more, and read by millions. And yet it would not occupy its present position if it were not for an event which took place shortly after the extermination of the Maccabees. This event was a turning-point in history. It was the birth of the Saviour, Jesus Christ.

6

THE NEW TESTAMENT

Jesus was born when he was six or seven years old. This is not nonsense; the fact is the early calendar-makers put the date of his birth six or seven years too late, and thus placed the whole of our system of time-reckoning on a false premise. They, of course, lacked the means to be able to calculate dates accurately; it is only during the last century that historians have been able to fix satisfactorily Jesus's birth-year by using the dates of Augustus's reign, Cyrenius's governorship, and Herod's death as guides. As early as 1603 the German court astronomer, Johannes Kepler, had guessed that the famous conjunction of Jupiter and Saturn in 7 BC must have been identical with the 'Star of Bethlehem' and deduced that Jesus must have been born in that year. But Kepler's work was quickly forgotten, and the old error had become too deeply ingrained in people's minds to be easily erased.

But why do we need to look for evidence of Jesus's birth in astronomy, mathematics, and contemporary history? Surely the Bible itself should be our first source of information about the dates of Christ's life

The answer is that from this point of view, as a reliable account of dates, names, numbers, places, and events the New Testament is a sad disappointment. In the whole of the four Gospels, for instance, there are very few references to the world outside Jesus's intimate circle. One example is when Augustus and Cyrenius are mentioned during the account of Christ's birth, and another is when Pontius

Pilate is named in connection with the Crucifixion. Otherwise the attention of the Gospel writers is concentrated on the words and deeds of the man who came to save the world and on what could be called the 'Jesus-phenomenon'. Whereas the Old Testament cannot be fully understood without some knowledge of contemporary events in the world in which it grew up, world-history is scarcely important to the New Testament. If a large part of the Old Testament is history, most of the New is super-history. Its events and characters belong not to one time or one people but to eternity.

In contrast to the Old Testament, which covers the history of more than one thousand years and the rise and fall of many nations, kings, priests, saints, and sinners, the New Testament spans the events of less than a century. And it was not even a century characterized by memorable incidents. During the whole of that time there was one ruling power—Rome—whose civilization dominated everybody and everything.

Jesus Christ lived and died under the shadow of Rome, and the light which he gave to the world was often in danger of being extinguished by the city on the Tiber. But, for good or evil, Rome's power is the one thing that links the story of Christ to world-history; otherwise that story is something quite apart from temporality, independent of time and place and all that is mortal.

Under the massive shadow of Rome, *Jesus was born, grew to manhood, and died. At His birth, Augustus* (left) *was Emperor. Tiberius succeeded Augustus in* AD 14. *In the forty years following the Crucifixion, the Emperors were: Claudius (41–54), Nero (54–68), Vespasian (69–79).*

The first part of the New Testament to be written was neither a majestic chronicle nor an awe-inspiring proclamation; it was a simple letter. This was not even the kind of letter which famous authors have been known to write, intended more for posterity than for the person to whom it is addressed, but a genuine letter written with no other purpose than to communicate with people far away from the writer. The first lines ran: 'Paul, and Silvanus, and Timothy, unto the church of the Thessalonians, in God the Father and the Lord Jesus Christ, Grace to you and Peace.' This was a conventional letter-opening and comprised the writer's name, the addressee's name, and a stock greeting. Yet these words are nothing less than the first lines of the first documents of the New Testament, Paul's Epistle to the Thessalonians. It was written in AD 51, about eighteen years after Jesus's death.

The Crucifixion was a thing of the past, like the bewilderment into which it had at first plunged Christ's disciples. They had long ago joined together to follow the teaching of the Lord and had gone out into the world to preach, convert, and baptize. The disciples had already become the apostles and, here and there, the first small Christian communities were forming. Years had elapsed since the conversion of St Paul from an antichristian to the most brilliant teacher and interpreter of Christ's words.

The earliest picture of the Crucifixion *is on an engraved gem of the 4th century. At that time of persecution and despair, Christ was not represented as nailed to the Cross; to encourage his followers He was always shown alive. Here He is seen standing before the Cross, with His apostles beside Him.*

Paul, who was probably born in AD 10 and had begun adult life as a tent-maker, was a pure-blooded Jew, but he had a considerable knowledge of the Greek language, literature, and philosophy—Hellenism in general. He was also a tireless traveller. He was the first missionary, the first man deliberately to spread the gospel abroad. He went to Cyprus and Attalia, Tarsus, Iconium, Antioch in the interior of Asia Minor, Troy, Philippi, and Thessaly on the borders of Macedonia, Athens, Corinth, Crete, and Rome. Wherever he went he made converts to the new religion, the religion of God's Son. He was able to visit some Christian communities several times, but even when he could go only once he did not let his interest wane. It was to keep in touch with these young churches that he wrote his Epistles.

Paul was preaching in Corinth when he heard that grievances had arisen in the Thessalonian community which he had visited with Silvanus and Timothy some years earlier. The apostles were being accused of selfish motives, doubts were being cast on the doctrine of life after death, and, above all, Christians were suffering oppression. So Paul set to and dictated a letter addressed to the Christians in Thessaly. In it he explained, cautioned, comforted—all with the particular needs of the Thessalonians in mind. There was no question of publishing this letter for a wider public, and Paul was not writing as an author or chronicler. It was entirely a *lettre d'occasion*, and Paul was later to write many more like it, whenever his help and advice were needed. Yet even now, 1,900 years later, these letters are among the most profound and significant of Christian writings, second only to the words of Christ himself.

This first Epistle of AD 51 was followed a year later by a second and, in the same year, a third. These were to the community in Galatia. The Epistle to the Galatians is the most determined of all Paul's writings, stretched taut with a passionate defence of his right to go his own way, independent of all other men, as the apostle of Jesus Christ. It also shows clearly how far Paul was from being a

St Paul was the first missionary—*the first man to travel widely spreading the gospel and making converts. This 12th-century enamel from Winchester shows him disputing with the Greeks. 'Ye men of Athens', he said, 'I perceive that in all things ye are too superstitious.' (Acts 17, 22.)*

professional author. For instance, he obviously meant to come to a close in the fourth chapter after his evocation of the 'holy time' when the apostles and the Christian communities were in complete accord. Then a new thought darted into his mind—an illustration from the Old Testament—and he told the story of Abraham, Sarah, and Hagar. And then there come, like hammer-blows, the ringing words of his denunciation: 'Now the works of the flesh are manifest, which are these, adultery, fornication, uncleanness, lasciviousness, idolatry, witchcraft, hatred, variations, emulations, wrath, strife, seditions, heresies, envyings, murders, drunkenness, revellings, and suchlike.' These are not the words of a polished writer who plans his work before he begins to write, but are those of a man who is telling his charges the unvarnished, undiminished truth, without regard for the literary consequences.

The two Epistles to the Corinthians, written in AD 57, are also strongly characteristic of Paul's mentality. When he wrote them he was in Ephesus and on his way to Macedonia. News of disputes in the Corinthian community which he himself had founded was brought to him—news that various factions had formed, some calling themselves followers of Paul, others followers of Peter or Apollo. Blood had been shed in these quarrels, and various novel ideas had sprung up. There had been an attempt to defend free love, and the Christian conceptions of married life and marital responsibility were in jeopardy. It was Paul's aim to reconcile these differences, untangle the confusions, and he set about the task as was his habit, without mincing his words. A clear picture of the first Christian communities emerges from what he wrote, a picture of confusion and dismay combined with fervent good intentions.

Paul was an inspired organizer who did not shirk the duty of bringing order out of chaos. It is difficult even to imagine the strength of conviction which must have sustained this small, delicate Jew from Tarsus, who never accomplished anything without rapidly seeing it undone by some bungler. Yet he never lost heart nor tired of recalling the strayed sheep to the flock. Paul's Epistles show a man of immense energy combined with wisdom and goodness and, above all, of strength of purpose.

Only once does the agony which he must have suffered show through his writing. This is in the second Epistle to the Corinthians, when he says: 'Out of much affliction and anguish of heart I wrote unto you with many tears.' Once again the style is utterly spontaneous. In the first part of the letter he defends himself passionately against the attacks which have been made on him, and then he gradually cools down and gives the Corinthians some concrete advice about a special tax-collection which he wishes his friend Titus of Corinth to make for Jerusalem. Then, suddenly, his painfully suppressed anger bursts out again and he attacks his opponents with renewed energy. He bitterly reminds the community of the hardships he has voluntarily taken on himself: 'Of

The sophisticated Athenians *must have found St Paul a very strange visitor.* '*And when they he of the resurrection of the dead, some mocked*' (*Acts 17, 32*)—*a scene that was illustrated by the illumina of a codex in the monastery of St Gallen in Switzerla*

ARGVMENTVM EPLE AD ROMANOS · PRESENS TEXTVS ·
HABET. MERITIS VT GRA DIFFERT. REDDENS CONCORDES
REBECCE VENTRE FREQVENTES·

PAVLVS

IVDEI ET GENTES

the Jews five times received I forty stripes save one. Thrice was I beaten with rods, once was I stoned, thrice I suffered shipwreck, a night and a day I have been in the deep; in journeyings often, in perils of waters, in perils of robbers, in perils by my own country-men, in perils by the heathen, in perils in the city, in perils in the wilderness, in perils in the sea, in perils among false brethren.' This is the one place where Paul really opens his heart and pours out the passion which must often have driven him to desperation. And his words had their effect. When he reached Corinth in AD 58 he found a chastened and improved flock.

Next he turned his attention to Rome, where there was a medium-sized Christian community. The Roman Epistle is entirely different in tone from those to the Corinthians and has been called 'the least letter-like of the Epistles'; it shows signs of having been carefully planned to give a comprehensive account of Christian doctrine.

Not long afterwards Paul went to Rome, but as a prisoner, not as a missionary. Even in prison he contrived to despatch four letters —to the Colossians, the Ephesians, the Philippians, and to his friend Philemon in Colossae who had gathered a small community around him from the members of his household. After Paul was released he may have undertaken more journeys, or he may, as some think, have been under police observation until he was re-arrested. In either event, it is doubtful whether he was the author of the Epistles to the Hebrews, Titus, and Timothy. When in AD 254 Origen, one of the early Fathers of the Church, was asked who was the author of the Epistle to the Hebrews he replied: 'God alone knows.'

The end of Paul's life is a mystery; even the date of his death is not known. All that can be said with certainty is that he was beheaded during the course of Nero's persecutions of the Christians.

Just as Paul was the most important of the missionaries, so his are the most important of the Epistles. Even the early Church recog-nized a distinction between Paul's Epistles and the so-called 'catholic Epistles', or joint letters, most of which are either written to a group of congregations or are not addressed to anyone in particular. The names of the authors are given as Peter, James, John, and Jude. None of these is as old as Paul's Epistles nor so marked by stylistic fervour, intellectual depth, and lucid beauty. One of the last Epistles to find a place in the New Testament was the 'Third Epistle of John'—a short letter from 'John the Elder' to his friend Caius, whose nationality is not disclosed. It was probably written in Ephesus around AD 100, but whether its author was the same man who wrote the first Epistle of John is not certain. But all these problems of date and place are matters for the specialist rather than

This portrait of St John, in an *Irish gospel of about* AD 800, *shows the evangelist holding in his right hand what seems to be a quill pen, dipped in a long, slender inkpot. This is some two hundred years earlier than any other drawing of pen and ink.*

for the general reader. It is not the writer who is important, whether he is Paul or John, but what he writes.

Externally, all the Epistles were alike. Each was written with a reed-pen on papyrus or, sometimes, parchment, which was then neatly rolled, put in a protective covering, and carried by the apostles' messengers along the roads which the Greek conquerors and Roman emperors had built for their military operations. Paul often employed a professional scribe to be his secretary, but he usually ended his letters with a greeting in his own hand. The Epistle to the Galatians alone has a longer ending, written by Paul himself, and he may even have written the whole Epistle.

As soon as the letters reached their recipients they began a new and exciting life of their own. The whole community read them, individually and in groups; they were passed from hand to hand, studied again and again, and finally copied. Since the word of the apostles was the greatest prize that any Christian community could possess, each wished to obtain copies of the Epistles; and so copies of all kinds were made—inaccurate copies, full of omissions and errors, hurriedly written out by eager young converts whose enthu-siasm outran their skill with the pen; and careful, copper-plate copies made by professional scribes whose livelihood depended on their accuracy and skill. In view of the intense hunger of the first Christian communities for anything relating to the new Gospel, and the way in which the copied Epistles were treasured and protected as though they were priceless jewels, it is surprising that a few disappeared entirely and left no trace except references to them in other writings. Paul, for example, wrote three, and possibly four, Epistles to the Corinthians, but only two are extant.

In this one instance there is a possible explanation of the loss. Paul had never toned down his language when deploring the dis-unity, sinfulness, and cruelty which were rife in Corinth, and it is possible that in the last Epistles he dealt even more harshly with the offenders. Naturally they were not proud of being denounced, and their shame may have induced them to suppress the letters.

Copied and re-copied and copied again, *the Gospels passed from hand to hand among the ea* *Christians. This one, found in Cairo in the early years of this century, is a complete set of the fo* *Gospels, written in Greek on parchment; the wooden covers are decorated with portraits of the evangeli*

The Epistles soon ceased to be letters in the strict sense of the term; they became general property, 'Holy Scriptures', appropriate to all men rather than the recipient to whom they were addressed. Contrariwise, the Gospels were never written for one group of people. They were composed as 'literature', to be read by everybody, studied, copied, and generally known. They were the 'good news' of the 'Word of God' (from the Old English *god spel*, 'good tidings').

The date of the first Gospel is not known. Some records of Jesus's teachings, set down in Aramaic, unlike the Epistles which were all written in Greek, may have been in existence by AD 50. Alas, they have been lost, if they ever existed. To us, now, it seems surprising that many years should have elapsed before the story of the Saviour was written down for posterity, but the people of that time looked on the matter differently. They were convinced that the end of the world was at hand. They took Jesus's words, 'Verily I say unto you, that there be some of them that stand here, which shall not taste of death, till they have seen the kingdom of God come with power', to mean that the end of the world would take place during that generation. The atmosphere was heavy with expectation of the return of the Lord and the coming of the kingdom of God. There was no need to write down Jesus's story for posterity; and, so far as the contemporary generation was concerned, there were enough men living who had witnessed his acts and heard his words to make a written record seem unnecessary. The apostles Peter, John, and James, men who had been Jesus's own pupils, were still preaching.

It was only when the hope of Christ's imminent return to earth began to fade, when the apostles began to meet with hatred and cruelty, and when those who had seen Jesus in the flesh began to die, that thought was given to preserving the Christian story in writing.

The first complete account of Jesus's life was written by Mark about AD 70. Mark was a Jew. Born in Jerusalem, he early adopted Christianity and followed the apostle Peter on his journey to Rome;

The four gospels *figure prominently in a mosaic of about* AD 450, *in honour of St·Laurence the mar*

MARCVS · LVCAS

MATTEVS · JOANN
ES

his account of Christ's life was based on what he himself had seen and what Peter had told him. He may also have been able to draw on the material written by the 'Hebrew' or 'Aramaic' Matthew, supposedly about AD 50. This Matthew was the first to write an account of the words and acts of Our Lord. Mark's style is concise, and he aims at an objective history without embellishment or personal emphasis. His one idiosyncrasy is the frequency of his allusions to Peter, and this is not surprising because he had been Peter's pupil and eager listener. He begins his Gospel with the appearance of John the Baptist, follows Christ into Galilee, tells some of the best-known of Jesus's parables and miracles, deals shortly with the quarrel with the Pharisees, relates the story of the Passion, and ends with the empty sepulchre. This ending comes in the eighth verse of the sixteenth chapter; the rest of the Gospel, from verse 9 to 20, was added later, possibly by a presbyter named Aristion, and does not appear in the earliest manuscripts. It seems unlikely that Mark himself stopped at this negative point; but if he ever added an epilogue it has been lost.

The second Gospel appeared shortly after Mark's. Its author was Matthew, called the 'Greek Matthew' to distinguish him from the 'Aramaic Matthew', though he was not a Greek but used the Greek language because it was then most widely understood. A Jew by birth, Matthew's writing differs considerably from Mark's. His Gospel begins with a long genealogical table of Jesus's lineage, and an account of his birth. It includes the Sermon on the Mount and, unlike Mark's, closes with the Resurrection. Matthew's prime purpose was to display Jesus as the fulfilment of the Law and the true Messiah of the Jews.

More is known about the third evangelist. Luke was not a Jew but a Gentile who had been converted to Christianity. He probably came from Asia Minor or Greece, and had certainly met Paul, if he did not actually accompany him on some of his mission journeys. He was a doctor by profession and an educated man who wrote for the educated, whether Jew or Gentile. He is the one evangelist

St Matthew's gospel, *though the first in the New Testament, was second to St Mark's in point of time. A 9th-century illumination shows Matthew writing his version of the story —the main purpose of which was to display Jesus as the long-prophesied Messiah.*

whose personality shows through his account which, incidentally, he dedicated to a friend named Theophilus, a rich and influential Roman whom he wished to convert. From the first the emphasis is laid on Jesus as the Christ, the Saviour of all men and all peoples. Luke is a poet, and his writing is always lucid and beautiful; his account of the Nativity has a particular tenderness and evocative power. Shortly after the appearance of his Gospel he wrote the Acts, the nearest approach in the New Testament to the historical books of the Old Testament, though it is scarcely history in our sense of the word. And even in the Acts Luke the man shines through his writing; much of the Acts is drawn from his own experience.

In this narrative he gives impressive accounts of the first Whit-Sunday, of the foundation of the first Christian community, of Peter's dramatic experience, and of Saul who later became known as Paul. Finally there are the journeys of Paul in all their variety. The reader is carried through the book almost in spite of himself, and it is only at the end that he realizes the skill which has gone into the writing. Luke was a consummate story-teller.

Scholars disagree about the date when Luke's Gospel was written. Some put it at AD 70; others assign it to 80–90; and a third school believe it to have been written in 100. But, even so, Luke was not the last evangelist. This was John, the most individualistic of the four. The first three books are sometimes called the 'Synoptic Gospels' because of their basically similar contents. The Gospel of St John, however, stands apart.

He begins: 'In the beginning was the Word, and the Word was with God, and the Word was God,' or, as the New English Bible translates this extremely difficult passage, 'When all things began, the Word already was. The Word dwelt with God, and what God was, the Word was.' Another recent translator, the Rev. J. B. Phillips, renders the statement this way: 'At the beginning God expressed himself. That personal expression, that word, was with God and was God, and he existed with God from the beginning.' But however it is translated, this opening marks John's Gospel as something quite different from the others. A philosophic generalization, it sets the tone for the whole book in which the story of Jesus is seen in a super-temporal context, a context where everything is reduced to its essence.

John has been accused of hating the Jews, but this view is now generally rejected. True, he represents the Jews as typical of those

'In the beginning was the Word.'
A richly decorated initial starts the
first chapter of the Gospel of St
John in the Latin Codex Aureus
of Echternach (late 10th-century).
This difficult philosophic statement
marks this gospel as quite different
from the other three: they simply
told the story, in basically similar
terms, whereas St John reduced it
to its philosophic essence and set it
in the context of eternity.

who refused to hear the Divine message, but this is only because the Jews, as God's chosen people, may be taken as representing all the peoples of the earth. The world's hostility to Christ is thus typified in his rejection by the Jews. This is probably the reason for the tradition that John was killed by the Jews, though in fact we have no certain knowledge about John's life. We do not know, to this day, who was the author of his Gospel. Was he, in fact, the John who was the son of Zebedee and reputed to be Jesus's favourite disciple? One of the Fathers of the Church, Ireneus, says: 'The last evangelist was John, the disciple of the Lord, who was close to his heart.' But another Father, Eusebius, writes of a 'presbyter called John'. From this it would appear that there were two men of the same name, one of whom was the disciple and the other the Elder of a community in Asia Minor. Which of them wrote the Gospel?

119

Some scholars say it cannot have been the apostle, who would have been at least one hundred years old when he wrote it. Others maintain that only the apostle, only a man who had actually experienced the events of which he wrote, could have written as John did. The first school replies that the apostle, a Galilean fisherman, could not have had the philosophic training which is evident in the Gospel. To this the opposing school retorts that the name of the author is actually mentioned in the Gospel. The last verse but one of the last chapter reads: 'This is the disciple which testifieth of these things, and wrote these things: and we know that his testimony is true.' But this is equally an argument on the other side, for John himself would not have written 'we know . . .' And so the problem remains unsolved.

On the whole, the pendulum of opinion seems to be swinging towards crediting the apostle John with the authorship of the Gospel. A piece of papyrus was found in 1934 which indicated that the book was in existence by AD 100. This makes it possible for the disciple to have written the fourth Gospel. But what does it matter who was the true author of a Gospel when the reality of his words is undisputed?

Who wrote the Gospel of St John? *We may never know for certain, but these fragments of papyrus, identified as part of the 18th chapter, prove that the book was written by AD 100, so the author may have been the apostle himself. This papyrus is the oldest existing manuscript of any part of the New Testament.*

'The third angel sounded, and there fell a great star from heaven, burning as it were a lamp ...' A 10th-century picture of the Apocalypse conveys vividly the nightmare, visionary quality of that astonishing book, the Revelation of St John.

INCIPIT EXPLANATIO SVPRASCRES ...

THE KEYS OF HELL AND OF DEATH

Whoever John was, he, or as some hold, still another John, wrote the Book known as Revelation. This is an astonishing work. Compounded of visions and nightmares, hot blood and sober thinking, it ranges over the whole cosmos from Heaven to Hell, from the terrors of the end of the world, to the mighty struggle between God the Word and the powers of darkness, to the Day of Judgment when all mankind, living and dead, shall be called before the throne of God to receive their final reward. This vivid pageant was probably written by John on the island of Patmos where he had been banished by the Emperor Domitian.

Revelation closes the New Testament cycle, the great cycle which reaches from the functional letters of the missionary apostles, through the Gospels, to this last dark tapestry which seems to have been woven by the light now of flashes of lightning heralding the end of the world and now of the glow of the new Jerusalem. The canon of the New Testament was closed soon after AD 100.

From the first, the Old Testament played almost as important a part in Christian thinking as the New. Jesus himself emphasized the importance of the Law and the Prophets, and the apostles frequently quoted from the ancient Scriptures and gave interpretations of these. The new Christian communities studied the synagogue scrolls minutely, seeking the word of God, mention of the Messiah, and, above all, a unifying line which would link all human history from the Creation to John's Revelation—a line which would bear witness to God's deep and eternal concern with Man, culminating in the sacrifice of His Son. That was what the Bible meant to the early Christians and that is still what it means to the Christian of today, whatever his Church, denomination or confession.

'And the earth shall be filled with the glory of God'

MARTYRS, MYTHS AND MARVELS

One hundred years after Jesus's birth there were Holy Scriptures in abundance but, as yet, no Bible. Before the emergence of the
Bible as we know it, the early Christian documents had to pass
through a number of stages.

We must understand that 'the Holy Scriptures' did not mean the
same thing to all the new Christian communities. Some books
were common to them all. Besides various long and sometimes
improvised prayers, all the Church services included readings from
the Psalms, the Prophets, and the Law, and such portions of the
Gospels and the Epistles as the congregation possessed. But alongside these generally acknowledged Scriptures there were many others
which some communities revered but others roundly repudiated.

These owed their existence to the intense hunger for spiritual
writings. Church leaders struggled and sacrificed to obtain such
scriptures for their flock. Men were ready to die for them if necessary.
Once a Roman legionary was found carrying a copy of the Gospels.
He was abruptly told to choose between death and renunciation of
his heresy. Unhesitatingly he chose death, and when his corpse was
later recovered the scroll of parchment was still clutched in his
stiffening fingers. Again, a Roman officer was seen with Paul's
Epistles. Because he was an officer of Caesar's empire, he was given
time to think and much good advice from his superiors. All in
vain. When it came to the simple choice between his life and the
Epistles, the officer chose the Epistles.

Thousands perished in the early days of the Christian Church, martyred for their belief. For hundreds of years, secular authorities of every kind clashed with the other-worldly stubbornness of Christian men and women, and in their often bloody conflict, saints and martyrs were born. One of the most famous, then and later, was King Edmund (left), put to death by Danish invaders for refusing to renounce his faith. St Kilian, 7th-century Irish missionary to Germany, and his companions were executed—all three, so tradition tells, with one sweep of the headsman's sword.

Thousands of Christians perished during the persecutions which harried the early Church. The scrolls owned by the dead were jumbled together and burned. The few survivors of the terror disappeared into hiding and took with them their treasured documents.

The lively demand for sacred books naturally produced its profiteers, who did a brisk trade in forged epistles, gospels, and other documents. One such forgery was a series of letters purporting to have been exchanged between Jesus and the king of Edessa, Abgar Uchomo. In these letters it was made out that the king had asked the Messiah to come to him to cure him of a severe illness. Jesus was supposed to have replied that after his Ascension he would send a disciple to heal him.

Another forgery purported to be a copy of an accidentally discovered letter from Lentulus, one of Pontius Pilate's friends, and included an exact description of Jesus's appearance. Other forgeries were supposed to be secret copies of Pilate's records of the trial.

126

dunc. Animam autem non possunt occide
re. His dictis. omnes pariter truncata sunt
capitibus. & martyrio coronati.

Adem & enim nocte cum omni celeritate
eodem in loco furam sepulta sunt. Sed & et
illorum capsae crux & euangelium aliaq

There must have been a considerable number of these fakes, for though most have perished many still exist. Usually these frauds were soon recognized as absurdities and were immediately destroyed, but some communities actually staked their lives on their authenticity.

Then there were other documents which did not pretend to be anything but what they were; these are still worth reading. They became grouped together under the name of Letters of the Apostolic Fathers. The most important is known as the Epistle of Clement. It was written before AD 100 and was sent to Corinth by the Christians in Rome at a time when quarrels were again threatening disunity. How this Epistle acquired its title is a mystery, because the name Clement is not found in the text and the work itself is undoubtedly the joint composition of the entire Christian congregation in Rome. Perhaps Clement was the name of the scribe or, somewhat less likely, the name could refer to the second Bishop of Rome.

There is no uncertainty about the authorship of another series of letters, those of Ignatius, Bishop of Antioch, who wrote to the Ephesians, the Romans, the Philadelphians, and the Smyrnians. He was imprisoned in Antioch for his religion and later taken to Rome where he was thrown to the lions in the arena of the Colosseum. During the journey he wrote a moving letter to the Roman Christians in which he begged them not to try to rescue him or to deprive him of martyrdom, the guarantee of eternal life. He died on the sand of the gladiatorial arena.

Other letters were written by Polycarp, who lived in Smyrna and was a close friend of Ignatius. The bishop corresponded with him, and Polycarp, on his side, sent his own letters and copies of Ignatius's to the Philippians. Lastly, there was the Epistle of Barnabas. This was generally respected by the early Christians but little is known about its author. To judge from his Epistle, he must have been a fervent enemy of the Jews. He denies them any connection with God and ridicules their pretensions to be 'the chosen people'.

The martyrdom of Polycarp, *Bishop of Smyrna, took place in* AD 125 *under the Emperor Antoninus Pius. A 15th-century woodcut illustrates the popular account of this Apostolic Father's death: when the flames left him unharmed, a gladiator was ordered to plunge his sword into the martyr's heart.*

At the same time, he gives an interesting interpretation of various Old Testament writings which he considers in an entirely Christian context. Like the Essenes, the Jewish sect which developed at the time of the Maccabees, Barnabas distinguishes between the Sons of Light and the Sons of Darkness, and he describes the two ways which lead to eternal happiness and to eternal damnation. His letter belongs to the first decade of the second century AD.

In contrast to these thoroughly honest, and often original, writings the numerous apocryphal gospels which form part of the literary output of this time only repeat well-known material with the addition of fanciful decorations. Some of these gospels were written for the adherents of Gnosis (the Greek word for 'knowledge') which was a mixture of Greek philosophy, Christian teaching, and

mysticism. Many of these gnostic gospels must have been written before AD 100. Luke expressly says in the preface to his Gospel that many before him had attempted the same work. There were the Hebrew Gospel, the Nazarene Gospel, the Egyptian Gospel, the Gospel of Peter—which had nothing to do with the apostle though it was much read by the Gnostics—and the so-called 'Infancy Gospels' which incorporated the legends that had gathered round the central figures in the Christian story. A Gospel of Thomas was found as recently as 1945. This included many hitherto unknown sayings which were attributed to Jesus. About the middle of the second century, Bishop Papias of Hierapolis in Phrygia wrote a five-volume *Exposition of the Lord's Oracles* which includes many gospel traditions not found in the New Testament canon. Almost none of this has survived.

Stories of the miraculous birth and life of the Virgin are found in the apocryphal Infancy Gospels. A 14th-century version in Latin rhyming couplets shows the Grace of God descending upon the unborn Virgin.

The theologian Thilo dismissed the 'Infancy Gospels' in 1832 as 'wholly regrettable fairy tales', but since then the tide of opinion has turned. What these stories lack in verisimilitude they make up in tenderness and beauty. They should be compared with the almost deliberately fanciful legends of the Middle Ages or even with Romantic literature rather than with the original Gospel accounts. In the Infancy Gospels Mary becomes an important figure with many miracles and wonders attributed to her. Marvellous tales were written about the birth of the Virgin, of what happened to her mother, and of her own pious sayings from the cradle upward. From the age of three she sang nothing but sacred hymns, and during her girlhood she surpassed all others in wisdom, humility, beauty, and purity. Her life-story was recreated over and over again

131

vmb d hie3 auch Joseph. vnd was getrew vnd erb. dā von w̄r
die chlag tester grö33. Nu chom das chint zu semem Joseph
vnd sp̄ch. Hast du nih3 vnome. vmb deinen genannen d ist
tot. Er sp̄ach. Ja herre. ich war3 e3 wol. vnd ist mir ga3 lait
wand er was vns alles des berait. des wir an in gerte. Do
sp̄ch das chint. wil du. so gench hin. vnd har3 in auf sten. v̄
wider lebe. den gewalt wil ich dir gebe. Des was Joseph v̄
vnd berant̄e sich v̄ lest. da3 auch zehant vō m̄ vnd gie zu
semem genanne. Do sah er michel wamen vnd chlage v̄
weiben. vnd auch von marne. Do sp̄ch Joseph dem tote. Jch
gebent dir pei semem name. d dich beschaffen hat vnd dir
das lebe hat gegebe. da3 du wid lebst. vnd auf stest. vnd ge
sunt stest. Zehant erchw̄chte sich d tot. vn stuent auf vnd
gie. sam ob er nie siech war worden. ⁊ chom ab eines
andn tages also. da3 Jesus m̄ andn chnd̄n schulen gie. als
noch am chint. gū pei dem andm ist. Nu chom̄e si mit em̄
and. auf ein hohe3 mueshaus. ich enwai3 wie sich ein chint
ga3. da3 e3 her ab viel. vnd was zehant tot. Do hueb sich m̄
ran̄. vnd chlag. von des chindes freunden. vnd begunden v̄
fragen. wer in her ab hiet gestozze. Do sp̄chen di andn chī
m̄ hiet Jhē Josephs sun. her ab gestozze. Do begunden si m̄
vaste dron. vnd entsneuten m̄ vngezogenleich. m̄ vil arge
red. Er langente fur sich. vnd gie to d tot lach. vnd sp̄ch zu r̄
Nu sp̄ch. vnd sag ga3 reht. han ich dich .... gestozze. Nar̄
du herre sp̄ch da3 chint dir sint mei fre ... vnde vmb su
vemt. vnd gehaz. si wizze selb nihr. vmb weu. Do sp̄ch da
chint Jhē. Seit du mich beredt hast. vnd hast mich vnschn̄
dich gesait. so stant auf vnd leb als e. wand ich tet dir v̄
gū lait. Do stuent da3 chint zehant auf vnd gie. sam ob
m̄ em̄ pam. nie gesw̄r. ⁊ Nu hör ab ein chrefteh w̄
der. da3 vns herre tet. Er nam di chint zu sich an ein̄
samtztag vnd gie zu einem wa3r da sahe si vische m̄
Jhē sp̄ach. wir schulen der vische vahen. als vil wir welle
Do sp̄chen di andn chint. wie schul wir das tuen. Jhē sp̄

us as a small boy *was
subject of many of the
ly Christian legends. The
h-century German manu-
pt opposite shows
attempt of one of his
panions to leap un-
med from a roof-top. In
4th-century gilt glass
ht) the young Jesus
ls the wedding crowns
r a bride and bridegroom
bless their marriage.*

in minute detail, and it culminated, of course, in the miracles of her virginity and the Nativity.

Jesus as a small boy came to be credited with every kind of miraculous power, and He is represented, delightfully, more as a boy magician than as solemn or staid. When a young boy he was playing on a roof with his companions, and he jumped to the ground unharmed, daring his friends to jump after him. One did, and was dashed to pieces. The Virgin reproved Jesus for this prank; with a laugh he touched the body of the dead boy with his foot and restored him to life. At six he made his loosely woven cloak hold water; at eight he was found with a pride of lions that had sunk upon their knees to pray to him. Later, he tamed a dragon, shattered Egyptian idols, and so on. . . . The story is one of a young boy with infinite power using it all for fun. If the Infancy Gospels are accepted for what they are, their simplicity becomes moving. They are the most comprehensive of the apocryphal gospels that

133

have come down to us; of the others only enough fragments remain to place them definitively in this period.

These were not the only early Christian writings to find wide currency. There were many visionary documents which describe Heaven and Hell, the Day of Judgment, and the Kingdom of God. The first of these apocalypses, such as those of Peter and Hermas, appeared shortly after John's Revelation, in the second decade of the second century AD. There are various references to an apocalypse by Paul and to different prophecies in the Judaeo-Christian sybillic writings. All these works originated in the same temper which produced the extra-canonical gospels—an unquenchable thirst for more and yet more wonders, an appetite which was not satisfied by the facts alone but craved more and more mysteries, regardless of whether the truth was distorted or not. Many of their authors must be credited with the best intentions, but the principle on which they appear to have worked, that the end justifies the means, cannot be upheld.

Some apocryphal stories about the apostles and martyrs vied with each other in depicting bigger and better miracles; they also show a strong Gnostic influence and can be dated from about AD 200. These include the Acts of Peter and Paul, a detailed account of the martyrdom of the two apostles, and the Acts of John, a collection of tales which bristles with miraculous resuscitations and exorcizings. Then there were the stories of Andrew and Matthew in the city of the cannibals, stories which were especially popular; and a highly poetic hymn about the 'Marriage of Sophia'.

The story of John by Leucius Charinus, which was in circulation shortly before AD 200, is highly entertaining. It too abounds in marvels of many kinds, some of which take place in the oddest circumstances. It tells of a certain Lord Callimachus who waylaid the pious and respectable wife of Lord Andronicus. The lady was so terrified that she fell down dead; whereupon, instead of repenting of his wicked ways, Callimachus gave way to his lust and made love to the corpse. Immediately it turned into a snake and strangled

Visions of the apocalypse *continued to appear after St John's Revelation, in response to a thirst for marvels and yet more marvels. A late 15th-century French MS shows St John on the island of Patmos, writing down his own unique vision. The Beast, rearing out of the sea, contrasts strangely with the idyllic beauty of the island.*

him. At this point John appeared, restored both bodies to life, and brought everything to a successful close with a severe sermon.

No less diverting is the story of John and the bugs. One night the apostle arrived exhausted at an inn where he proposed to spend the night. The moment he went to bed an army of bugs marched out of every crack in the furniture and advanced upon him. But John did not lose his head. He gave an order, and lo! the bugs retreated, unit by well-drilled unit, to the door, where they took up sentry-positions and guarded the room throughout the night. They did not move from their posts until morning when John commanded them to return to their quarters in the bedroom furniture.

The adventures of Thekla, *though pure invention, were so successful that even in the Middle Ages the fictional Thekl*

All these inventions were outdone by an Elder in Asia Minor who wrote the exciting story of Paul and the beautiful Thekla. Although Thekla was already engaged to a distinguished and wealthy young man, she was converted by Paul and sworn to life-long continence and celibacy. Accordingly she renounced her attractive young man in his elegant villa and attached herself to the apostle. And to emphasize the extent of her sacrifice, the author points out that Paul was ugly, a small bent man with a twisted

still revered as a saint. A frieze in Tarragona Cathedral graphically illustrates the main episodes of her enthralling story.

figure, bandy legs, a gleaming bald head, and a nose like a potato. The subsequent life of the beautiful Thekla is as full of incident as that of a strip-cartoon heroine. Condemned to be burnt at the stake, she escaped from the flames at the last minute, only to be drowned —almost, for an angel saved her. Later, after Providence had rescued her from a particularly ferocious lion, she was baptized by Paul. Thereupon she began her work as a missionary, converted many heathen, healed the sick, restored the dead to life, and

137

attained, by the grace of God, her seventieth year. At this advanced age she was set upon by a band of ruffians who tried to rape her. Before their eyes she scampered up a sheer cliff-face which suddenly opened, let her in, and closed again behind her. The rapists were left standing in front of the mountain like the forty thieves in Ali Baba.

Not everyone appreciated the gallant author of this story. Soon after his tale began to circulate he was accused of being an out-and-out liar, and although he strongly defended himself, on the grounds that he had written to the greater glory of the apostle Paul, he was deprived of his post as Elder. But nothing could stop the success of his tale. Its impact was so great that Thekla, an entirely fictional creation, was still revered as one of the outstanding saints as late as the Middle Ages. Indeed, she ranked nearly as high as the Virgin herself and was considered to be a shining example of absolute purity.

It is difficult for the modern reader, accustomed to our habit of scepticism, to realize just how avidly such stories were listened to and prized by the early Christians. Their insatiable hunger for anything that was even remotely connected with the Gospel message made them uncritical. Just as the most ludicrous objects became revered relics, so the most questionable writings became the literary treasures of the early churchmen and women. They were simple people, with untutored, unsuspicious minds. Many of them accepted fiction as willingly as they did fact. But credulity, if not the deep seriousness which underlay it, began to decline in the second century AD.

Congregations had sprung up everywhere—in Rome, Greece, and Asia Minor. Some were small, scarcely more than individual households, like that at Lullingstone in Kent; others were more important and produced major figures from among their members. Each chose an Elder or Presbyter to lead it, held regular church services, and above all cherished the Holy Scriptures.

By this time there was a corpus of Gospels, Epistles, Revelations, various apocalypses, uncanonical letters, fantastic tales, and unsubtle

Even the wild beasts bowed down to Thekla, or so the story ran and so it is perpetuated in a 12th-century Greek menology. This tells the story of (to quote the Greek caption under the picture) 'the martyrdom of the holy and glorious Thekla, martyr and apostle'.

forgeries—all jumbled together in one indiscriminate mass, without system or order. Some communities had faithful copies of the Gospels or the Epistles; others had only forged writings; most possessed documents of both kinds. The educated among the Christians knew it was becoming more and more imperative that the manuscripts should be carefully sifted and classified. They needed some kind of standard text, a canon, like that which determined the form and content of the Old Testament, because only such a canon could protect the less-educated from error and confute those who were the chief danger to the young Church—the people who mingled truth and falsehood in their teachings and threatened to confuse and divide the simpler members of the community. The hold of such people could be dislodged only by a fixed, unalterable canon which distinguished between the genuine and the mythological.

8

THE CHURCH GROWS UP

Before the leaders of the early Church were ready to create a canon for the New Testament they were forestalled by a heretic, a man named Marcion, who came to be hated by all orthodox Christians. Marcion was born in Asia Minor, at Sinope on the Black Sea, probably about AD 100. As a young man he was banished from his native town, on the ground of heresy, by the bishop, who was also his father. Marcion made a fortune as a shipowner and went to live in Rome, where he made over all his money to the Christian community and devoted himself to writing, his object being to reform the Church in accordance with what he believed to be the true doctrine. First, he determined to eradicate from Christianity every trace of Judaism. The true God was not Jehovah, the God of the Old Testament and of the Creation, but the loving heavenly Father acknowledged by Jesus. It was a cardinal point in Marcion's doctrine that God in His goodness sent His Son to deliver mankind from the evil God of the Jews. This complete break with the Old Testament, this spurning of the visible, material world as the creation of an evil spirit, was a radical contradiction of the message of Jesus and the apostles, and naturally was seen as a mortal danger for all the Christian communities. But Marcion had no desire to found a new religion; all he intended to do was to remould the existing one on his own lines. For this he needed a canon.

He soon grasped that such a canon could not be put together in the same way as the canon of the Old Testament. There the accent had been on collecting the existing books together and filling in any gaps; with the New Testament the principal need was to get rid of all the questionable material. Marcion did not believe in half-measures. He threw out all the Gospels except Luke's, which he kept because it had been written by Paul's pupil. Luke's Gospel made up Part I of Marcion's canon; Part II comprised ten of Paul's Epistles. And that was all. So far as Marcion was concerned, Matthew, Mark, John, the Acts, Revelation, and the rest of the Epistles did not qualify.

Once he had begun to prune he got carried away. Out came everything in Luke and the Epistles which had any reference to Judaism. He had no compunction in doing this, for he held that he had the reformer's duty to restore the true and unadulterated teachings of the early Church.

Contemporary Christians were unanimous in stigmatizing Marcion as an impostor, though they followed the main lines of the skeleton canon he had laid down, chiefly because nobody else had proposed one.

The only man who made any approach towards tackling the problem was the martyr Justin, who died in 165 in Rome. Justin was an 'apologist' or champion of the faith. But although he wrote along orthodox lines and interpolated long passages from the Gospels and apostolic writings, he took pains to point out what was genuine and what was false. He paved the way for a more thorough investigation of the problem of the New Testament canon.

There was another man who did work of this kind. His name is not known; indeed, it was not until the eighteenth century that fragments of his writings about the correct order of prayer and the Scriptures which ought to be read by true believers were found. These are generally known as the Muratorian Fragments, after their discoverer, a librarian from Milan named Muratori. In these fragments the writer discriminates quite unambiguously between 'the official Gospels' and the writings which should be rejected. He classifies as genuine the four Gospels, the Acts, Revelation, the Epistles of Paul, John, and Jude; but he does not recognize the

Part of an altar-piece *from a Catalan church (about 1120) shows an early representation of St Philip, St Jude and St Bartholomew.*

Epistle to the Hebrews, the Epistles of Peter and James, or the third Epistle of John. This unknown author writes in extremely poor Latin, and he lapses into many mistakes. We can assume he was an uneducated man, though the poor style may equally well be the fault of the medieval scribe who copied the work.

In the East there were a number of important thinkers, such as Athenagoras, Melito of Sardes, Theophilus of Antioch, and Papias of Hierapolis, who were teachers and interpreters rather than

143

A Syrian Christian, *Tatian, attempted in the 2nd century to weld the four gospels together into a consecutive story without repetitions, and recast them in Greek of a more colloquial style. Except for later translations, not complete, a fragment of papyrus, excavated at Dura Europos, is all that remains of this early venture in popularization.*

codifiers. They wrote long commentaries, and quoted freely from the Gospels and Epistles, but they did not collect their writings systematically or make any attempt to give a ruling on true and false documents. Papias, for instance, laid more stress on oral tradition than on written doctrine. He searched widely for anyone who had talked personally with the apostles, because, as he said, 'I was of the opinion that what I could glean from books was less important than the testimony of living men.'

About this time a remarkable work was being created in Syria by a man named Tatian. He did not restrict himself to collecting documents but went on to weld them into a consecutive whole. He made a single narrative out of parts of all four Gospels and recast

144

The four evangelists *had their symbols, which can be seen (opposite) on the cover of a lav ornamented 12th-century gospel manuscript. St Matthew's is an angel, St Mark's a lion, St L a bull and St John's an e*

the whole in a more colloquial style. The result, he admitted, was not meant for scholars or for specialist studies but for the common reader. It was to be the sole authority for the ordinary layman and provide a clear text for use in church services. Tatian's work continued to be used for two centuries, and as late as 360 the scholar Ephraim wrote an exhaustive commentary on it. In 450, however, the Chief Priest of the Syrian Church, Theodore of Antioch, declared it invalid, and said: 'We have four Gospels, not four in one. Four Gospels, like the four winds and the four points of the compass.'

Theodore was not the only authority to place so much importance on the four Gospels. Two hundred years earlier it was expressed in almost the same way by Irenaeus, Bishop of Gallia. He quotes, in his writings, from the Gospels and the Epistles of Paul, the Acts, Revelation, the first Epistle of Peter, and the first and second Epistle of John. Another of the second-century Fathers of the Church, Tertullian, follows much the same lines, though Clement of Alexandria is not quite so definite. There is also the 'Gospel of Truth' found at Nag Hammadi in Egypt in 1947, together with a mass of other Gnostic writings, from which we learn that a New Testament canon, not so very different from the one we have today, existed as early as AD 150.

'WHOLLY ABSURD AND UNGODLY WRITINGS'

After AD 200 the history of the New Testament canon developed along two distinct lines, the one among the Greeks and the other among the Latin-speaking races, which comprised a large part of North Africa as well as most of civilized Europe.

The Greeks produced perhaps the most important scholar of the time. This was Origen, a much-travelled man who was acquainted with most branches of learning and had the breadth of vision of the born scholar. His birth-place was Alexandria and he became the greatest theologian of his century. He approached his work logically and with energy. First he discarded all that was immediately recog-

Among the 'doubtful' books *the great Greek scholar Origen placed the Epistle to the Hebrews, perhaps working from a papyrus roll such as the one from which this fragment came. It shows verses 1–11 of the twelfth chapter.*

nizable as fiction or forgery. Next he divided the remaining writings into two groups, those that were 'generally recognized' and those that were 'doubtful'—the *homologoumena* and the *amphiballomena*. In the first category he placed the four Gospels, the thirteen Epistles of Paul, I Peter, I John, Revelation, and the Acts; the second comprised II Peter, II and III John, the Epistle to the Hebrews, and the Epistles of James and Jude.

Another early theologian, Eusebius Pamphili, carried the work a stage further. He became Bishop of Caesarea in Palestine in 314 and enjoyed the confidence of the Emperor Constantine, who allowed him access to all the Church archives. Thus encouraged, he set about making a precise, dated account of all the events of early Christianity. Unfortunately for the modern reader, Eusebius's style is extremely forbidding, sometimes unbearably dry and wooden, then suddenly breaking out into repellent sentimentality. His biography of the Emperor Constantine is particularly gushing, per-haps for reasons all too human.

But whatever his style, Eusebius's scholarly thoroughness, both in his historical work and in his canon of the New Testament, makes up for it. Mostly he follows Origen, but he divides the writings under review into three instead of two groups. Like Origen he places the four Gospels, the Acts, Paul's Epistles, I Peter and I John in the *homologoumena*, but though he also includes the Epistle to the Hebrews he questions Revelation. Eusebius divides the second group into two, the 'less' and the 'more doubtful'. His third group comprises the 'wholly absurd and ungodly writings' and contains most of the known forgeries.

Eusebius's treatment of Revelation is interesting. This book appears in two different places in his canon, in the first group and in the 'more doubtful' sub-division of the second group; and in both places it is qualified by a question mark. He explains that some scholars regard the book as unquestionably genuine, while others reject it completely. This uncertainty about Revelation was indeed common among Greek scholars in the first centuries. Origen him-self had no doubt about it, but his pupils were continually debating its authenticity. Eusebius left himself uncommitted, though it is plain that as a book, Revelation was foreign to his quiet, dry nature. Apart from this single query, his canon agrees in every par-ticular with the one which is in use today. His first group and the first division of his second group make up our New Testament. By the authority of the Festival Letter of Athanasius in 367, Revelation finally gained unquestioned admittance to the canon.

The Latin scholars took no part in this quarrel over Revelation, which they accepted from the first. But they took longer to accept

The strangeness of the book of Revelation *was foreign to many of the early scholars. Some accepted it as genuine, others denied it. An illuminated commentary of the 10th century strikingly conveys the flavour of the saint's apocalyptic vision.*

BHEVGIENSSPVSCOFLANTEREVERTITVR

Ambrose, Bishop of Milan *in the 4th century, was one of the early Fathers of the Church. A relief in his church in Milan illustrates his summons by the Holy Ghost to take up the office of bishop.*

the Epistle to the Hebrews. Scholars such as Cyprian, Hilarius, and Ambrose, who was governor and later Bishop of the Province of Milan, mostly followed the canon which is indicated in the Muratorian Fragments. Their work largely resembled that of the Greeks. though they had noticeably less background knowledge, but they made up for this by being more systematic and more insistent on logical order.

Cyprian, Bishop of Carthage, *martyred by the Romans, was a convert to Christianity late in life. A Greek miniature of the 9th century shows him in his pagan days, surrounded by heathen idols and magic utensils.*

The canon followed a different course of development in Syria, where for a long time Tatian's 'integrated Gospels' were used. It was not until the beginning of the fifth century that the bishops joined together to devise a 'standard Bible', the *Peshitto*, which has remained ever since the standard work for the Syrian Church. It differs little from the other versions and was brought into line with the Greek and Latin Bibles in the sixth and seventh centuries.

Except in Syria, the canon of the New Testament has not changed since the end of the fourth century. In his Festival Letter of AD 367, Athanasius, Bishop of Alexandria, proclaimed the canon to be fixed and unalterable, and so it has remained. Then, as now, it contained the four Gospels, the Acts, Revelation, the thirteen Epistles of Paul, I and II Peter, I, II, and III John, James, Jude, and the Epistle to the Hebrews. These twenty-seven books have remained the final authority and last court of appeal for the whole Christian Church. It is one of the most miraculous features of the miraculous history of Christianity that the New Testament canon managed to establish itself, however slowly, despite the political tangle of the times and the dangers which more than once threatened to wipe out Christianity altogether.

The New Testament in its prese form was proclaimed in AD 367 Athanasius, Bishop of Alexandria (posite, from a mosaic in St Mar Venice) as fixed and unalterable. T Syriac church followed its own cou but their authorized version, the 'Peshit differs but little. On the left is part o MS. version of this, written in AD 464 the earliest precisely dated Bible manusc in any language.

The persecutions of the early Christians equalled anything that the Inquisition was to do later. The first campaign against the Christians conducted by Nero in 64 was only a foretaste of what was to follow. In this campaign the Roman Christians were consistently hounded, thrown to the lions in the arena, burnt alive, tied to pitch-covered stakes in the Emperor's garden, crucified, stoned to death, left to starve. The apostles Peter and Paul were martyred, together with hundreds of other Christians. But this campaign was confined to Rome. Fifty years later it is evident from a well-known exchange of letters between the Emperor Trajan and the younger Pliny, then Governor in Bithynia, that Christians were suspect and liable to torture. From 132 to 135 Bar Kochba combined with his short-lived revolt against Rome a furious attack on the Jewish Christians in Palestine, who would not accept his claim to be the Messiah, and he almost succeeded in exterminating them. In 180 the persecutions spread to North Africa, and twenty years later they reached Alexandria. In 250 the Emperor Decius instituted a large-scale persecution of Christians, and under his successor Valerian Christians everywhere were threatened with immediate death. Fifty years later Diocletian undertook the same work and concentrated especially on Christian writings, which were burnt as fast as they could be found, sometimes to heat the Emperor's bathwater. A little later came the persecutions of Venturius, a military commander, which lasted until 298, followed by those of Maxentius and Severus in the west and Maximinus Daia in the east. Maximinus Daia in particular became notorious for his inhuman cruelty. In short, members of the early Church faced an endless chain of terror, hunger, sorrow, and death. But through it all they continued to follow Christ; and steadily their numbers increased and their beliefs crystallized.

At last, in 313, Constantine issued his Edict of Tolerance. This guaranteed safety for the Christians and permitted them to teach and to attend their religious services freely. There were still minor

Constantine the Great, *whose Edict of Tolerance ended the persecution of the Christians. A genera* *later, Christianity became the state religion of Ro*

outbreaks of persecution—in Persia from 343 to 383, and under Julian the Apostate in 361—but none of these equalled the earlier campaigns in cruelty and horror. The Church, and with it the Holy Book, had won.

The survival of the Christians is not more miraculous than that of Jesus's original teachings through all the internal disagreements and quarrels of the early Church. In these initial years there sprang up hundreds of different dogmas, heretical and otherwise, from out and-out absurdities which had scarcely anything to do with Christianity, to more dangerous subtleties in which truth and falsehood were so mixed that they were scarcely to be distinguished. There were, first, the Gnostics, a general term which embraced the Basilides, the Valentinians, the Ophites, the Encratites, and the Marcionites. There was also Ebionitic Gnosticism, which comprised the Elkhasaites and the Sampsaeans. There was Manichaeism— an element within Christianity influenced from the East—Hyposta-sianism, Monarchianism, and Alogism. There were Theodotianites, Aremonites, Noaetians, Hippolytans, Chiliasts, and Montanists. There were splinter groups under Felicissimus in Carthage, Meletus in Egypt, and Novatian in Rome. In 255 a quarrel over baptism arose between Rome and Carthage under Stephen, and later a further quarrel broke out between Arius and Athanasius on whether Christ was God's Son or not. This last very nearly des-troyed Christianity altogether. At another time the Pelagians and Massiliensines challenged the orthodox doctrines and even opposed St Augustine, then Bishop of Hippo in North Africa. There were more and more arguments, in Palestine, Italy, Alexandria, more and more sects—Monotheletes, Priscillianists, Andrians, Apostolics, Donatists . . . The list goes on and on.

The history of these disputes is full of furious passages of arms. Indeed, if the first centuries can be called the Church's infancy and the Middle Ages the prime of its life, then the fourth and fifth cen-turies were certainly its adolescence, with all the gaucherie and rebelliousness which the word implies. Distressing accounts exist of the judgments of different synods before which doctrinal quarrels were brought. From the time of Constantine onwards synods were set up to act as ecclesiastical courts of enquiry. They were called together by the Emperor and presided over by his agent, called a prelate, and bishops were appointed with power to give judgment. The state paid all expenses. Thus constituted, they often found themselves called upon to act in cases which were entirely beyond their capability to judge.

The most notorious of these trials was the Council of Ephesus in 449. It was significantly nicknamed the 'Robber Synod'. After a stirring and dramatic debate the Emperor's representative, Dioscurus, lost his temper and called in the guards who were followed into the council chamber by a mob. The synod dissolved in wild disorder. The outcome was that the Emperor not only broke with the Pope but also turned his Empress and one of his ministers on to the street because he blamed them for bringing the whole business upon him.

There were many incidents of this kind during the Church's adolescence, for adolescence is, after all, a time of violence and confusion. But it is also the prelude to manhood.

Despite everything, the Church went on from strength to strength, thanks less, perhaps, to the bishops and synods than to the mute masses, who left doctrinal hair-splitting to their betters. Perhaps it was them, and not their spiritual teachers and pastors, whom Jesus had in mind when he said: 'Ye are the salt of the earth.'

9

THE QUIET SCHOLARS

THE NEED FOR AN AUTHORIZED BIBLE

One of the most venerated of the old Jewish rabbis, Rabbi Akiba, maintained that 'there is nothing new under the sun'. Yet during his lifetime he saw something entirely new, something entirely without precedent—the birth of Christianity. Akiba ben Joseph lived in Palestine from about AD 55 to 137, and he was among the many orthodox Jews who viewed the steady growth of the new faith with mounting repugnance. He did his best to counteract its influence, and even took an active part in Bar Kochba's military campaigns against the Christian congregations who refused to support his revolt against the Romans because the rebel leader asserted he was the Messiah. But although Rabbi Akiba opposed Christianity, he nevertheless did it an inestimable service. He had a hand in the final canon of the Old Testament and, like many another Jewish scholar of his time, devoted almost the whole of his life to a study of Old Testament writings.

To Jewish scholars, the preservation and illumination of the Torah came before everything else—the Torah which is as much a part of the Christian as it is of the Jewish heritage. The rabbis worked quietly, and caused no great stir in the world at large. They shunned synods, councils, and committees. But the result of what they did was probably of more importance than anything achieved by their more publicized contemporaries.

Not only did the Hebrew script lack vowels but the individual words were not separated from one another, and there was neither punctuation nor capital letters. Consequently, any reader who was

Without vowels, without punctuation—*such was the old Hebrew script, as in this manuscript letter signed by Simon ben Kochba. But Hebrew scholars, to preserve the Scriptures and make them easier for the ordinary reader, introduced vowels and punctuation and separated the words. The 14th-century MS. opposite shows the reformed script, and a young pupil learning it from a rather formidable teacher.*

not well acquainted with the language had to struggle to produce a correct reading and, with the best will in the world, tended to corrupt the text he read. Only the priests and scholars who used the Scriptures daily were able to read the unpointed text fluently and without making mistakes; most Jews could not even begin to do so. Their mother-tongue was now Aramaic, and Hebrew was used only for religious purposes, just as Latin is in present-day Roman Catholicism. As for the early Christians, they could approach the Old Testament only at second-hand through the Septuagint—an unsatisfactory solution for anyone who wished to study delicate

וּבְהַבִּיא וּבְשָׂרָהּ אֲחֻזָּתוֹ לֹא יִמְכֹּר וְלֹא יִגָּאֵל כָּל חֵרֶם קֹדֶשׁ קָדָשִׁים הוּא לַיהֹוָה כָּל חֵרֶם אֲשֶׁר
יָחֳרַם מִן הָאָדָם לֹא יִפָּדֶה מוֹת יוּמָת וְכֹל מַעֲשַׂר הָאָרֶץ מִזֶּרַע הָאָרֶץ מִפְּרִי הָעֵץ לַיהֹוָה
הוּא קֹדֶשׁ לַיהֹוָה וְאִם גָּאֹל יִגְאַל אִישׁ מִמַּעַשְׂרוֹ חֲמִשִׁיתוֹ יֹסֵף עָלָיו וְכָל מַעְשַׂר בָּקָר
וָצֹאן כֹּל אֲשֶׁר יַעֲבֹר תַּחַת הַשָּׁבֶט הָעֲשִׂירִי יִהְיֶה קֹדֶשׁ לַיהֹוָה לֹא יְבַקֵּר בֵּין טוֹב לָרַע וְלֹא
יְמִירֶנּוּ וְאִם הָמֵר יְמִירֶנּוּ וְהָיָה הוּא וּתְמוּרָתוֹ יִהְיֶה קֹדֶשׁ לֹא יִגָּאֵל אֵלֶּה הַמִּצְוֹת אֲשֶׁר
צִוָּה יְהֹוָה אֶת מֹשֶׁה אֶל בְּנֵי יִשְׂרָאֵל בְּהַר סִינָי

חזק

סִימָן סְכוּם פְּסוּקֵי דְּסִפְרָא נְטֹרָה

shades of meaning or linguistic effect. To do this it was necessary to study the original text.

Jewish scholars were not concerned with Christian difficulties but with the demands of their co-religionists. The rabbis who could still read Hebrew perfectly joined together to provide a text which could be read by the non-specialist. The worst stumbling-block to be removed was the lack of vowels. How could these be inserted without radically changing the language in its written form? It was done by means of small marks, mostly dots, which were placed over or under the consonants.

The rabbis made no alterations to the text itself; they added nothing and took nothing away. Their sole aim was to make it accessible, so that anyone who knew any Hebrew could read it. In the end they became slaves to exactitude and pursued it for its own sake. They were so in love with it that they counted the number of separate letters there were in the Old Testament as a check against posterity's dropping a single character. They even worked out which word and which letter formed the precise middle of the Torah. The word was 'search' and its middle letter was the equivalent of V. The rabbis became so fascinated by calculations of this kind that they were nicknamed the *Sopherim* (auditors). All the same, they did not confine themselves to such work and to punctuating the text but wrote many valuable commentaries on it. These commentaries were known as the *Masora*, and so they also became known as the Masoretes and their work was termed the masoretic writings.

The Masoretes began their work in the fifth century AD and formed academies in Palestine, Babylon, and Cairo. Each academy differed slightly in its method of punctuation; some put the vowels above the consonants and others below; but their aims were the same. For more than one thousand years they and their successors continued the great task and some of their members came to be known outside Judaism—ben Asher, for instance, and ben Naphtali, and Jacob ben Chaim who was a contemporary of Martin Luther and published the first printed rabbinic Bible.

For more than a thousand years, *Hebrew scholars continued the work of purifying, preserving and commenting on the sacred texts. In the 15th century Moses Maimonides, a Jewish scholar from Spain, wrote the 'Mishneh Torah', a collection and codification of the Mosaic laws. This beautifully illuminated title and contents list heads its fifth book.*

Whatever period they belonged to, the Masoretes attained a level of scholarship and thoroughness which was rarely equalled by Christian scholars. And so, just as Christianity owed its first canon of the New Testament to a heretic, so it owed the major part of its Old Testament scholarship to the Jews.

The Masoretes were not the only men to devote their lives to the Bible. There were also the many translators, who first began to make themselves felt in the second century AD. Until then, the only non-Hebrew version of the Bible was the Septuagint, which had been intended originally for the Greek-speaking Jews of the Diaspora. It was not long before another Greek translation was made,

163

this time by a pupil of Rabbi Akiba, named Aquila. This version suffered from Aquila's excessive thoroughness, which led him to translate the Hebrew word for word with a painful disregard for Greek idiom. Nothing had to be altered—not even the position of the words or the construction of the sentences, and this made his Greek wellnigh unintelligible. Aquila, however, was much admired by his contemporaries, who felt that they could rely on him not to cheat them out of a single syllable of the Torah.

A little later Symmachus also translated the Torah into Greek, and as he aimed at being not only faithful but felicitous his translation comes off better. At the end of the second century Theodotion made yet another translation or, rather, an amended edition of the earlier ones.

By the middle of the third century there were thus a number of Greek translations of the Bible in use. The question was, which was the 'best'? A need was felt for an authorized Bible, especially when

The Masoretes not only punctuated the texts and wrote commentaries on them (left-hand column) but embellished them with illumination and illustrations. A page from the Pentateuch of 1310 shows Samson grappling with the lion.

discussions arose about meaning or interpretation. There was still, of course, the Hebrew original, but few people could read it and so it was of little help in settling such questions.

The problem was solved by Origen. He first mastered Hebrew and then undertook the onerous task of collating all the existing translations in one comprehensive work. He laid out his left-hand page in three columns: the first contained the Hebrew text, the second a transliteration of it into Greek to indicate pronunciation and to help the reader unfamiliar with Hebrew, and the third column contained Aquila's word-for-word translation. Origen so arranged the columns that the lines exactly corresponded and could be easily compared. On the opposite page he put Symmachus's translation, the Septuagint, and Theodotion's version, also arranged in three equal columns. In this way the reader could compare six versions of the text by merely flicking his eye along the line. The book came to be known as the *Hexapla*, or six-fold Bible.

Origen was a model of thoroughness. He not only set out the six texts side by side, but he provided them with marginal comments and a seventh reading where none of the others satisfied him. If he found a word in a translation which did not appear in the original he bracketed it, and if a word was missing he inserted it with a suitable comment. It is daunting to think of the labour all this must have meant, but it resulted in a text which superseded all others and could be trusted by the most demanding scholar.

There was, indeed, only one thing wrong with the Hexapla. It was so large and ran into so many volumes that only a professional man of letters could use it. Consequently few copies were made and only thirty-five fragments of these are extant. Origen seems also to have compiled a Tetrapla, or four-fold Bible, in which four Greek translations were similarly dealt with, but nothing is known of this book, not even whether it was an abridged edition of the Hexapla or an independent work.

Extracts from the Hexapla probably had a wider circulation than the whole book. The fifth column, the Septuagint, was especially popular, for besides being the oldest and still the most reliable of all the translations it was also readable. With Origen's emendations and additions it became the most widely read of all Greek translations of the Old Testament. Again and again scholars published new editions of it and compared it with other texts. Lucian, the martyr of Antioch, published one edition, and so did Bishop Hesychius, who died in Diocletian's persecutions of the Christians.

The remarkable thing about all the scholars of this period is that they accomplished their exacting work not in some tranquil haven of learning or scholastic backwater but in the midst of fighting and upheaval, often in danger of their lives. Their courage and perseverance often exceeds that of many popular heroes.

The number of translations grew from decade to decade. First came the *targums*, translations into Aramaic, which was the language of the Persian empire and continued to be current after that empire had fallen. These *targums* had begun to appear in preChristian times; Rabbi Gamaliel, Paul's teacher, owned a *targum*scroll of the Book of Job. In the fifth century the *targums* of Onkelos and Jonathon were well known and were considered to be standard texts, though their Aramaic was as stilted as Aquila's Greek. Fragments of fourth-century translations into various Coptic dialects, such as Sahidic and Bohairic, still survive. At about the same time the King of Abyssinia's conversion to Christianity occasioned a translation into Ethiopian for the use of his subjects. In the fifth century the Bible was translated into Armenian and in the tenth into Arabic.

But none of these translations, however zealously and perseveringly made, was as important and far-reaching in its effects as the Latin translation. Latin was the language of Rome, southern France, and North Africa—the language of power. In quite early Christian times there were Latin translations, of which fragments survive. All such fragments from before the time of St Jerome and

The nearest approach to a world language *in early Christian times was Latin. The great scholar St Jerome, at the orders of Pope Damasus, produced the Latin version known as the Vulgate—the basis of the authorized version for the Roman Catholic church. An 11th-century gospel MS. shows the saint dictating to a scribe.*

his Vulgate translation are called the *Vetus Latina*. Little is known about them; they may have been the work of a single hand or of a group of scholars. Their style is similar to that of the Muratorian fragment—popular, sometimes primitive and often slangy, with a tendency to drop into grammatical and other mistakes.

In 382 Pope Damasus commissioned the famous Christian scholar Jerome to make a complete, exact, and yet readable revision of the Latin versions of the Bible. Jerome, working first in Rome and later in Bethlehem, where he was head of a monastery, worked also straight from the original Hebrew of the Old Testament and the

Greek of the New, using many other versions for comparison, and incidentally scandalizing ecclesiastics by ignoring the Septuagint, which by then had become almost sacrosanct. His new Latin translation occupied many years, but it was worth all the labour. It became the basis of all Bible studies in the Middle Ages, and in 1546 the Council of Trent declared it to be the authorized Bible for the Catholic Church and conclusive in all matters of doctrine and ethics. Eventually it acquired the name of 'the Vulgate', meaning the book of the people.

WULFILA THE GOTH

All these early translations, even the Vulgate, pale beside the Gothic Bible of Wulfila. This is an astonishing work, for Wulfila had to create his own script before he could begin to translate.

During the second and third centuries the Goths had left their original home to find land in the area which is now filled by the Balkan states. The Goths were not noted for their sensitivity to the feelings of the local inhabitants; whoever opposed them was speedily removed, and whoever hesitated to give them obedience or money was severely punished. From time to time the Goths would enslave whole towns and take the people forward with them in their further conquests. Wulfila's ancestors were slaves of this kind and he himself was born in captivity in 311. His name meant 'Little Wolf', and he must have had something of the wolf's cunning, for he soon mastered several languages, including Greek, and rose to be an official at the Gothic court. When the Goths sent a legation to the Emperor Constantine, Wulfila accompanied it as interpreter and stayed for some years in Constantinople. His family had been Christian for three generations. Wulfila took orders and became bishop of the Danube Goths when he was only twenty-nine years of age. And in 350, in what is now Bulgaria, he began to translate the Bible into Gothic.

The Goths had no usable written script. Their rune-script was wholly inadequate for Wulfila's purpose. So he fashioned a com-

The most astonishing of the early translations was Bishop Wulfila's Gothic version. Not only did he have to invent a script (relying heavily on Greek), but he had somehow to make an essentially concrete language capable of expressing highly abstract ideas. This page from the Gothic Bible contains part of the first chapter of St Luke's Gospel.

pletely new script. He took the Greek alphabet for his model and adapted it to meet the needs of Gothic. But when this had been done and he had supplemented his alphabet with some runic signs he was still unable to begin translating because Gothic, essentially an unwritten and concrete language, lacked most of the words he needed for the Bible's abstract concepts. This was Wulfila's chief difficulty. To create a written alphabet suited to the sounds of a language is a difficult enough task, but to expand a vocabulary so that hundreds of new ideas can still be communicated to those who speak the old language calls for linguistic and philosophic genius. Wulfila had to create, single-handed, the first Germanic language.

169

Moreover, he had to be a skilled psychologist. If his Bible failed to make a good first impression, his work would go for nothing. So he deliberately omitted the two Books of Kings lest these should excite the imagination and warlike instincts of the Gothic warriors. The work was finished in 380. It was the first written monument of a northern people and the first appearance of the Bible in a country cut off from the Mediterranean basin. Wulfila's work marked the beginning of Christianity's move northwards, towards the land-mass of Europe. And it opened the way for the many Bible manu-scripts which soon poured out over Germany, France, England,

With intricate designs *and rich, glowing colours, the scribes adorned their manuscripts to the g glory of God. Above: an Irish crucifixion (8th century); opening initial of the Book of Daniel (G*

and Ireland—manuscripts which became works of art in themselves because of the glow of their rich colours and the intricacy of their designs. These were, of course, manuscripts in the true sense of the word, for they were still written by hand. They consumed years and even decades in the lives of the scribes who laboured to produce them in monasteries. There are roughly three million letters in the Bible, but to the patient monks in their cells each letter was a labour of love, an offering to God, and they rarely wearied of the contribution they were making in this way to the wider acceptance of the true faith.

10th century); the entry into Jerusalem, from a 13th-century Syriac gospel; and a French version
e Apocalypse, early 14th century.

10

IN LETTERS OF GOLD

TO PRAY, TO WORK, TO TEACH

It took two hundred lamb-skins to make one copy of the Bible. It took gold and silver, red and blue paint, intricately intertwined like exotic gossamer. It took a lifetime of patiently acquired skill. It took a mentality in which piety and diligence, craftsman's pride and Christian humility were equally mixed.

What do we know of the Middle Ages? No country is so foreign as a bygone era; no species so remote as the humanity of a few centuries back. How can a modern man, with his jet-travel and newsprint, television, and psycho-analysis, put himself in the place of Francis of Assisi or the Venerable Bede?

He can only guess, and sometimes his guesswork is falsified by patronage, sometimes by harshness. The notion, which was once common, that the Middle Ages were the 'Dark Ages' was based on ignorance, which sprang mainly from the over-emphasis which was formerly given to classical antiquity. This mode of thinking saw in every Greek cattle-drover an Achilles and in every medieval northerner a superstitious savage, and was blind to the towering Romanesque and Gothic cathedrals, the fervour of the saints, the poetry of the troubadours, and the fruitful union between religion and the creative urge. This culture flowered exquisitely in the illu-minated manuscripts of the period.

It is true that most people in the Middle Ages were not particularly well-off, either intellectually or materially. It is also true that at the early universities scholarship often meant absurd quibbles. And it is likewise true that the religious passion of both men and women

173

often exceeded all reason, as did the passions of vengeance, lust, and greed. They could be foolish, superstitious, and credulous. It was a time of emotional excess, though people deluded themselves that they prized 'restraint' above all other courtly ideals. Concealment and self-consciousness were not practised. The medieval man did not try to hide his deepest feelings either in his words or in his actions, and least of all in the Bible manuscripts which so faithfully portray yet another side of his mentality.

The general level of education was very low, and more than one reigning monarch could neither read nor write. But it is completely false to infer from this that the Bible was unknown except to priests and the religious in the Middle Ages. On the contrary, it was the best-known book of the whole period. The general knowledge of Biblical writings was relatively far greater and considered more important than it is today. Parents often made their children learn whole pages of the Bible by heart; even when they themselves could not read it they had it read out to them again and again until they had memorized it. In this way many people could repeat whole books of the Bible word for word.

Such learning by rote is, of course, no criterion of general culture. But the lives of the people of the Middle Ages were bound up with their faith, and their thought and emotion sprang from religion in a way which we can scarcely imagine.

Without the Bible the Middle Ages might well indeed have been the Dark Ages. When Christianity had once struggled its way into Europe it became the driving force of the people. It reached its highest creative peak in the monasteries. Names like St Gallen, Cluny, Fulda, Corvey, Speyer, Worms, and Cologne shine out like the coloured capitals in the manuscripts that were written there. In Luther's time the Benedictines alone, with their offshoot orders, had 37,000 religious houses.

The monasteries existed to pray and to work, to study and to teach. Their number proves that religious knowledge and culture were far wider spread than was once supposed. Many of them had

Craftsman's pride and Christian devotion *were expressed in the manuscripts produced by medieval monasteries—and most particularly in their wealth of decorated in*

their own schools and taught not only young men training to become priests but also children of all classes who later took their acquired knowledge out into the secular world. Out into the world, too, went the many copies of the Bible which were so painstakingly made in the silent monastery-cells. More than 12,000 manuscripts and fragments of manuscripts survive today from this prolific activity, and these must be only a small fraction of what was once produced.

'PRESERVE ME FROM THIS EVERLASTING WRITING!'

During the early Middle Ages script was confined to capital letters and was written without spaces between the words or sentences, like the various scripts of antiquity. From the time of Charlemagne small letters came to be used; these were more easily read and took up less room. They were developed in the palace school at Aix-la-Chapelle which Charlemagne, extremely interested in scholarship of all kinds, founded for his courtiers and their children. Shortly afterwards a cursive script was evolved in which the letters of each word were joined together as in modern handwriting. At the same time the scribes discovered how to draw lines across the parchment to keep their writing straight. The page was usually divided into two or three columns or 'rubrics', so called because the capital of the first word of each column was often illuminated with red, or *ruber* in Latin.

The sheets of parchment were sewn together to form a 'codex' or book, and these soon grew to an intimidating size. Generally they measured about eight inches by one foot, but sometimes they were as much as two or more feet in length. They were objects of impressive visual beauty. The *Codex Argenteus*, or Silver Codex, was so called because it was written in silver and gold letters on crimson parchment. It was made in the sixth century in a north Italian monastery. The *Codex Carolinus* followed a little later and was arranged in two columns, the first in Gothic and the second in Latin. The *Victor Codex* of Fulda is older and contains the New

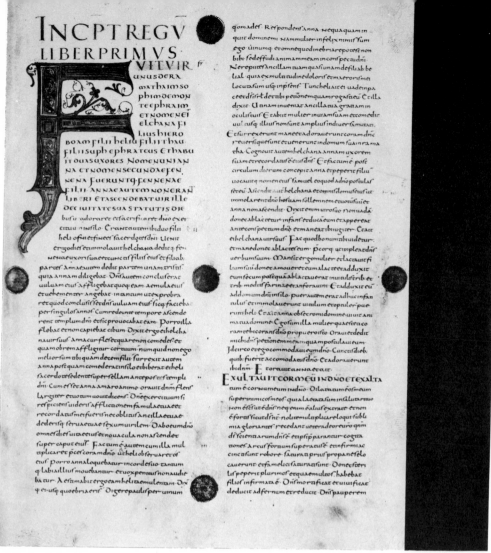

Made for Charlemagne in the 9th century, Alcuin's beautifully illuminated manuscript of the Vulgate is a fine example of an early cursive script. This page shows the decorative opening of the first Book of Samuel.

Testament in Latin. It was taken to Germany by St Boniface. One of the most beautifully illuminated of the codices is the manuscript made by a monk named Alcuin for Charlemagne in the ninth century. The Stuttgart Bible Psalter, dating from the same period, though less well written, is most wonderfully illustrated with pictures in vivid, glowing colours.

Calligraphy reached one of its peaks in the tenth century with the works which came from the St Gallen monastery. One of these is a German translation of the Psalms by a monk called Notker and nicknamed Labeo because of his full underlip; this one is still in existence.

More and more manuscripts were produced during the following centuries. Some of these are so regular in every detail that they appear to be printed. The loving decoration of the initials and ornamental detail are witness to an astounding skill and fervour on the part of the scribes.

Later, some of the monasteries became expert in business efficiency. Where there were more scribes than documents for them to copy, one monk dictated the text to ten or even twenty others, so that, by a kind of mass production, several copies of the Bible, or portions of it, could be made at the same time. This practice had the disadvantage of allowing more mistakes to creep in than when a monk could take his own time with his copying, and as these copies were sometimes used as models for others a chain-reaction of unreliability was set up.

The zeal of the monks began to wane in the later Middle Ages. Bishop Richard of Bury complained that 'the monks of today care more about drinking beer than writing books'. Unforgivably careless manuscripts were scribbled down by some of the more indifferent brothers, and occasionally they even added marginal comments which gave vent to their feelings. On the last page of a Codex from St Gallen there is a drawing of an outsize tankard and some rather clumsy hexameters by the bored writer. The verse can be rendered into English in this way:

If, Grimoal, you drink from this or a similar flagon,
May the good liquor it holds, like vinegar, choke you and burn you,
So that, coughing and gasping, you stay everlastingly thirsty!

In another manuscript there are Irish glosses by the side of the Latin text. The writer, a monk from Ireland, relieved his tedium with

The workshop of a scribe *is illustrated in a medieval French MS. Jean Mielot, a canon of St Pierre de Ville, is copying from the book held open on the stand. In his left hand he has a pointed instrument for ruling the lines; beside him and on the shelf at the back are bottles of ink and colouring materials.*

such heartrending cries as, 'God be praised, 'tis growing dark', 'St Patrick of Armagh, preserve me from this everlasting writing', and 'Oh, if I only had a nice glass of old wine in front of me!' Modern scholars naturally suspect the reliability of manuscripts like these; it is a pity we do not know what medieval readers thought of them.

179

The monks of the Middle Ages did new work besides copying old writings. The manuscript Bible on parchment ran into many volumes and was not easy to read except from a lectern, so selections were made—short anthologies of the Psalms or the Gospels. One of these acquired more than ordinary importance; it became used as the book on which the German Emperor swore his coronation oath. Written in gold on crimson parchment in the palace school at Aix-la-Chapelle, it was prized as one of the treasures of the empire.

Many of these little books are priceless works of art. Kings, princes, and nobles had them made, as elaborately as possible, for themselves and their families, and into them went the finest parchment, the most careful writing, gold and silver for the lettering, and delicate miniatures. The bindings were equally artistic. Sometimes they were made of chased silver or copper; often they were gilded. Sometimes they were of solid gold set with jewels and precious stones; sometimes of carved ivory; sometimes of rare woods laced over with silver-filigree. In short, the best and most expensive of everything—skill, artistry, and materials—went into them.

New translations were also made. These were intended mostly for the pupils in the monastery schools, but they soon reached a wider public. In 830 Hrabanus Maurus, head of the monastery school at Fulda, made a translation from Latin into Old High German of Tatian's Syrian 'integrated Gospel'. His pupil Otfried von Weissenburg made his own free version of the Gospels in Old High German verse. Notker Labeo of St Gallen translated the Psalms into German with exceptional power and beauty. The Abbot of Ebbersberg, who had studied at Fulda, made a trilingual translation of the Song of Solomon; in the middle column was the Vulgate text, on the left a paraphrase in Latin, and on the right a free German translation which is one of the most charming to survive from this period.

Translations, paraphrases, and new versions continued to be made throughout the Middle Ages. These included Rhyming Bibles written in the twelfth and thirteenth centuries, translations

Craftsmanship of rare beauty *was devoted to the bindings as well as the writing of the early B\
manuscripts (opposi*

of the Vulgate into verse for easier memorizing. To our taste they are stiff and unpleasant doggerel, without literary merit, but they follow the text closely and may have served their purpose when they were written. So, no doubt, did the 'story Bibles' of roughly the same time. These presented the Bible stories in colloquial language and were intended to be text-books and story-books. The 'story Bible' of Petrus Comestor, the chancellor of a church in Paris, was for two hundred years the widest read book in northern France and stimulated many imitations; it was translated into German, Dutch, Portuguese, Czech, and even Old Norse.

BIBLES FOR THE POOR

Eventually books began to be made with wood-blocks because of the ever-increasing demand for cheaper editions than those produced by hand. Many copies could be made by printing off one woodcut on parchment or paper, which was introduced into Europe from the Orient in the thirteenth century. The wood-engraver began to rival the scribe. He became extremely skilled in devising illustrations and symbolic ornaments for the text. Indeed, the pictorial side of these books came to be more important than the writing, which was reduced to headings for the pictures.

Among these woodcut books were the *Biblia Pauperum*, or Bibles for the Poor. In these, abstract ideas and long passages of text were deliberately excluded and, instead, each page was given up to a pictorial representation of one theme. In the middle of the page there would be a picture of an event from the New Testament; to left and right of it Old Testament illustrations which had a similar theme; and above and below these were portraits of Biblical charac-ters or symbolic drawings. The pictures were separated by single lines of text relating to the main theme. Even an illiterate could gather the meaning of the page from the pictures, and would also glean some exegetical knowledge from seeing how one part of the Bible was related to another. In the *Biblia Pauperum* of St Florian in Austria these pictures were grouped together: Herod's massacre of the innocents with Saul's and Athaliah's deaths; Jesus's Ascension with Elijah's and Enoch's entries into heaven; the Last Supper with the sacrifice of Melchizedek. In this way the inner structure of Christian teaching could be presented in a form understandable to the simplest person. These books were intended for the poor in learning rather than for the poor in material goods, for the uninstructed among the laity (and even for the religious, for that matter)

The simplest reader could gain greater understanding of the Bible message from the 'Biblia Pauperum' with their woodcut illustrations. This page from a 1370 version shows Joseph thrust into the pit by his brothers, Jonah being cast into the sea, and the body of Christ placed in the sepulchre.

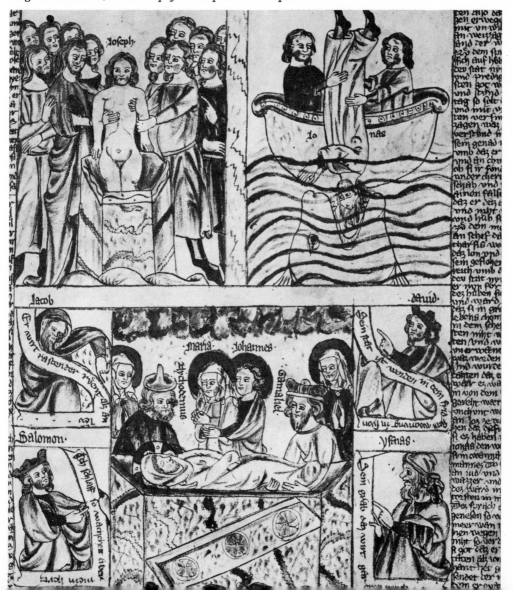

who could not read. They were, in fact, expensive and accessible only to the comparatively wealthy.

As for the hand-written manuscripts, only nobles and whole communities could afford them. In 1309 the nuns of Wasserler in the diocese of Halberstadt sold to Herr von Stein a complete Bible in four volumes for sixteen pieces of silver. Three years later the same nuns were given five pieces of silver and were able to buy with this half a 'hide' (120 acres) of land, two farmhouses, a wood, a whole farm with two acres of woodland, and another quarter of a hide of land. This gives some idea of the price that a Bible fetched in the fourteenth century. In 1388 the abbey of Johannisberg bought a Bible for seventy florentines, and asked for leave to pay over a term of four years. At this time the price of a fat ox was two florentines at most; so that the abbey was called upon to make a considerable sacrifice for its Bible.

Libraries were so limited that one complete Bible and a few writings of the patriarchs made a magnificent collection. The largest library in the world, that of the Vatican, had no more than 1,100 books at this time.

Voletes fibi oparare infrafcriptos libros mag̃
cũ diligẽtia correctos. ac in hmói lra mogũntie
impffos. bñ otinuator. vemãt ad locũ habitatio-
nis infrafcriptũ.

Primo pulcram bibliam in pergameno.
Item scõam scõe beati thome de aquino.
Item quartũ scripti eiusdẽ.
Ite tractatũ eiusdẽ de eccie sacris a articlis fidei.
Ite Augustinũ de doctrina xpiana. cum tabula
notabili pdicantib multũ pficua.
Ite tractatu de róne et osciétia.
Ite mgrm iohãnẽ gerson de custodia lingue.
Ite osolatoriũ timorate oscie venerabilis fratris
iohãmis nider sacre theologie pfessoris eximij.
Ite tractatũ eiusdẽ de otractib mercator,

To guard against thefts and damage, churches and monasteries chained their books to the wall or shelf. In St Emmeran in the fourteenth century there were 240 books and each one was attached, by a strong chain running through the spine, to an iron bar. They could be read standing up, but they were proof against the light-fingered. In 1378 Thomas of Farnilaw, Chancellor of York, directed in his will that his Bibles and prayer-books should be given to the churches at Newcastle 'there to be chained up so that all men may use them'. And to this day a small library of chained books may be seen in the church of All Saints in Hereford. There are others elsewhere in Britain.

In accordance with the prevailing anti-medievalism it used to be thought that, before the Reformation, Bibles were chained to prevent laymen from using them. This is a typical misconstruction. There has never been a period when men have been so eager to spread the message of the Bible abroad, and to as many people as possible, despite all obstacles. Cost, labour, trouble—all these shrivelled away before the burning religious passion of the Middle Ages. The Bible was paramount.

First, a fine Bible on parchment ... The catalogue of a medieval library lists a total of twenty books. When books were made wholly by hand they were an expensive luxury, to be carefully listed, perhaps chained to a reading desk as a precaution against theft.

11

PRINTING TAKES OVER

WHO WAS THE INVENTOR?

The story goes that one day Johann Gutenberg was sitting in his workroom engaged on an intricate wood-block. One of his pupils ran past and knocked it out of his hand, so that it was shattered into hundreds of tiny fragments. Whereupon Gutenberg boxed the pupil's ears and told him in lurid polysyllables what he thought of him. But after the heat of the moment had passed, Gutenberg went down on his knees to save what he could out of the wreckage; and it was then that the idea came to him that he could use individual letters, like the fragments he was picking up, for printing.

This anecdote is, no doubt, fiction. Very little is known about the beginnings of European printing; it is unknown who invented it, let alone how and when he conceived it. It could have been a certain Waldvogel of Prague, who lived in Avignon from 1444 to 1446 and was rumoured to have developed a system of 'artificial writing' based on the casting of single letters in metal. But so far as we know he did not leave one example of his invention to posterity, and nothing further was heard of him after he left Avignon in 1446. It could have been Laurens Janszoon Coster of Haarlem, who certainly made experiments along these lines, but he does not seem to have had any success until 1454 when Gutenberg was already established. It could have been Johannes Brito of Bruges, an example of whose work is in the *Bibliothèque Nationale* in Paris. But a watermark in the paper would seem to place this book considerably later than Gutenberg's first achievements. Panfilo Castaldi of Feltre, Baldassare Azzoguidi of Bologna, Filippo of

Lavagna, and Antonio Zaroto of Parma all claimed that they had invented printing, but probably this means no more than that they introduced it into their cities.

THE PRINTERS OF ASIA

Gutenberg's only serious rivals are the printers of Asia. In 1392 a method of casting pieces of type in copper was invented in Korea, and eleven years later a state printing-works was founded by T'ai Tsung; this was equipped with several hundred thousand pieces of type and could turn out forty pages in a day. But, generally speaking, printing was hampered in the Far East by the number of different characters needed—more than 40,000 in some instances.

Even earlier than the fourteenth century, between 1041 and 1048, the Chinese craftsman Pi Sheng had made thousands of single letters out of pottery which he baked, stuck on wood, coated with ink, and used to print words on paper—the first recorded use of movable type. Earlier still, the Chinese had used wood-blocks for printing text, in the same way as these were used in Europe to print pictures. In 868 Wang-Chieh printed the Diamond Sutra, an illustrated account of the teachings of the Buddha.

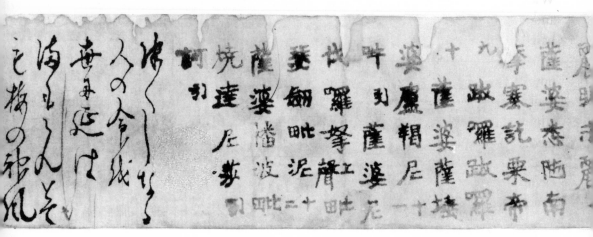

The ancestors of printing *came from the east. Not yet made from movable type, the Buddhist charm above is one of a million copies ordered by the Empress Shotoku of Japan in* AD 767.

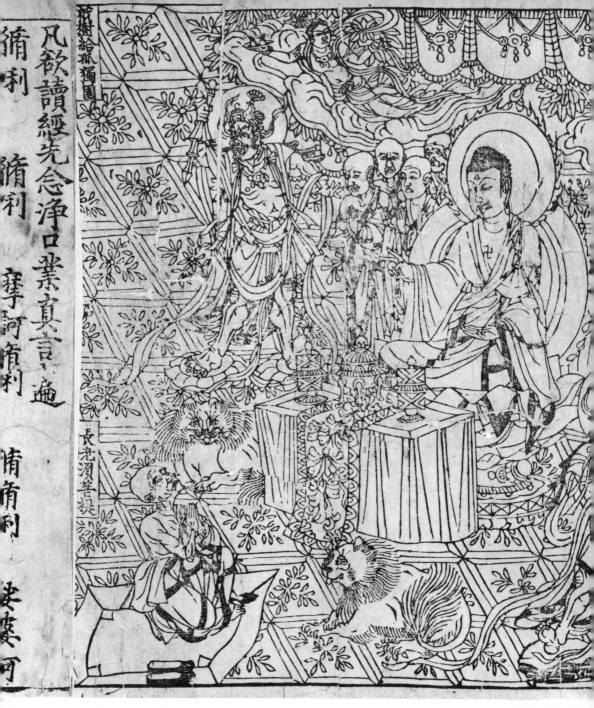

The first dated book *to be printed by the wood-block method was the Diamond Sutra, an illustrated account of the teachings of the Buddha. It was printed in China in 868.*

Paper was a Chinese invention. According to legend, a eunuch named Ts'ai Lun, a self-made man who rose to become Treasurer of the Empire, invented it in AD 105. There is no evidence to corroborate this, but it is at least certain that paper was in use in China during the second century. In 1901 Sven Hedin, the traveller, discovered paper in a desert town in Tibet; this paper could not have been made later than AD 252. Paper was not seen in Europe until one thousand years later. The first paper-mill in Germany was founded during the thirteenth century. Paper was as important to the development of printing as type. It was only by using both in conjunction that books could be produced cheaply.

Not until the invention of paper *by the Chinese had spread to Europe were the conditions right for the produc*

Gutenberg has as good a right to be called the European inventor of printing as any man. What kind of a man was he? What were his interests? How did he hit upon his invention? We should like to know the answers to these questions. But all we know about him personally is that he was always in financial difficulties; that he frequently borrowed money to continue his researches; and that he was often unable to pay his debts. These details can be gleaned from the numerous lawsuits he was involved in.

His real name was Johannes Gensfleisch, and he came of a good Mainz family. He took the name Gutenberg from his father's

beap books. This 14th-century Dutch relief shows processes of manufacture in an early water-powered paper-mill.

estate, on which he was born. The date of his birth must have been during the last decade of the fourteenth century, but exactly when, and exactly how he spent his early years, is not known. To judge from his later achievements, he may have picked up some knowledge from the skilled goldsmiths and silversmiths of Mainz, but, again, this is merely surmise.

Mainz at this time was a troubled town. Feuds raged between the old families and the upstarts who sought to rival them. Perhaps this prompted Gutenberg to move to Strasbourg in 1434. From this city he carried on a protracted lawsuit with a magistrate in Mainz who demanded payment of a debt. Gutenberg seems to have prospered in Strasbourg, despite being sued for breach of promise by a lady called Ennelin. So far as we know, he never married. The breach of promise action led to a legal skirmish with Claus Schott who, in the course of a speech for the prosecution, slandered Gutenberg. He retorted by calling Schott a fool and a rogue, and suggested that his skill in vilification was equalled only by his taste for debauchery. Whereupon Schott sued Gutenberg and was awarded substantial damages. What is more, the lawyer obtained his money. Gutenberg was no pauper. His house on the outskirts of Strasbourg had a cellar stocked with 4,000 bottles of wine for his personal consumption. He gave generous presents to his friends, mixed with the leading citizens, was respected as a goldsmith, attracted many pupils, and, generally, flourished.

By 1442, however, he was so deeply in debt that he had to borrow more than £400 from the monastery of St Thomas. He sank from affluence to insolvency in one year. But this was no rake's progress. Gutenberg's inheritance was swallowed up, not by drinking, dandyism, or debauchery, but by his research work. He was the kind of man who nowadays would be given a government grant and set up in well-equipped laboratories. Or would he? Almost nobody recognized his genius then, because it would have needed another genius of equal calibre to do so. Would his fortunes have been different today?

Gutenberg, the first to make, and print from, movable type. In his right hand he holds a type-punch, symbolic of the new invention that brought him honour and fame and a crushing burden of debt.

According to the legal records, Gutenberg was manufacturing small trinkets at this time—crosses, medallions, and jewellery knick-knacks. But he was simultaneously carrying on secret researches. He was using up vast quantities of lead and had bought a large wooden press, together with other oddments which seemed to have no use. All this cost a great deal of money, far beyond his own means, and he borrowed frequently from three business partners. But when, after a long interval, he seemed no nearer success, his backers lost interest and demanded their money back. Gutenberg was unable to pay. Lawsuits followed, witnesses testified on both sides, and the dispute dragged on interminably. The one piece of evidence which was not submitted to the court was the nature of the work Gutenberg was engaged in. Various kinds of apparatus were mentioned—presses, metal punches, moulds, smelting bowls, and lead—but what these were all for was left to the magistrate's imagination. The purchases were attributed to a whim. The trial ended in recriminations and general dissatisfaction, and in 1444 Gutenberg left Strasbourg for Mainz where he resumed his work. Next year he reaped the reward of his perseverance: he printed his first words.

At first he printed small calendars and a short Latin grammar by Aelius Donatus. The finished products were clear, legible, and pleasing to the eye; above all, they were cheap enough to be bought by the ordinary man who had never before been able to afford books. Gutenberg achieved a small reputation. He was given testimonials, illuminated addresses, everything but the means he needed to go on with his work. His debts grew. First he borrowed 150 guilders at an exorbitant rate of interest from a professional money-lender; then he looked round for a new business partner. He found one in Johannes Fust, who gave him 800 guilders. Now he could start work on his real ambition—the first printed Bible.

THE 42-LINE BIBLE

The preparations took two years and enormous labour. Gutenberg had to devise and make everything for himself, from the individual pieces of type to the ink. Moreover, the idea of economizing on labour never occurred to him. He made all twenty-six letters of the alphabet, together with their capitals, and also abbreviation signs, intricately wrought double-letters, punctuation marks, and numerals. His invention had to be better and clearer than the best and clearest handwriting. It had to be so good that the most skilful calligraphers would not be able to better it. In the end, Gutenberg decided that he must have 290 different characters. Since each page of his Bible had 42 lines of type, this meant 2,600 characters to a page and 46,000 pieces of type to keep three pages going. Each one of these 46,000 pieces had to be finished by hand after it had been rough-cast.

Gutenberg decided to print his first Bible in two editions, one on parchment and the other on paper. Each copy would have 340 sheets of parchment, or the equivalent of 170 calves' skins. Parchment alone would cost him 450 guilders. Not surprisingly, he soon found himself once more in financial straits. Another 800 guilders from Fust tided him over for a short while—he was paying his assistants 30 guilders a year—but then it, too, was gone. Another

The 42-line Bible *of Gutenberg—the world's first printed Bible. With abbreviation signs, dot* *letters and punctuation marks, 290 different characters were needed, all made and finished by h*

Lucas sirus · natõe anthi
ocensis · arte medic9 · disci
pulus apostolog · postea
paulu secut9 usqʒ ad con
fessionẽ ei9 seruiens dño sine crimine :
nam neqʒ vxorem vnqȝ habuit neqʒ fi
lios : septuaginta et quatuor annoru
obijt in bithinia · plen9 spiritu sancto.
Qui cũ iam scripta essent euãgelia · p
matheũ quidẽ in iudea · p marcũ aut
in italia : sancto instigante spiritu in
achaie partibʒ hc scripsit euangeliũ :
significans etiã ipe in principio ante
suũ alia esse descripta . Cui extra ea q
ordo euãgelice dispositionis exposcit
ea maxime necessitas laboris fuit : ut
primũ grecis fidelibʒ omni pfectati
one venturi in carne dei cristi manife
stata humanitate ne iudaicis fabulis
attenti : in solo legis desiderio teneren
tur : vel ne hereticis fabulis et stultis
solicitationibʒ seducti excideret a ve
ritate elaboraret : dehinc · ut in princi
pio euangelij iohãnis natiuitate pre
sumpta · cui euangelium scriberet et in
quo elect9 scriberet indicaret : cõtestãs i
se cõpleta esse · q essent ab alijs inchpa
ta . Cui ideo post baptismũ filij dei a
pfectione generationis i cristo implere
repetende a principio natiuitatis huma
ne potestas pmissa ê : ut requirentibʒ
demonstraret in quo apprehendens e
rat per nathan filiũ dauid introitu re
currentis i deũ generationis admisso
indisparabilis dei pdicãs in homini
bus cristũ suũ · pfecti opus hois redire
in se p filiũ faceret : qui per dauid patrẽ
venientibus iter phebat in cristo . Cui
luce non immerito etiã scribẽdorum
actuũ apostolog potestas i ministerio
datur : ut deo in deũ pleno et filio pdi
tionis extincto · oratione ab apostolis

facta · sorte domini electionis numer̃
cõpleretur : sicqʒ paulus cõsumma
tione apostolicis actibʒ daret · quẽ diu
cõtra stimulũ recalcitrante dñs elegis
set . Quod et legentibʒ ac requirentibʒ
deũ · et si per singula expediri a nobis
vtile fuerat : sciens tamẽ q operantem
agricolã oporteat de suis fructibus e
dere · vitauim9 publicã curiositatem :
ne nõ tã volentibʒ deũ demõstrare vide
remur · qm fastidientibus prodidisse.
Explicit pfacio] Incipit euangelium
secundũ lucam : Prologum ps
sans beati luce in euangelium simul

Quoniã quidẽ multi co
nati sũt ordinare nar
rationes q i nobis com
plete sũt rer · sicut tradi
derũt nobis q ab inicio
ipi viderũt · et ministri
fuerũt sermonis : visum ê et michi assecuto
omnia a principio diligẽter ex ordie tibi
scribere optime theophile : ut cognoscas
eoꝝ verboꝝ de qbʒ erudit9 es veritatẽ . l.

Fuit in diebus herodis re
gis iudee sacerdos quidam
nomine zacharias de vi
ce abia · et vxor illi de filia
bus aaron : et nomen eius elizabeth.
Erant autem iusti ambo ante deum :
incedentes in omnibus mandatis ʒ
iustificationibus domini sine quere
la . Et non erat illis filius · eo q es
set elizabeth sterilis : et ambo proces
sissent i diebz suis . Factũ est aut cũ sa
cerdotio fungeretur zacharias in ordi
ne vicis sue ante deũ : scdm cõsuetudi
nem sacerdotij sorte exijt ut incensum
poneret ingressus in templũ domini.
Et omnis multitudo ppli erat orãs fo
ris hora incensi. Apparuit autem illi
angelus dñi : stans a dextris altaris

The many crafts and trades *that Gutenberg's invention brought in its train are illustrated in*

request to Fust brought about a quarrel, the inevitable lawsuit, and further money troubles.

One way or another, Gutenberg managed to begin printing by 1452. He now had six assistants. Together they set about a work of extraordinary size. It took a full day to set up one page, and an hour to print off ten copies. Everything was done by hand—inking the type, pressing the sheets on to it and hanging them up to dry. Although the hours of work were twelve a day, and sixteen in summer, it took two years to bring out the first edition, and this comprised only 150 copies. The parchment edition cost twenty guilders (roughly the equivalent of £400), the one in paper a little less. This was not as cheap as Gutenberg had hoped, but it sold fast. This may have been due to Fust's commercial ability; anyway,

a series of 16th-century woodcuts. From left to right: paper-maker, typefounder, printer, binder.

he amply recovered the 1,600 guilders he had sunk in the venture. But for Gutenberg, and for most of his customers, the new invention was much more than a successful commercial enterprise: it was the beginning of an era.

The new Bible was a work of art. It was published in two large volumes, beautifully bound by hand. There were 648 pages in the first volume, and 634 in the second. Each page was divided into two columns. The first letter of each chapter and the headings were written in red by a skilful illuminator. The printing was even, clear, and beautiful. Only forty-five copies survive, and some of them are incomplete, but their present-day value is incalculable.

In 1457-8 Gutenberg began work on a new Bible. By this time he had broken with Fust and set up his own works in Bamberg.

The new Bible was to have thirty-six lines to the page instead of forty-two and be set in larger type. This meant that it would have 1,768 pages instead of 1,282, and it overflowed into three volumes. Gutenberg could not obtain all the paper he needed from one mill and had to use ten different kinds. On the whole, the result was less successful than the first Bible, but still it was a remarkable achievement.

These two Bibles, in the Vulgate translation, were the only full-sized books that Gutenberg printed. A large number of calendars, letters of indulgence, Psalters, prayer-sheets, a papal bull, and a *Missale Romanum* are ascribed to him, but these may not have come from his presses. By this time the new art of printing had been taken up by craftsmen, especially goldsmiths, all over Europe. It was an art which was peculiarly satisfying to the medieval mind, since it combined skill with taste, and craftsmanship with technical mastery. Above all, it was an art devoted to the service of religion, because books meant primarily at that time the Bible and prayer-books.

Fust founded a printing-works in Mainz after he had broken with Gutenberg. One of Gutenberg's pupils, Albrecht Pfister, started up in Bamberg and produced one Latin and two German 'Poor Bibles' between 1462 and 1464. Two years later Mentelin of Strasbourg brought out the first German Bible, a much smaller and cheaper work than Gutenberg's Bibles. Pfister crammed sixty-one lines on to a page and packed the whole work into one volume; it sold for 'only' twelve guilders, or £240. A little later another German Bible was published at Strasbourg, this time under the imprint of Heinrich Eggestein. This was followed by an illustrated Bible produced by Joducus Pflanzman. At the same time other printers were producing books in Nuremberg, Cologne, and Hamburg. Printing-works were now springing up in Europe and cheaper Bibles followed one another on to the market.

The printers demanded new translations, besides the Latin Vulgate, to work from. Within a short time, Bibles in High German, Low German, Dutch, French, Italian, Catalan, Czech, Polish,

Russian, and Ethiopian were brought out. The creative excitement mounted almost to a frenzy; there was a glut of Bibles—large, imposing volumes, pocket selections, richly bound New Testaments, polyglot versions like the one compiled by Alcala, the *Bible en françoys* of Paris, and the *Biblja Ruska* of Prague. Altogether, 70,000 Bibles were printed in Central Europe alone before the Reformation. A total of 120,000 Psalters and other Old Testament extracts also belong to this period, and so do about 100,000 New Testaments. And yet each edition ran to, perhaps, no more than 300 copies.

With their fanatical zeal and patience, these early printers were, in the truest sense of the word, what George Bernard Shaw called 'Bible-worshippers'.

New printing-works *sprang up all over Europe in the last years of the 15th century, printing cheaper Bibles in countless new translations, such as this Bohemian Bible of 1489.*

DOCTOR · MARTINVS · LVTTER · AVGVSTINER · WITTENB ·

12

THE NIGHTINGALE OF WITTENBERG

'I CANNOT WITHDRAW WHAT I HAVE SAID'

The year 1521 saw Central Europe in an uproar: Martin Luther had defied both the Pope and the Emperor. Four years earlier he had nailed a manifesto to the church-door in Wittenberg. Two years later had come his famous defiance: *The Pope and the Councils can err.* Then in 1520 he had published three polemics: *Address to the German Nobility*; *The Babylonic Captivity of the Church*; and *The Freedom of a Christian Man.* The Pope had retorted by threatening Luther with excommunication, but he had thrown the papal bull in the fire.

Then there had been his encounter with the Diet of Worms. Luther, a poor, lowly monk, had dared to defy Charles V, by the Grace of God Emperor of the Holy Roman Empire, Lord of the Netherlands and of Burgundy, King of Spain and Aragon, Lord over Austria, Bohemia, and Hungary—the most powerful ruler in the western world. Luther had spoken to the monarch as though he had been simple Charles Schmidt. 'The Holy Scriptures and my conscience are my emperor,' Luther had said. 'I cannot, and will not, withdraw what I have said. God help me. Amen.' The Emperor had raged, called down the imperial ban on his rebellious subject, outlawed him, ordered his writings to be burned, his supporters to be imprisoned, his name wiped out of human memory. It was all in vain. Luther was not to be blotted out by an imperial decree.

Pamphlets were written on both sides. Luther was hailed as the man who had freed Germany from the Roman yoke, who had unthroned the Pope with a stroke of his pen. He was an archangel

When Luther nailed his defiance *to the cathedral door, Duke Frederick the Wise, who had appointed him professor of theology, must have felt he was nurturing a viper in his bosom. An allegorical painting shows the Duke in his bedchamber, dreaming of the unruly monk, whose pen was mightier than the sword—or even than the hammer that drove in the nails.*

struggling with the powers of darkness, 'the nightingale of Witten-berg', as Hans Sachs called him. Erasmus was ironical and wrote: 'He has committed two unpardonable crimes. He has attacked the Pope's authority—and the monks' dinners.' In Luther's name church-doors were broken down, statues smashed, and crosses hacked apart. It was thought that a new era was beginning when falsehood and corruption would be banished from the world for ever.

In reality, Luther's greatness lay not in rebellion but in scholar-ship. In 1521, while the world around him was aflame with attack and counter-attack, he was forced to hide from the Emperor's soldiers in a tower in the Wartburg, an isolated castle-fortress. And there he began his greatest work, which would outlive all the hubbub which seemed so important at the time. This work was his translation of the Bible.

The idea had been fermenting in his mind for years. During his journeys through Germany he had seen how Germans in different regions no longer understood one another, how the Bavarian dialect was as foreign to the Hessian or Westphalian as French or Italian. The German Bibles then in use were equally foreign to Bavarian, Hessian, and Westphalian alike. Luther knew the Bible, even the awkward, almost incomprehensible German translations of it, through and through. That was mainly why, in less troubled times, he had been chosen by Duke Frederick the Wise to be Professor of Theology in the new university of Wittenberg. Luther knew that the one way to make the Bible acceptable to the German people was to present it to them in an entirely new way.

What was needed was a 'mean German', a language which could be understood by Saxon and Silesian, scholar and peasant. But such a language could not be created in a study; it needed to be culled from the ordinary day-to-day life of the people, from the cries of market-women, the talk of children, the backchat of work-men at their jobs. How could he get this material when he was an outlaw? He did it by disguising himself and risking his life in a property tunic and beard while he pretended to be a country squire. Death would be the penalty if he gave himself away. It was a gamble that a professional spy might have quailed at; and he was not a professional spy, only a small, rather delicate, and extremely sensitive scholar.

He collected his findings in a *Letter on Translating*. 'It is no use,' he wrote, 'consulting the Latin letters to find out how German is spoken. Rather should one listen to the mother in her house, the children in the street, and the ordinary man in the market-place, and write so that they will understand and know that they are reading German. . . . To write real German the translator must not be led by the Hebrew words; he should make sure that he really understands the sense and ask himself: "What would the German say in such-and-such an instance?"' These observations hold good for any translator at any time.

203

He began his task in a small uncomfortable room furnished with nothing but a table, a chair, a chest, a bed, and his lute. His health was not good, and he was constantly in danger from other, less natural, causes. He was forced to take precautions when he wrote to his friends, and addressed his letters from 'a town' or 'the Wilderness' or 'the Isle of Patmos' to allay suspicion. Once, when news of his hiding-place leaked out despite all his subterfuges, Luther contradicted the rumour by writing a letter which was intended to be lost. It said: 'I hear that people are saying that Luther is in the Wartburg near Eisenach. They probably think so because I was once captured in the woods thereabouts. But I am here, safe and sound. . . . It is strange that nobody thinks of Bohemia.' Unfortunately we shall never know whether the plan came off and the

Erasmus of Rotterdam *made the fi* *attempt at a scientifically correct text of* *Greek New Testament, working, as he s* *'with all possible diligence and faithfulne.* *In 1516 he produced a parallel Greek* *Latin version, which Luther used as a basis* *his own work. Opposite: a page from t* *showing the beginning of the Epistle to* *Romans.*

letter fell into the intended hands; but it does illustrate the hazards which Luther faced when carrying out a work for which a life-time of peace and quiet would scarcely have sufficed most men, however learned, brave, and indomitable.

All Luther had to work with were two translations of the New Testament by Erasmus, a Greek New Testament published by Frobenius of Basle in 1519, a Latin edition, and one or two German translations. Erasmus's translations were based on such Greek texts as he could find, and they were not the best. The other editions were not distinguished and Luther used them little.

Luther began the work in December 1521 and finished the whole of the New Testament four months later—a fantastic achievement possible only to a man of complete single-mindedness, inexhaus-

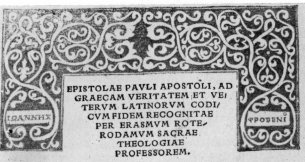

tible energy, and formidable learning. Once the translation was finished he did not give much thought about how it was to be printed and bound. 'I have no time,' he wrote, 'to see what paper and ink, letters and pictures the printer chooses.' Later, experience taught him to pay more attention to the appearance of his books.

The first edition appeared in September 1522 and was entitled *Das Newe Testament Deutzsch. Vuittemberg.* It was illustrated with twenty-two woodcuts from the studio of Lucas Cranach. Melchior Lotter was the printer. The only name omitted from the cast-list was that of the star, Luther himself, who dared not risk disclosing his whereabouts. But Germany quickly guessed that there was only one man who could have achieved this notable work. Three thousand copies were run off and were sold out within three months. Each copy cost $1\frac{1}{2}$ guilders, a sum which would support a student for two months. The salary of a young professor at that time was no more than twenty to thirty guilders a year. And yet readers grasped at the book as though it were the only diet that could save them from starvation. Perhaps in a sense it was.

The *German New Testament* passed from hand to hand, from professor to student, from townsman to farmer. According to a contemporary account, many people carried it around like a talisman and learnt it by heart. Duke George the Bearded, whom Luther called the Dresden Hog, feared the power of the book so much that he made it a criminal offence to buy it, and offered to purchase it back from anyone who owned a copy. But in the whole of Leipzig only four people surrendered their German Bibles.

Scarcely had the first edition been published than Luther set about preparing a second. He made 576 corrections to the earlier text. This edition was ready by December 1522, and was followed by several more in swift succession. Luther made seventeen corrected editions, and altogether eighty-three printings rolled off the Wittenberg presses. With printings in other towns the total rose to 336. Three years after the book first came out, 128,000 copies were in circulation.

'I have no time', said Luther, 'to see what paper and ink, letters and pictures the printer chooses'. But the first edition of his New Testament in German—here is an illustration to the Book of Revelation—was a handsome volume, with its twenty-two woodcuts from the studio of Lucas Cranach.

'HOW WE SWEATED AND STRAINED'

Luther presently turned his attention to the Old Testament. During his stay in the Wartburg he had written to his friends in Wittenberg: 'I cannot begin the Old Testament until you are present and can work with me.' After his return he set to work while his New Testament was still being printed. He was probably helped by his friends Melanchthon, a born philologist, and Matthaus Aurogallus, a Professor of Hebrew. But even with their help it was arduous work. Luther's reference books were a copy of the Vulgate of 1494 and a Hebrew Bible of 1488; with these resources, it took him twelve years to complete his task.

His letters and other writings contain many moving accounts of his labours on the Old Testament. The difficulty of the project, and the painful searchings for the right words, the appropriate form, and the exact equivalent come out clearly in his own words: 'We have often spent a fortnight, or even three or four weeks, over a single word. We were working on Job, Master Philippus (Melanchthon), Aurogallus, and I, for four weeks before we had finished three lines. Now that it is finished anybody can read it easily and smoothly, without ever stumbling over a word or a phrase, as though he were sliding over a polished floor. Little does he realize how we sweated and strained to remove those obstacles which would have tripped him up.'

He went to endless trouble to find the exact word which would make everything clear to the German reader. In Leviticus 11 and Deuteronomy 14 there are the names of many animals. The Latin of the Vulgate gives 'crocodylos', 'mygale', 'cameleon', 'tragelaphus', 'pygargus', 'oryx', and 'camelopardus'. None of these meant anything to Luther, let alone to the average German. So he wrote to his friends who knew more about zoology than he did and asked: 'I beg you to lend us your aid and describe the following animals according to their name and kind. Birds of prey: kite, vulture, hawk, sparrow-hawk. Game: roe, chamois, ibex, antelope or *Hircus silvestris*. Reptiles: Is *stellio* the same as a salamander? *Lacerta limaria* = toad? The Hebrew, Latin, and Greek are so confused that we have to guess these animals by their descriptions. So I would be grateful for the names of all birds of prey, all game, and all poisonous reptiles.'

He was often dissatisfied with himself and with the progress of his work. Even in those days, lack of time was a common complaint. In 1522 he wrote: 'Nobody would believe how letters, business, and friends have held up my work. But now I have promised myself that I will shut myself up at home and make sure that the five books of Moses are ready for the press in January. I will publish these separately, and then the historical books, and finally the prophets. I think this division is permissible, considering the size and value of the books.'

Luther's impatience is not easily understood because he seems to have completed his work on the Old Testament in an astonishingly short time. The Law was published in 1523, Samuel, Kings, and

Twelve years of arduous work *went into Luther's translation of the Old Testament. But when it was done, he had made from the German of the common man a literary language, subtle, flexible and expressive. The whole Bible ran to 1,816 pages.*

Chronicles in the following year, and the Prophets in 1534. Thus the whole canon of the Old and New Testament had been trans-lated. The Prophets gave him the most trouble, as they have done other translators; this is no doubt because they are more subjective, and therefore more obscure, in character than the rest of the canon.

The complete Bible, all 1,816 pages of it, made a deep impression on the German mind. It easily surpassed all previous translations and it opened up new possibilities in the way of a unified, literary German language. He wrote in the vernacular, that is, common or 'mean' High German. He did not originate this. It was the tongue of children at play and of men gossiping in taverns. What Luther did was to establish it as a literary language, a foundation on which a literature could be built. Whatever gaps he found in the vocab-

209

ulary he filled largely from his native East Middle German, and the outcome was a highly subtle, flexible, and expressive language.

Luther's Bible probably did more to unite the German people, for good or evil, than any other single factor. But this did not prevent many of his contemporaries from protesting loudly against his 'freedom of translation', even what were called his 'lies'. One scholar wrote: 'This is not the Bible. It is a piece of outright heresy which seeks only to blaspheme against God and the Pope.' Another, with slightly less hysteria, said: 'Luther has warped the original to suit his own doctrine.' One critic pointed out that whereas chapter 3 verse 28 of the Epistle to the Romans ought to read, 'Therefore we conclude that a man is justified by faith without the deeds of the law,' Luther, by adding 'alone' after 'faith', had changed the emphasis of the statement. He defended himself by saying, 'the word "alone" is indeed not in the original, but it comes naturally to the German tongue to use it in a comparison between two things.' When his friend Doltzigk reproached him with using vulgar abbreviations and contractions, Luther replied that he had chosen these deliberately to convey the vulgarities in the original. Similarly, when he was attacked for mistranslating the names of animals, he explained that he did so only where it could in no way affect the sense of the passage and where an exact translation would mean absolutely nothing to anybody but a zoologist or philologist. A chameleon, for instance, might have been a kind of elephant or snake for all the sixteenth-century German knew to the contrary; so he felt justified in translating it as 'weasel', which was an animal that meant something to his readers, even though a weasel is not a chameleon.

Admittedly there were errors in Luther's translation, but many of these stemmed from the poor originals at his disposal. He said to the quibblers, 'I know, but you have no idea, how much skill, perseverance, and understanding are needed for a good translation. You have not tried. . . . If you have to put the first two verses of the Gospel of St Matthew into German you would be baffled at once.

Luther had a powerful protector *in the Elector John Frederick of Saxony, seen here in a group by Lucas Cranach the Elder. Luther is on the Elector's right. Bare-headed, with right forefinger raised, is Philip Melanchthon, who was Luther's valued helper in the translation of the Bible.*

. . . If you do not like the way I do it, do it better yourselves. . . . There is nothing to stop anyone improving on my version.'

Luther continued to improve his own translation until he died. A school of disciples grew up around him; all its members were dedicated to the scrupulous search for German equivalents of Greek or Hebrew expressions. At the same time, Luther lectured on theology, preached, taught, wrote, and argued. He published a catechism, pamphlets, dissertations, and hymns. When he died on 18 February 1546 he was recognized as the greatest German who had ever lived.

While Luther was still alive, his Bible spread in translation to nearly every European country. There were then no copyright laws and, even if there had been, it is questionable whether Luther would have invoked them. The more people read his Bible the better he was pleased. What angered him was when those who abused him as a heretic and a liar stole large portions of his translation and passed these off as their own work. In practice, these plagiarisms enjoyed little success. In Germany, at any rate, Luther was para-mount and no substitute was acceptable.

Abroad, however, matters were different. Luther had to be translated into the language of the country if he was to be under-stood. The first of these translations was made by the German-Swiss theologian Juda. It followed quickly the publication of the German New Testament but it ran into an unusual difficulty. The printer, Froschauer, stirred up trouble by giving his workers, who put in a twelve-hour day, sausages for their breakfast during Lent. This sacrilege horrified the town council of Zurich, who were not to be mollified by Froschauer's explanation that his men could not complete the work on time if their stomachs were empty, and he could not afford to give them fish. It was not until the great Zwingli came forward with a masterly tract, elaborately entitled *On the freedom of the table. On evil minds. Whether anyone has the right to proscribe food at a given time*, that Zurich's councillors gave way and allowed the work to go on.

In the succeeding years Luther's Bible was translated into Dutch, English (by Tyndale), Danish, Swedish, and Hungarian. Gott-skalksson, who made the Icelandic translation, had been one of Luther's pupils, and King Christian III of Denmark and Norway stipulated that the Danish translation must keep as close to Luther's version as possible. A little later, Bartholomaus Willent and Johannes Breker translated the Bible into Lithuanian, and Johann Sioklucki into Polish. Soon Rumanian, Bohemian, and Slovenian versions appeared. Often enough, these translations marked the

Translations poured out *in the period immediately after Luther's pioneer work. Some early versio[n] include (left) Danish—which King Christian III stipulated should keep closely to Luther's tran[s]lation—Welsh, Hungarian; (right) Slavonic and Romansch (Italian-Swis[s]*

Top-left quadrant (Danish)

I.

Er kong, Dauid vaar
gammil och ved alder / da kunde
hand icke bliffue varm / end dog ath
mand lagde Klæder paa hänem. Da
sagde hans Tienere til hannem / La-
der dem oplede min Herre Kongen
en Pige som er Iomfru / som hun skal
staar Kongen oc tæcte hannem / och
soffue i hans arm / oc verme min Herre Kongen. Oc de oplete en deylig Pige inden alt Israels landemercke / oc
de funde Abisag aff Sunem / oc før-
de hende til Kongen. Och hun vaar
en meget skøn Pige / och hun tæcte
Kongen oc tiente hänem / a'en Kongen befende hende icke.

Adonia Hagiths søn opffør-
re / och laff credesinds tiue / Hend til Dauanteres saat sich / oc
hand berede sig Vogne oc Reysene
hannem i sin nid / at hand maatte haffue sagt / Hui gør du saa? Oc hand vaar oc saa en meget
deylig Hand / och hand haffue affter hannem nest effter Absalon. Och hand haffue sit Raad.

Abisag
staar effter
Regis.

Adonia
staar effter
Regis.

Lower-left quadrant (Welsh)

16 Bellach nid fel gwâs, eich wuch-law
gwâs, [sef fel] braud annwyl yn henhenbeig i
mi: pa saint mhwy i ti yn y cnawo, ac yn yr Ar-
gluwydd hefyd?

17 Os wyf gan hynny yn fyng-hymmeryb
yn y gymmybeith, derbyn ef fel yb fum.

18 Os gwnaeth efe niwed iti, neu fod yn
dy byled, cyfrif hynny arnaf.

19 Myfi Paul a scrifenais [hyn] â'm llaw
fy hun, myfi a daluf, megis ni boswedaf wrthit,
dy fod yn fy-aghel am danat sy hun.

20 Ie frawd, myfi a'th fwynhaf di yn yr Ar-
gluwydd: llonna fy ymraceroed yn yr Ar-
gluwydd.

21 Gan pwnhybied yn dy wyds-dod yn y scrifenais i atat, gan wybod y gwnei hwy nag a
ddywedwch.

22 Ond hefyd paratoai mi let: canys yr
ywyf yn gobeithio trwy eich weddiau
chwi i'm rhoddir i chwi.

23 Y mae ynby annerch Epaphras fyng-
hyd garcharor yng-Hrist Iesu.

24 Marcus, Aristarchus, Demas, [a] Lucas fyng-gyd weith-byr.

25 Gras ein Harglwydd Iesu Grist [fyb-
ded] gyd â'ch yspryd-chwi. Amen.

O Rufain yr scrifenwyd hwn at Philemon gyd â'r gwâs
Onesimus.

Epystol Sanct Paul at yr Hebræaid

PENNOD. I.

Dangos y mae efe rhagor-fraint Crist goruwch yr angelion, 7 ac am eu swydd hwythau.

DUW lawer gwaith a
llaveir modd gynt i penboddiaurod â'r tadau trwy y'proph-
wydi:

2 Y dyddiau di-
wedaf hyn efe a
penboddiaurod â ny-
ni trwy ei Fab, yr hwn a wnaeth efe yn etifedd
pob peth, trwy'r hwn hefyd y gwnaeth efe yr by-
doedd.

10 Ac * ydwyt yn y dechreuad ô Arglwydd a
feiliaist y ddaiar, ag gwaith dy dwylaw di yw y
nefoedd.

11 Hwynt-hwy a ddarffwdant tiche a thân-
bentiw hwynt hwy oll â heneiodaint fel dilleyn

12 Megis y wisc hefyd y plegi di hwynt, ac
hwy a newidiwnt: eithr yr wyt ti a'th hy-
nyddoedd ni phallant.

13 Wrth bwn y'r angelion erioed y dywe-
dodd efe * : eistedd ar fy llaw dehau hyd oni
osodwyf dy elynion yn troed-fainge i'th draed?

14 Onid yspryiion ghafnaethgar ydynt
hwy oll, y rhai a danfonir i wasanaethu, er
mwyn y rhai a gânt etifeddu iechydwriaeth?

Top-right quadrant

Lower-left quadrant (Hungarian)

SUMMAJA AZ NEGY
EVANGELISTAKNAC.

AZ NEGY EVANGE-
LISTAC MEGIRJAC AZ JESUS CHRI-

stusról ez világnac id verítéjérol valo históriát : tudniillic nemzetségét, fo-
gantatását, születését, beszédét, cselekedetit, szenvedését, halálát, eltemet-
tetését, feltámadását, és menyben mentelit. Melly részeket egyic bévebben,
másic rövidebben, vagy egy az egyiket másíc másikat beszélli meg. Ugy
mindazáltal hogy ha szinte nem azon igékhelis, de az értelemmel mind
négyen egyezzenek. Melly dolog mindeniknec el-számálálásában
bizonyisbá és hihetóbbe tesza.

SZENT MATHE
IRASA SZERINT
valo Evangelium.

Az EVANGELIUM Görögige, és Magyarol annyit tészen mint
örvendetes szenet. Es ez igen az szent Irasban értetic az Isten kegyelmét-ce,
bününc boczánattyánac és az örök életnec az Christusban kijelentese és hir-
detése. Itt pedig az Evangeliumnac igéje vétetic az Christusnac lett dol-
gaijért : Tudniillic mint lett embërré, mit szenvedet, mit cselekedet és
mit tanitot, kivaltképpen mint lett meg az mi büneinkért és mint tá-
madott fel igazalásunkért. Szent Mathe ki volt legyen lásd meg
ez könyuec 9.Cap.v.9 es 10.cap.v.3.

ELSŐ RESZ.

Christus nemzetséginec el számálása : fogantatásánac és születésénec históriaja.

JESus Christusnac, David és
Abraham fianac nemzetsé-
gérol való könyv. 2 A-
braham nemzé * Isaacot. I-
saac nemzé Jacobot, * Jacob
nemzé * Judat, és az ó atya-
fiait. 3 Judas nemzé Pharestés Zarat Thá-
mar ól. Pharest nemzé Esromot, Esrom
nemzé Aramot. Aram nemzé Aminada-
bot. Aminadab nemzé Naasfont. Naaf-
són nemzé Salmont. 5 Salmon nemzé
Boozt Rachabtol, * Booz nemzé Obe-
det az Ruth asszonytol. Obed nemzé
Jessét.

Lower-right quadrant (Romansh)

IL SANCT
EVANGELI
DA
NOSSEGNER
IESV CHRISTO
segund
S. MARCO.

Ls velgs Doctturs dalla Baselgia tegnen, è vöglian commü-
namaing, chia quaist Marco, uschlio eir nominá Joanne, fa-
la stat ün filg da Maria, Act. 12. 12. ün parains da Barnaba,
Col. 4. 10. ün cumpaing da Paulo, è Barnabá, Act. 12. 25.
ün dfai Coulavurant da Paulo, 2. Tim. 4. 11. Il qual eir
Petro nomna seis filg, 1. Pet. 5. 13. El aü in secund Evangelist : è traita dal Battaisem è predgias da Joan Battista. E
Lhura davart Christo nos Salvader, sia combatta cun Satan.
Item sia doctrina, miraculs, è sanct deportamaint. Lhura co 'ls Iudeus l'hajan cruci-
fichá, è 'l sco Princip dalla vita, in il terz dí saja resüssá, apparí, & it à schel.

CAP. I.

Joannes battizand, è predgiand, dá
per dута da Christo, è 'l battaja : Christo
vain tentá, predgia, è guarescha amalads.

IL PRINCIPI DAL E-
vangeli da Jesu Chri-
sto, Filg da Dieu.

2 Segund chi 'l ais
scrit in 'ls profets; *Me-
ra, eug tramet meis An-
guel avaunt tia fatscha, il qual vain à
drizar tia via avaunt tai.

3 *Qua aís üna vusch d'ün chi bra-
gia in 'l desert : Chiönfchá la via dal
Segner, fat sias semdas plaunas.

4 †Joannes battizava in 'l desert, è
predgiaiva 'l battaisem dalla penitenza,
in remissiun dals puchiads.

5 E tuot il pajais dalla Judea, è quels
da Jerusalem, giaivan oura pro el, è

givan tuots battizads da d'el in 'l süm
Jordan, confessand lur puchiads.

6 Mo Joannes eira vestí cun peus d'
chamél, & haveiv' üna tschinta d'chü-
ram intuorn ils fianchs ; è mangiava la-
lips, è meil sulvadi.

7 E predgiava, dschant : †Davo mai
vain quel ch'ais plü ferm co 'eug, dal
qual eug nun sun deng, m'inclinand,
da slargiar la curaja dallas scarpas.

8 †Eug s'ha battizads cun agua ; mo
quel s'battizará cu 'l Spirt sanct.

9 E dvantet in quels dids, chia Jesus
vain da Nazaret da Galilea, è fuo bati-
zá da Joanne, in 'l Jordan.

10 E sübit, cur el venn sü our dall' a-
gua, vazet el s'fender ils tschels, è 'l
Spirt gnir giü our sur el, in sumgienscha
da columba.

11 E venn üna vusch da tschel,
dschant : *Tü est il meis chiar Filg, in 'l

Mal. 3. 1.

Es. 40. 3.

Mat. 3. 1.

Luca
3.
14.

Mat.
3.
11.

Es. 42.
Mat. 3.

beginning of a literary language in their countries of origin, just as Luther's had done in Germany.

France, Spain, and Italy remained outside this widespread move^ment which Luther had begun, but in these countries also new translations of the Bible were made. In 1530 the Venetian humanist Brucioli published an Italian translation of the New Testament, and of the whole Bible two years later; because of its Lutheran tendencies this was placed on the *Index Expurgatorius* in 1559. But in 1536 a monk named Zaccheria produced another Italian New Testament, and another monk, Santi Marmocchino, published a complete Bible in Italian in 1538. None of these was bad, but none equalled Luther's. A translation by Giovanni Diodati, however, is worthy to take its place alongside the best of all translations of the Bible. It was only because Latin was still the chief language of religion in Italy that these translations did not match in importance Luther's Bible in Germany.

The first Spanish translation of the New Testament was published in 1543, and of the whole Bible in 1569; these were by Francesco de Enzinas and Casiodoro de Reina respectively. Portugal had to wait another one hundred years for her first New Testament, and the full Bible in Portuguese did not come out until 1719. An oddity was the New Testament in Basque, made in 1571 but not printed until 1900.

France, however, abounded with translations; so much so, that to this day no one of them has been singled out as the authoritative, generally accepted version. Since Le Fevre's translation in 1523, there have been versions by both Catholics—Besse, Frison, Veron, Benoist, Corbin, Marolles, and Godau—and Protestants—Olive^tan, Bertram, Diodati, and Desmarets.

One French Bible has a particular significance in that it was the first to divide the chapters—a device adopted by Stephen Langton, Archbishop of Canterbury in the thirteenth century—into verses. The story goes that Robert Estienne (Stephanus) was reading the proofs of his Greek New Testament as he rode from Paris to Lyons,

The verse^arrangement *we know today was seen for the first time in this Vulgate (Latin) printed Robert Stephanus in 15*

and whenever his ass stumbled Stephanus made a division in the text. The senselessness of some of the divisions might seem to lend support to this story, but it is entirely apocryphal. Stephanus, indeed, was not the first to use this expedient. As early as 1448 the rabbinical scholar Nathan divided the Hebrew Old Testament into verses. Nathan's edition was printed in Venice in 1524 and verse division was adopted in the Latin Bible edited by the Dominican Santes Pagnini and printed at Lyons in 1527. But the New Testament of Pagnini made a different arrangement; and the 1550 Greek New Testament printed by Stephanus was certainly the first to set out the verses that we know today. Verses have proved a most useful device for scholars all over the world. They make it possible to check a reference within seconds. Their disadvantage is that they break up the text in a way that disconcerts the ordinary reader, and mark off the Bible as though it were an oddly presented textbook.

The Roman Catholic authorized version did not appear until the sixteenth century. Until then, the Vulgate had been the most used, but more and more divergences had crept in between one edition and the next. This was felt less by the Roman Catholics than it would have been by Protestants, because the former emphasize the Sacraments more than they do the Word. All the same, Roman Catholics began to call for a more reliable text.

In 1546 the Council of Trent decided to take the Vulgate as the basis for all future work, and in 1588 Pope Sixtus V set afoot work on a revised version of the Latin text. This was published two years

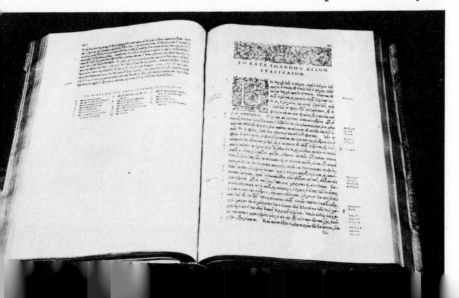

later. Sixtus, however, was so bitterly opposed by the Jesuits that this edition was withdrawn, and it was not until he was succeeded by Clement VIII that revisions were made to meet Jesuit objections. The Sixtine-Clementine Bible which emerged is to this day the authorized Latin text on which all Roman Catholic translations are based.

In Germany, although Luther's Bible continued to be far and away the most widely read, other versions were prepared from time to time. A polyglot Bible containing the Hebrew, Chaldean, and Latin texts was published in Wittenberg; another, in Nuremberg, contained twelve different languages. In 1597, two Protestant scholars, Olivianus and Piscator, brought out a new translation in which they aimed at greater accuracy than Luther had been able to attain. Their translation was the official Bible of the Swiss Church until 1790.

Suddenly the whole face of Germany was changed. The Thirty Years War swept through the towns and villages; soldiers billeted themselves on unwilling peasants, killed the men, raped the women,

The Council of Trent *met in 1546, and the deliberations of the assembled bishops were not completed until eighteen y*

and terrified the children. Hundreds of thousands of Bibles were destroyed, relentlessly searched out and offered on the altar of Roman Catholic immaculacy by the Spaniards who fought in the war. Incidentally, a good many Roman Catholic Bibles went the way of the Protestant ones—literacy was not the strong point of the Spanish army. Beautiful old manuscripts, precious codices, and plain functional Bibles—all were seized and burned as soon as the invaders caught sight of them.

A Bible became a rarity. For a time it seemed that all Luther's work, all the diligence of the monks, translators, and printers through the centuries was to go for nothing and be lost for ever. Presently the lack of Bibles was so deeply felt by Duke Ernest the Pious, of Saxe-Weimar, that he was impelled to replace them, when the fighting died down, with a vast number of new Bibles printed at his expense and issued at a price that most of his subjects could afford. It was the first move towards putting the Bible within the means of most people. Out of the ashes of the Thirty Years War sprang a new objective—the Bible for the People.

. One of their first decisions was to make the Latin Vulgate the basis of an authorized Bible for Roman Catholics.

de þinne· mon gum þ[er]an· rpide undeɽ regle
runum ⁊ dohtrum· oð þ[æt] knom cyme· rolde pforded
þ[er]d lond monig· þine gefylled·

13

THE ENGLISH REFORMERS

In their enthusiasm for the Bible and in the sacrifices they have been ready to make for it, the British have a record that few other people can match. The story begins long before Bibles in the mother tongues of the other countries of Europe began to appear during the Reformation.

In Anglo-Saxon times, before the Norman Conquest, there were few books and little learning in England, save that to be found in a few of the monasteries and abbeys of the land. Yet even then a beginning was made by one or two monks whose missionary zeal incited them to spread some knowledge of the gospel of Christ among the ignorant laity outside their gates. In the Bodleian Library at Oxford there is a tenth-century Anglo-Saxon manuscript containing in verse a paraphrase of parts of the books of Genesis, Exodus, and Daniel. They are thought to have been the work of Caedmon, of whom this story is told: 'One day, asleep in the stables where he had charge of the horses, there stood by him in a dream a man who saluted him and greeted him, calling on him by name, "Caedmon, sing me something." "What shall I sing?" asked Caedmon. He said, "Sing to me the beginning of all things." So Caedmon sang first of the earth's creation and the beginning of man and the story of Genesis, which is the first book of Moses and afterwards about the departure of the people of Israel from the land of Egypt and about many other stories in the books of Scripture.'

He became a member of the community at Whitby, where he learned something of the Bible-story which he turned into Anglo-

'I have passed all my life *within the walls of the monastery,' wrote the Venerable Bede, and it is thanks to his devotion and scholarship that we know as much as we do of the early days of Christianity in England. A 10th-century illuminated MS. shows him in his cell, writing his life of St Cuthbert.*

Saxon verse. He is also credited with the authorship of the fine poem *The Dream of the Holy Rood*.

Part of this poem was cut in runic letters on the stone cross set up at Ruthwell in Dumfriesshire towards the end of the seventh century, when Caedmon may still have been living in the monastery at Whitby.

The only early reference we have to him is that in the *Ecclesiastical History* of the most famous writer of Anglo-Saxon times, the Venerable Bede, who lived at Jarrow between AD 673 and 735, in the generation after Caedmon. He was an accomplished scholar who said of himself, 'I have passed all my life within the walls of the monastery devoting myself entirely to the study of the scriptures.' He

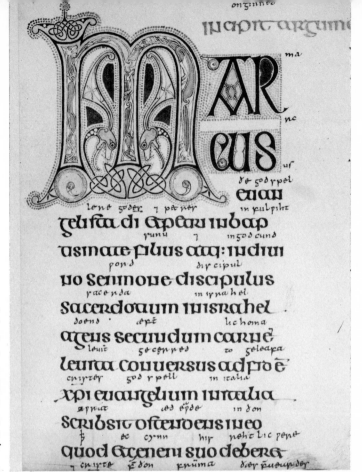

No complete Anglo-Saxon version of the Bible was ever made, though the Venerable Bede translated large parts of it. The monks of the Abbey of Lindisfarne, however, did provide help for those who had no Latin, by writing Anglo-Saxon equivalents above the lines of a Latin translation of the gospels.

wrote a great deal in Latin on many books of the Bible and the best-known story about him tells how, as he lay dying, he succeeded with his last breath in finishing the dictation of the last verse of his translation of the Gospel of St John into Anglo-Saxon. This work has perished.

There is in fact no complete Anglo-Saxon Bible, not even a New Testament. Monkish industry, apart from the honourable exception of Bede, does not seem to have extended to translating the Scriptures. The most that some monks achieved was to provide 'cribs' or word-for-word Anglo-Saxon equivalents for the Latin, which they wrote between the lines of a Latin text, as can be seen in the famous Lindisfarne Gospels now in the British Museum. It was left

221

to King Alfred at the end of the ninth century somehow to find time amid his wars against the Danes and his longer translations of Bede and Boethius, to translate the Psalms as part of his valiant effort to educate and guide his people. As he himself recorded: 'I, Alfred, by God's grace dignified with the title of King, have perceived and often learnt from the reading of sacred books, that we, whom God hath given so much worldly honour, have particular need to humble and subdue our minds to the divine law.'

Little more seems to have been done until long after the Norman Conquest of England in 1066. A later translator was the poet and mystic, Richard Rolle of Hampole, writing in Middle English in the thirteenth century, who turned the Psalms into the vernacular.

In the following century, in the Age of Chaucer, we have a great advance with the first English translation of the Bible as a whole, which bears the name of John Wycliffe. Long before the Reformation he sought to reform the Church as he knew it and his whole work for reform was based upon the Bible. Despite his great renown and tremendous personal influence upon the men of his day and those in the succeeding generations, Wycliffe remains a shadowy figure. It is said that he was emaciated, the result no doubt of his fasting and abstinence, for he was very troubled lest by over-eating and drinking he took sustenance needed by the poor; 'held by many the holiest of all in his day, he was lean of body, spare, and almost deprived of strength', wrote one of his followers (Lollards). His spirit was fiery enough, and it is significant that in spite of the tremendous conflicts which he stirred up by his life and teachings, none of his enemies dared attack him. He died in his bed at Lutterworth after a stroke while hearing mass in his own church, on 31st December 1384.

By 1400 the 'Lollard' Bible, the first English translation of the Bible as a whole, was completed, having been revised by John Purvey, who became leader of the Lollards after Wycliffe's death.

Did Wycliffe in fact do the translating? Certainly men of the time who were his enemies regarded him as the translator. Knighton,

The first English translation *of the Bible as a whole was John Wycliffe's. A beautifully decorated* *of about 1380 (near the end of Wycliffe's life) belonged to the Duke of Gloucester, son of Edward*

Þisofe þou þe
opitile first þ mad
asermoun. or þost
of alle þe þuigɛ
þat iesus bigan
for to do ꝛ teche·
til in to þe day
in þe whiche he comaudede to þe
a postlis bi þe hooly goost: whið
he chese was taken vp. To whom
ꝛ he ȝaue hym self aliue or quic
after his passioun· in many ar
gumentis or preuyngis bi fourti
days: apperinge to hem ꝛ spekyinge
of þe reume of god. And he etynge
to gyder comaudide to hem þat
þei schulden not depte fro ierusalē
but þei schulden þe abide þe biheeste
of þe fadir· þe ȝe herden he seiþ bi
my mouþ. Soþeli iooin baptizide i
water: but ȝee schuln be baptizid
in þe hooly goost: not after þes ma
ny days. Therfore þei camen to gi
dre· axeden hym seyinge. Lord ȝif
in þis tyme: schalt þou restore þe
kyugdoue of ꝛrael· forsoþe he sei
de to hem. It is not ȝoure for to
haue knowe þe tymes or momē
tis· þe whiche þe fadir haþ putte
in his þiler. But ȝee schuln take
þe vertu of þe hooly goost amuȝge
fro aboue in to ȝou ꝛ ȝee schulnbe
witnessis to me in ierm̄ in al iu
dee and samarie: ꝛ vnto þe vtmeste
of þe erþe. And whenne he hadde
seide þele þigges hem seeyinge: he
was lifup and acloude reeyued
hym fro þe eeien of hem. Whāne
þei biheelden hym goyinge in to
heuene· loo two men stooden niȝ
beside hem in whitt clodis þe
whiche and seyden. a ȝen of galilee·
what stonduȝee biholdinge m
to heuene· þis iesus þat is take
vp fro ȝou in to heuene· so schal
coume as ȝee sawe hym goyinge in to

heuen. Þan þei turneden aȝein
to ierm̄ fro þe hill þat is clepid
of oliuete þe whiche is bisidis
ierusalem· hauyuge þe iourneye
of a saboth. And whanne þei had
den entrid in to þe soupinge place
þei wenten vp in þe laȝer þuiges·
wher þei dwelten petir ꝛ iooin ia
mes ꝛ audrew· philip· ꝛ thomas·
bartholomewe· ꝛ mathu· iames of
alpheus· and Symoielotes· ꝛ iudas
of iames· alle þes weren dwellinge
or lastyuge to gidre in preier. wiþ
wymmen and marie þe moder of ie
su. And wiþ his breþeren. In þo
dayes petir risynge vp in þe mid
dil of breþeren· seide· fforsoþe þer
was a cōpanye of men to gidre: al
mest an hundrip and twenty men
þei breþeren it bihoueþ þe scripture to
be fulfillid. whiche þe hooly goost
before seide þe mouþ of dauyþ· of
Judas þat was leder of hem· þat
token iesu þe whiche was nounh
brid in vs: ꝛ gat þe sort of þis mi
nystre. And forsoþe þis weldide a
feeld of þe hiur of wickidnesse and
he haugid· to brast þe middil· and
alle his entrailis ben scheed abrood
ꝛ it was maad knowen to alle me
dwellinge in ierusalem· so þat þe
ilk feeld was clepid acheldemac in
þe lauguge of hem: þat is þe feeld
of bloode. fforsoþe it is writte in
þe booke of psalmys. The habita
cioun of hym be maad diȝert and
be þer not þat dwelle in it· And
an oþer take þe bischopriche of
hym· þerfore it bihoueþ of þis me
þat maad ben gadrid to gider wiþ
vs in alle tyme· in whiche þe lord
iesu entrede in ꝛ wente out amōg
vs bygynnynge fro þe baptyme
of iooin vnto þe day in whiche
he was taken vp fro vs: oon of
þese for to be maad a witnesse

writing in about 1400, accused him of scattering evangelical pearls before swine by allowing the eternal word to become a jest and a plaything of the people. Archbishop Thomas Arundel in a letter to Pope John XVIII about 1412 cursed Wycliffe for turning the sacred books of the Church into the mother tongue, calling him 'that miserable, pestilential John Wycliffe of damnable memory, son of the old serpent, forerunner and disciple of Antichrist'.

Wycliffe's Bible attained a considerable circulation, for those days, when many priests were unable to read and very few had Bibles in Latin. Nearly two hundred copies, not all now complete, of the Wycliffe version made before 1450 still survive, despite the fierce opposition of the Church. In 1401 Archbishop Arundel got

'That miserable, pestilential John Wycliffe', *as Archbishop Arundel called him, handed on the torch to his followers, the Lollards, and his translation of the Bible was revised after his death by their leader, John Purvey. Left: the last verses of Isaiah 40 in the 'Lollard Bible'.*

The Golden Legend of de Voraignes, a 13th-century collection of lives of the saints, illustrated with woodcuts, was one of Caxton's most ambitious productions. With this and similar books he was able to make the main Bible stories available to the common reader at a time when the Church forbade the printing of Wycliffe's Bible. The woodcuts opposite show (left) the Resurrection, and St Jerome and his grateful lion.

Parliament to pass an Act condemning heretics to be burned. In 1407 a Council at Oxford condemned and forbade translations of the Bible. In spite of such steps and yet further prohibitions, the Lollard attitude persisted, and Wycliffe's Bible was treasured and circulated.

Because of the fierce opposition of the Church William Caxton was not able to print Wycliffe's Bible after he had set up his first printing press in England in Westminster in 1476. He did, however, print a translation of de Voraignes' *Golden Legend* in 1483 and other similar books telling the main stories of the Bible, and in this way much of the substance of the Scriptures became part of the oral tradition of the English people.

¶ Here begynneth the Resurrection

Here foloweth The lyf of Saynt
Iherome And first of his name

Iherome is layd of
Ierm that is holy / And
of nemus / that is to saye a
wood / And soo Iherome
is as moche to saye as an holy wood

As yet the Bible text was by no means accurate. Wycliffe and his helpers were forced to translate from the Latin Vulgate edition, for they knew no Hebrew or Greek. The first waves of the New Learning were, however, on the way. In 1498, when Erasmus paid a visit to England, John Colet gave a series of lectures based upon a fresh approach to the Greek text that were to make him the first Englishman to attempt a scholarly approach to the interpretation of the Bible.

Among his students was William Tyndale, who later went to Cambridge in 1522 where Erasmus had been Lady Margaret Professor of Divinity. After translating *The Manual of a Christian Soldier*, a protest of Erasmus against the ungodly lives of many of the monks and friars, Tyndale resolved to turn the whole Bible into English. However, the help Erasmus told Tyndale to expect from the Bishop of London (Cuthbert Tunstall) was not forthcoming; in fact, Tyndale was forced to flee to Hamburg. In a matter of months he had completed his translation of the text which Erasmus had edited of the Greek New Testament after conferring, so the story goes, with Luther at Wittenberg.

Barely had the printing begun at Cologne when Tyndale's enemies got wind of it, so he had to escape in a great hurry to Worms, taking such printed pages as were ready. There Peter Schoeffer completed an edition of 600 copies. They were smuggled into England despite the determination of Wolsey and Henry VIII to exclude them. Out of this large number only two imperfect copies have survived. The Bishops denounced the new English Testament with great violence, speaking against it at St Paul's Cross in London, and any copies they could detect were publicly burned. They complained that Tyndale not only translated but also added marginal notes and glosses of his own, favouring such heresies as the right of private judgment in religious matters.

Meanwhile, still in Germany, Tyndale began to study Hebrew so as to be able to translate the Old Testament as well. With the aid

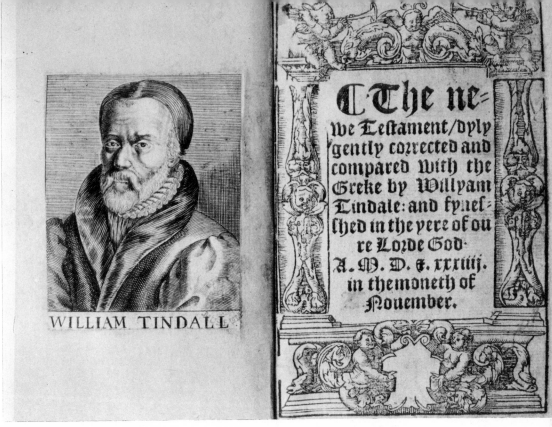

WILLIAM TINDALL

𝕮The ne=
we Testament/Dyly
gently corrected and
compared with the
Greke by Wyllyam
Tindale: and fynes=
shed in the yere of ou
re Lorde God·
A.M.D.ꝭ. xxxiiij.
in the moneth of
Nouember.

'Dylygently corrected', *Tyndale's first revision of his New Testament was printed in Antwerp in 1594, and, like the first edition, smuggled into England.*

of Miles Coverdale he succeeded in publishing, probably in Antwerp, an English version of the Pentateuch in 1530. In 1535 he was kidnapped by his enemies, shut up in a castle near Antwerp and strangled and burned at the stake on 6 October 1536 at the command of Charles V. Meanwhile his disciple Miles Coverdale was more fortunate, despite Henry VIII's proclamation of 1530, *For the damning of erroneous books and heresies and prohibiting the having of Holy Scriptures translated into vulgar tongues.* Using and somewhat revising Tyndale's work, and supplementing it by translating the rest from 'Douche and Latyn', that is to say from the German of Luther and from the Vulgate, he brought out, probably in Cologne, in 1535 the first complete Bible to be printed in English.

It did not encounter the ban that had fallen upon Tyndale's work. On the contrary, it was dedicated to the King. Two years later, in 1537, another complete Bible appeared but apart from its use of what are believed to be unpublished fragments of translation left by Tyndale, it did not do more than print what Tyndale and Coverdale had done. It was put out as being 'truly and purely translated into English by Thomas Matthew'. It was probably the work of John Rogers, a close friend of the martyred Tyndale, and may have been printed at Antwerp. This 'Matthew's Bible' is substantially Tyndale's work.

To Coverdale we owe such phrases as 'She brought forth butter in a lordly dish', and 'Man goeth to his long home'. From Tyndale comes such magnificent English as 'Until the day dawn and the day-star arise in our hearts'; 'In Him we live and move and have our being'; and 'For here we have no continuing city but we seek one to come'. Anne Boleyn had a copy of this Bible, bound in vellum and with gold edges, in her room. It belongs now to the British Museum. According to the present Archbishop of York, Dr F. D. Coggan, it has been reckoned that 90 per cent of Tyndale's work stands unaltered in the King James Authorized Version of 1611.

'EXHORT EVERY PERSON TO READ THE SAME'

Tyndale's personal tragedy is all the more poignant because within ten years of his martyrdom the cause for which he gave his life at last triumphed.

Among the regulations known as The Ten Articles which Cromwell issued in 1536 for the abolition of popish practices, was a rule that children and servants should be taught the Paternoster and the Ten Commandments in English.

In 1538, Cromwell, with the approval and authority of the Archbishop of Canterbury, Cranmer, commanded all the clergy to provide before Christmas 1538 'one book of the whole Bible of the largest volume in English, and the same set up in some con-

228

'Truly translated out of Douche and Latyn', Coverdale's version was the first complete English printed Bible (1535). Opposite; the New Testament contents page.

The new testament.

The gospell of S.Mathew.
The gospell of S.Marke.
The gospell of S.Luke.
The gospell of S.Jhon,
The Actes of the Apostles

The epistles of S.Paul.

The epistle vnto the Romaynes.
The first and seconde epistle to the Corinthians
The epistle to the Galathians.
The epistle to the Ephesians.
The epistle to the Philippians.
The epistle to the Colossians.
The first and secóde epistle to the Tessalonians
The first and seconde epistle vnto Tymothy.
The epistle vnto Titus.
The epistle vnto Philemon.

   The first and seconde epistle of S.peter.
   The thre epistles of S.Jhon.
   The epistle vnto the Hebrues.
   The epistle of S.James.
   The epistle of S.Jude.
   The Reuelacion of S.Jhon.

venient place within the said church that ye here have cure of, where your parishioners may most commodiously resort to the same and read it'. The clergy were expressly instructed that 'ye shall discourage no man privily or apartly from the reading or the hearing of the said Bible, but shall expressly provoke, stir and exhort every person to read the same'. Of the two printed English Bibles then allowed to circulate, that of Coverdale was often inaccurate, while Rogers's version, or 'Matthew's Bible', was accompanied by some tendentious notes. In giving their blessings to Coverdale's book and to the later translation by Rogers, and getting Henry VIII to license them, the Archbishop of Canterbury and the Secretary of State were putting Henry in the very foolish position of approving Tyndale's work, a man whom the King had condemned as a seditious heretic, for both Coverdale and Rogers had incorporated Tyndale's work in their versions.

To cover up this very awkward situation, Cranmer and Cromwell instructed Coverdale to produce a new text with all speed. Coverdale and his printer Grafton were forthwith sent to Paris to put the work in hand, but the work of printing had not got very far before the Inquisition heard about it and both Grafton and Coverdale had to beat a hasty retreat. Their work would have perished but for the cupidity of the man responsible for confiscating the printed sheets. He sold some of them to a tradesman from whom they were bought and shipped to London, where Grafton and Coverdale were able to finish the work by April 1539.

Coverdale's new Bible of 1539 followed Tyndale even more closely. But this edition, the first 'Great Bible', was the one that Cromwell wanted to set up in churches. It appeared with a handsome title page said to have been designed by Hans Holbein on which Henry VIII, Cranmer, and Cromwell were depicted distributing Bibles.

In 1524 Tyndale had boasted to his clerical enemies 'If God spare my life, ere many years I will cause a boy that drives a plough to know more of the Scriptures than you do.' That vow was being

230

The Great Bible *of 1539. The title-page, said to have been designed by Holbein, shows King Henry VIII, Archbishop Cranmer and Thomas Cromwell distributing Bibles to the people.*

❧ The Byble in

Englyshe, that is to saye the con=
tent of all the holy scrypture, bothe
of ỹ olde and newe testament, truly
translated after the veryte of the
Hebrue and Greke textes, by ỹ dy=
lygent studye of dyuerse excellent
learned men, expert in the forsayde
tonges.

❧ Prynted by Rychard Grafton &
Edward Whitchurch.

Cum priuilegio ad imprimen=
dum solum.
1539.

¶ The second parte of the Byble contaynyng these bookes.

realized, for Cromwell's Bible of 1539 included all Tyndale's work, extended and completed by Miles Coverdale and Richard Taverner. Within four and a half years of the appearance of Tyndale's transla-tion in 'Matthew's Bible' of 1537, ten folio and two quarto editions were printed in English, so adding some ten thousand copies to a largely bookless land.

A royal proclamation of 14 November 1539 conferred upon Cromwell the exclusive right to allow the Bible to be printed in English for the next five years. So Bible printing in England became a monopoly controlled by the Crown. Renewed and estab-lished by Queen Elizabeth I in 1589 to confer an exclusive privilege upon the Queen's Printers and the Universities of Oxford and Cambridge to print the Bible in England, it alone of all the Tudor and Stuart monopolies has operated to this day.

Royal enthusiasm for Bible reading did not last long. Despite Henry VIII's new proclamation of 1540 again requiring a Bible to be made available in all churches at a price of 10s. unbound or 12s. bound, no more Bibles were allowed to be printed in England after 1541. In 1543 it was ruled that the gentry were allowed to read the Bible in private; women, artificers and apprentices were forbidden all access to it, a prohibition which created burning resentment. Henry VIII evidently thought that indiscriminate Bible-reading promoted too great diversity of belief. After his evil life had come to an end early in 1547 a number of printers profited by the renewed encouragement given to the Bible by the Protector Somerset in the name of Edward VI. A new set of Injunctions were issued in 1547 on the lines of those of 1538, and in six years thirty-five editions of the New Testament and fourteen editions of the complete Bible were published.

'PROPAGATING VERY GREAT AND DETESTABLE HERESIES'

Not a single Bible was printed in the English language in the reign of the Catholic Queen Mary from 1553 to 1558. Reading the Bible in public was prohibited by a royal proclamation of 18 August

233

Each part of the Great Bible had a separate contents page, with woodcuts illustrating the main incidents in it. Opposite is the opening of the second part, Joshua to Job, in the 1539 edition.

1553. In June 1555 it was forbidden to import the works of Tyndale, Coverdale, and Cranmer, of whom only Coverdale escaped a martyr's death and died in his bed. Rogers had been one of Mary's first victims.

The London Company of Stationers owed its first Charter in 1557 to the determination of Queen Mary and King Philip to provide 'a proper remedy against seditious and heretical books . . . propagating very great and detestable heresies against the faith and sound Catholick doctrines of Holy Mother the Church'. In return, the Company, under its first Catholic master, was empowered to search the workshops of all printers to ensure obedience, and heavy fines were imposed for failure to carry out this obligation. Catholic animosity grew more bitter and more vicious until 1558. A cruel death was the fate of any caught concealing the writings of the Reformers in their homes. It was a brutal age, for which evil precedents of burning and beheading for religious opinions had been set by Queen Mary's odious father, Henry VIII; she, however, soon made him seem an amateur in the business. Many English Protestants, men and women, to whom the Bible was a priceless possession, suffered imprisonment and torture. Nearly three hundred of them were burned at the stake in holocausts which made the English indelibly resolve that never again should the Roman Church be allowed to regain political power in the British Isles. The memory of these martyrs was kept alive by the *History of the Acts and Monuments of the Christian Martyrs* by John Foxe. Undaunted by its 2,154 pages of closely printed black-letter type in two columns, the Elizabethans bought four editions before Foxe died in 1587, and most of them were thumbed to pieces. It has been said of Foxe's *Martyrs* that 'it is impossible to exaggerate its influence upon English feeling and opinion'. While 'Bloody Mary' was earning her title, English Protestants in Geneva undertook the production of a Bible in English. The revised English translation of the New Testament which appeared there in 1557 was the work of William Whittingham, who had succeeded John Knox as

THE HOLY

GOSPEL OF IESVS
CHRISTE, VVRIT
by sainct Marke.

* *
*

THE FYRST CHAPTER.

*The office, doctrine, and life of Iohn the
Baptist. Christ is baptized and tempted, he pre
acheth, and calleth the fishers, Christe healeth
the man wyth the vncleane Spirite, helpeth Pe
ters mother in lawe, clenseth the leper, and hea
leth diuers others.*

A

Malac.3.a.

THE ᵃBE-
gynnyng
of the Go
spel of Ie
ſᵇChriſte,
the Sonne
of God .
2 As it is
writtē in
the Pro-
phetes ,
* Behold
I ſend my

ᵇ In Greke,
Angel, or am
baſſador .

ᵇmeſſenger before thy face , ẃ ſhal prepare thy way before thee.

a Chriſte begyn
neth the Goſpel
by the preaching
of Iohn Baptiſte

As a Protestant weapon *against Catholic
Queen Mary, Whittingham produced the
Geneva Bible in 1560. The text, broken up
into verses for the first time, was printed
in a readable Roman type instead of the
old black-letter Gothic.*

chaplain of the English community in Geneva. Calvin popularized
the edition by providing an introduction. It was printed in handsome Roman type instead of in the black-letter Gothic type of the
Great Bibles; and for the first time it broke up the text into numbered
verses on the Continental model.

Whittingham's New Testament of 1557, newly revised, was
reissued in 1560 together with the Old Testament in a new translation which has ever since been known as 'The Geneva Bible' (or

235

The Bishops' Bible *unsuccessfully tried to supplant the Geneva Bible, whose Calvinistic footnotes were too popular for the Church's liking.*

'Breeches Bible', because of its statement in Genesis that Adam and Eve sewed fig leaves together and made themselves 'breeches'). Three Biblical scholars spared no pains in their three years' toil to make it more accurate and more reliable than previous versions. The translators were Reformers, and they made many marginal notes designed to score points in favour of the Reformed Church of the Calvinists. They were scornful of episcopal government of the Church, and so the book's great popularity was mortifying to the authorities of the Church of England. Tyndale's work had been of the same stamp. He translated 'congregation' instead of 'Church'; 'elder' instead of 'priest'; 'repentance' instead of 'penance'.

The Geneva Bible was so popular that the bishops decided to produce another translation, free from the objectionable Calvinistic features with which reformers had so freely interlarded the word of God. A great effort was made to render the 'Bishops' Bible' attrac-

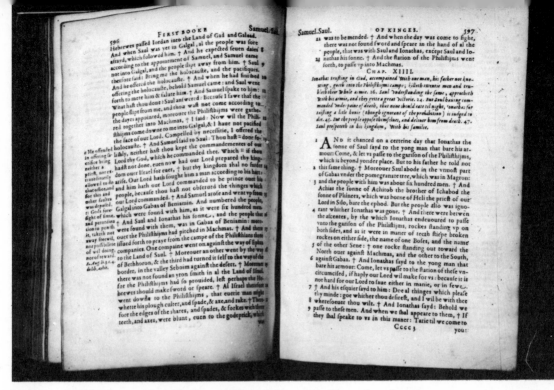

The Douai Bible of 1609, *the Catholic counterblast, made no concessions to the unlearned, using many unfamiliar words, and had little influence.*

tive by woodcuts and engraved portraits of Queen Elizabeth, Burleigh, and the Earl of Leicester. But the bishops did not succeed in supplanting the Geneva Bible, whose text indeed they used freely without acknowledgment. The Bishops' Bible of 1568 was reprinted twenty times; an insignificant number compared with the hundred or more editions of the Geneva Bible in the first eighty years after its publication. It was the Geneva version also that long held the field without a rival in Scotland. When between 1576 and 1579 the printing of a vernacular Bible was undertaken in Scotland by a public subscription from every parish, it was the text of the Geneva Bible that was used. Later it was to become equally popular in America, where it accompanied many who exiled themselves from Britain for conscience's sake.

When Queen Mary died, fears that her widowed husband, Philip II, would mount a mighty invasion to restore Catholic

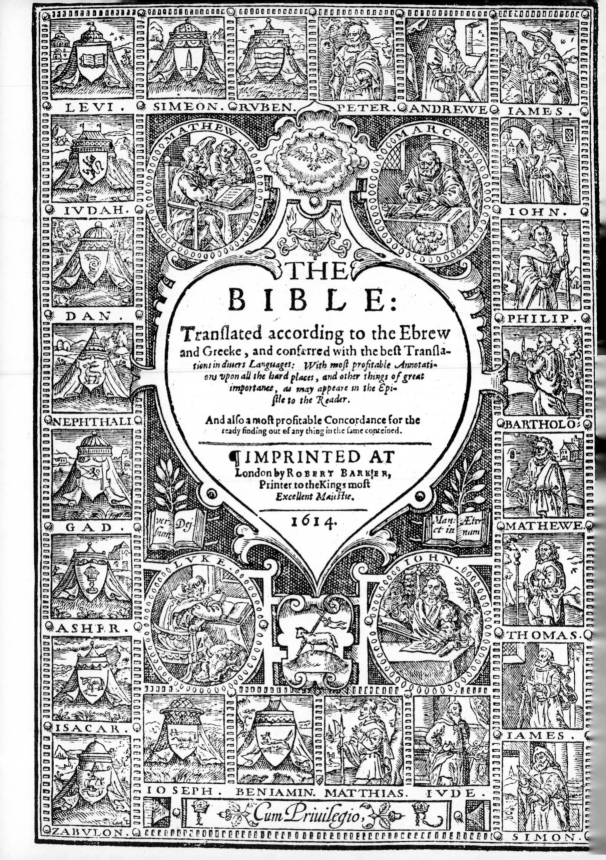

LEVI. SIMEON. RVBEN. PETER. ANDREWE IAMES.

IVDAH.

DAN.

NEPHTHALI.

GAD.

ASHER.

ISACAR.

ZABVLON.

MATHEW. MARC.

IOHN.

PHILIP.

BARTHOLO.

MATHEWE.

THOMAS.

IAMES.

SIMON.

THE BIBLE:

Translated according to the Ebrew
and Greeke, and conferred with the best Translations in diuers Languages: With most profitable Annotati-
ons vpon all the hard places, and other things of great
importance, as may appeare in the Epi-
stle to the Reader.

And also a most profitable Concordance for the
ready finding out of any thing in the same conteined.

¶ IMPRINTED AT
London by Robert Barker,
Printer to the Kings most
Excellent Maiestie.

1614.

verbum Dej

Manet in Æternum

LVKE. IOHN.

IOSEPH. BENIAMIN. MATTHIAS. IVDE.

Cum Priuilegio.

supremacy made active Catholics a menace in England, altogether different from and more sinister than the middle class and poor Protestants whom Mary had tortured and burned. Many Catholics fled abroad to escape the consequences of the open war declared upon England by Pope Pius V in his Papal Bull of 1570, *Regnans in Excelsis*. Later, some Catholic seminary priests, trained in Douay, began to infiltrate into England where they became vulnerable to the Act of Parliament of 1571 which sought to protect the Queen and country from the consequences of the Pope's hostility. One was executed in 1577, two more in 1578. In 1580 two more sinister and determined men arrived in England on the same errand. They were the Jesuits Campion and Parsons. Campion was caught and executed in 1581, Parsons fled the country. There had been provocation enough before the weapons of the rope, the block, and the stake, which the Catholics had first used on a great scale, were at last turned upon one or two of their ringleaders of sedition.

Towards the end of Queen Elizabeth's reign, some English Catholic refugees produced at Rheims in 1582 a new translation of the New Testament. Afterwards at Douay they completed the translation of the rest of the Bible, but it did not appear until 1609. It was not very successful, as no effort was made to translate some of the more difficult words. The Catholic Church had never shown much enthusiasm for vernacular translations of the Bible and the Douay version did not benefit by support from the Hierarchy of the very active kind which Cromwell and Cranmer extended to the Great Bible of 1539. The Latinity of the style of the Douay Bible was in places so excessive that it was almost unintelligible to the ordinary churchgoer. To meet this objection a glossary of fifty-eight unusual words was included. Some of these words have passed into current English and no one today would boggle at 'victim', 'co-operate', 'adulterate', 'allegory', and 'acquisition'. But what would a modern reader make of 'prefinition' if confronted with it in the text, 'azymes', 'scenopegia', 'exinanited', and 'the parasceve of the pasch'? The Douay Bible was of no great influence.

239

THE ACTES OF
the Apoſtles.

CHAP. I.

1 Chriſt preparing his Apoſtles to the behol-
ding of his aſcention, gathereth them together into the mount Oliuet, commaundeth
them to expect in Hieruſalem the ſending
downe of the holy Ghoſt, promiſeth after few
dayes to ſend it : by vertue whereof they
ſhould be witneſſes vnto him, euen to the vt-
moſt parts of the earth. 9 After his aſcen-
ſion they are warned by two Angels to de-
part, and to ſet their mindes vpon his ſecond
comming. 12 They accordingly returne,
and giuing themſelues to prayer, chuſe Matthias Apoſtle in the place of Iudas.

He former treatiſe
haue I made, O
Theophilus, of
all that Ieſus be-
gan both to doe
and teach,

2 Untill the
day in which he
was taken vp, af-
ter that he through the holy Ghoſt had
giuen commandements vnto the Apoſtles, whom he had choſen.

3 To whom alſo hee ſhewed him-
ſelfe aliue after his paſſion, by many in-
fallible proofes, being ſeene of them for-
tie dayes, and ſpeaking of the things

ſons, which the Father hath put in his
owne power.

8 *But ye ſhall receiue ‖ power after that the holy Ghoſt is come vpon
you, and ye ſhall be witneſſes vnto me,
both in Hieruſalem, and in all Iudea,
and in Samaria, and vnto the vtter-
moſt part of the earth.

9 * And when he had ſpoken theſe
things, while they beheld, he was taken vp, and a cloud receiued him out of
their ſight.

10 And while they looked ſtedfaſtly
toward heauen, as he went vp, behold,
two men ſtood by them in white ap-
parell,

11 Which alſo ſaid, Ye men of Galilee, why ſtand yee gazing vp into heauen? This ſame Ieſus, which is taken
vp from you into heauen, ſhall ſo come
in like maner as ye haue ſeene him goe
into heauen.

12 Then returned they vnto Hieruſalem, from the mount called Oliuet,
which is from Hieruſalem a Sabbath
dayes iourney.

13 And when they were come in, they
went vp into an vpper roome, where a-
bode both Peter and Iames, & Iohn,
and Andrew, Philip, & Thomas, Bartholomew, and Matthew, Iames the

14

THE AUTHORIZED VERSION

Zeal for the House of the Lord had eaten up the ministers of the
Kirk, as the Church was called in Scotland, and had devoured
whatever good manners they might otherwise have developed.
James VI of Scotland, now James I of England, learned early that
they were no respecters of persons. His tutor was that extraordinary
man and great scholar, George Buchanan (1509–1582), a Catholic
turned Protestant, the traducer and vilifier of the character of the
King's mother, Mary Queen of Scots. Under his guidance James
became able 'to read a chapter out of the Bible out of Latin into
French and out of French after into English'.

The real rulers of the Scottish people at that time were the Pres-
byterian ministers, through the Kirk sessions in which the lower
classes of the community were able to make their voices heard.
Ministers shared the poverty of their flocks, but led them in an
intense piety and devotion to Bible principles that was exceeded only
by their passionate hatred of anything resembling the teaching and
ritual of the papal Church. One of them, Andrew Melville, told
James to his face that he was 'but God's silly vassal'. Memories of
such incidents, and there were many, caused him in later years to
say that 'a Scottish Presbytery agreeth as well with monarchy as
God and the Devil. Then Jack and Tom and Will and Dick shall
meet and censure me and my Council.' The uneasy life which he
then led as James VI of Scotland, in fear of the lairds and nobles, in
resentment of the pretensions of the Kirk and in a dependence upon

England which forced him to connive at his mother's execution, all conspired to damage his character and disposition which had never been robust or resolute.

When therefore in 1603 he inherited the English throne, he very cheerfully escaped from his turbulent capital, as he is reported as saying, 'Into the Promised Land where I sit amongst grave, learned and reverend men, not as before, elsewhere, a King without a State, without honour, without order where beardless boys would brave us to the face'. Troubles soon met him in England. He was met on his way south by a deputation bearing a petition from seven hundred and fifty English ministers pleading to be allowed to modify church services in a way to satisfy their strong puritan scruples.

The result of this appeal was a meeting at Hampton Court Palace on 14 January 1603 between four representatives of those against conformity; nine bishops including Whitgift, Archbishop of Canterbury; eight Deans; and four other eminent clergymen. James I presided as Moderator before a public audience of the Lords of the Privy Council. The Hampton Court Conference lasted three days. William Barlow, who was one of the four eminent clergymen present at the Conference, published shortly afterwards 'The Sum and Substance of the Conference at Hampton Court', which, selective and tendentious as it seems to have been, remains the only account of what went on. Thomas Fuller in the next generation relied upon it in his much-quoted *Church History of Britain* (1655).

The leader of the four puritan divines, the learned and saintly John Rainolds, President of Corpus Christi College, Oxford, seems to have failed through diffidence or the implacable hostility of his opponents, to make the impact upon the meeting that his talents, his character, his learning, and his deep sincerity deserved. He had, however, one or two triumphs. 'May your Majesty be pleased', he asked, 'that the Bible be new translated, such as are extant not answering to the original.' Bancroft, the Bishop of London, tried to squash him by saying 'if any man's humour might be allowed, there would be no end of translating.' The King, however, sided

King James I of England and VI of Scotland, 'God's silly vassal' as a Scots minister called him, set on foot the great work of the Authorized Version, saying that he 'could never yet see a Bible well translated in English'. He gave it his royal authority, but not a penny towards the cost of it.

with Rainolds. 'I profess,' he said, 'I could never yet see a Bible well translated in English but I think that of all, that of Geneva is the worst. I wish some special pains were taken for a uniform translation which should be done by the best learned of both Universities, then reviewed by the Bishops, presented to the Privy Council, lastly ratified by royal authority, to be read in the whole Church and no other.' Trimming his sails to the royal wind, Bancroft interjected 'But it is fit that no marginal notes be added thereunto.' James was pleased. 'That caveat is well put in, for in the Geneva translation, some notes are partial, untrue, seditious and savouring of traitorous conceits, as when from Exodus 1, 17 disobedience to kings is allowed in a marginal note.' The King did not seem to know that the Bishops' Bible contained a note to the same effect: 'It is better to obey God than man.'

243

As a result of this discussion forty-seven learned men, among whom Rainolds was included until his death in 1607, divided into six groups, two at Oxford, two at Cambridge, and two at West- minster, and parcelled out the work between them. Two companies worked on the New Testament, three on the Old Testament, and one on the Apocrypha. The Dean of Westminster, whom James's mandate had appointed to be one of the 'directors', was at that time Lancelot Andrewes, of whom it was said that he 'might have been interpreter-general at Babel . . . the world wanted learning to know how learned he was'. The translators included a future Archbishop of Canterbury (Abbot), and six bishops, as well as an array of dis- tinguished scholars from Oxford and Cambridge. An unexpected foreign name was that of Adrian de Saravia, prebendary of Canter- bury, who had found in England the middle road he sought between the extremes of Rome and Geneva.

The work of translating was spread over three years and a further nine months was spent on revision. 'The work has not been huddled up in seventy-two days', says the preface, 'but has cost the workmen, as light as it seemeth, the pains of twice seven times seventy-two days and more: matters of such weight and consequence are to be speeded with maturity: for in a business of moment a man feareth not the blame of convenient slackness.'

'HONOURED BE THEIR NAME THAT BRAKE THE ICE'

The Authorized Version of the English Bible is easily the most renowned and extraordinary exception to the general truth that it is impossible for a committee to produce good prose. Such were its felicitous choice of words, its cadences, its clarity and simplicity that it made its way into the minds and hearts of generations of English men and women by its outstanding merit. It had no other aid, for no ecclesiastical recommendation, no royal command, no parliamentary authority promoted its circulation. Other translations were not prohibited or discouraged except by the terms of the royal patent of Queen Elizabeth conferring exclusive rights of printing

Bibles upon the Queen's Printers. While this patent did not say that the royal printers should issue none but the Authorized Version after 1611, they concentrated upon it. During the Protectorate the patent lapsed, but the Authorized Version survived, to command the field when under Charles II the King's Printer's Patent was restored.

It was also without royal financial support. There is no evidence that James ever undertook to pay for the Authorized Version, and it seems clear that he never provided a farthing towards it. Such were his colossal debts and financial embarrassments that it was most unlikely that he would make any contribution. The expense, which was said to have amounted to £3,500, a very heavy outlay in those days, was probably found by the King's Printer, Robert Barker. In the following reign, probably as a result of sabotage by one of his ill-disposed employees, Barker and his associate Lucas, the King's Printers, produced the 'Wicked Bible' of 1631, so-called because of its reading of Exodus 20, 14, as 'Thou shalt commit adultery' for the Seventh Commandment. Every copy that could be located was called in and burnt. The King's Printer was ruined. Charles I put all the Bible printing costs upon them because they were, he said, 'great gainers by this patent'.

The translators of the Authorized Version gave proper credit to their predecessors. In their epistle to the Reader they said 'We are far from condemning any of their labours that have travailed before

The King's Printer, *Robert Barker,* *probably had to find the whole cost of the* *Authorized Bible—a considerable outlay* *for those days. Barker's imprint is here* *seen on a psalter of 1639, with corrections* *made in 1661, probably when* *other associates joined him in his privileged* *but expensive position.*

us in this kind, either in this land or beyond sea, either in King Henry's time or Queen Elizabeth's—that we acknowledge them to have been raised up of God for the building and furnishing of his Church and they deserve to be had of us and of posterity in everlasting remembrance. Therefore blessed be they and honoured be their name that brake the ice . . .'

To none can this generous tribute be directed with greater justice than to William Tyndale. His racy, vigorous style which did not disdain colloquialisms such as 'Tush, ye shall not die', and 'The Lord was with Joseph and he was a lucky fellow', had also a fine feeling for the use of words and at times a poetic felicity. He too had the Lollard Bible to provide him with a first draft. Those who produced the Authorized Version truly declared, 'Good Christian Reader, we never thought from the beginning that we should need to make a new translation, nor yet to make of a bad one a good, but to make a good one better; or out of many good ones one principal good one.' In so doing they were able to preserve language that had already become slightly archaic, the language of the Lollards, of Richard Rolle and of Sir Thomas More, and to forge an indestructible strand which has ever since helped to preserve the continuity of English prose.

A happy comparison has been made between their work and an English cathedral, as the product not merely of one particular period but of several ages. Fuller's verdict of over three hundred years ago may still stand: 'wheresoever the Bible shall be preached or read in the whole world, there shall also this that they have done be told in memorial of them.' It is not given to many to have such a memorial, one whose great merits have had superlative praise over the years. Macaulay said that 'if everything else in our language should perish it would alone suffice to show the whole extent of its beauty and power.' Not long ago it was described as 'the greatest of all translations . . . the greatest of English books, the first of the English classics, the source of the greatest influence upon English character and speech.'

Hough I spake with the tonges of men and aungels, and haue no loue, I am euen as soundyng brasse: or as a tynklynge cymball.

And though I coulde prophesy, and vnderstande al secretes, and all knowledge: yea, yf I had a* all fayth, so that I could moue moū-is out of their places, and yet had no loue, I were no-ge. And though I bestowe all my goodes (to fede the poore) though I gyue my body euen that I burned, and yet : no loue, it profeteth me nothynge.

✝The pistle on the sonday called Quinquagesima.

Math.vij.c
Luke.xiiij.c

Hough I speake with the tongues of men ⁊ of Angels, and haue not charity I am become as sounding brasse or a tinkling cymbal.

2 And though I haue the gift of prophesie, and vnderstand all mysteries and all knowledge: and though I haue all faith, so that I could remooue mountaines, and haue no charitie, I am nothing.

The growth of our language *as an organic, living thing is mirrored in the many versions of the Bible in English that have appeared over the centuries. Above are Tyndale's translation (1525) and the King James version (1611) of the beginning of 1 Corinthians 13.*

Nile ȝe tresoure to ȝou tresouris in erthe,
where ruste and mouȝte destrieth, and
where theues deluen out and stelen; but
gadere to ȝou tresouris in heuene, where
nether ruste ne mouȝte destrieth, and
where theues deluen not out, ne stelen.
For where thi tresoure is, there also thin
herte is. The lanterne of thi bodi is thin
iȝe; if thin iȝe be symple, al thi bodi shal
be liȝtful, but if thin iȝe be weiward, al
thi bodi shal be derk. If thanne the liȝt
that is in thee be derknessis, how grete
schulen thilk derknessis be? No man may
serue tweyn lordis, for ethir he schal hate
the toon, and loue the tother; eithir he
schal susteyne the toon, and dispise the
tothir. ȝe moun not serue God and
richessis. Therefor I seie to ȝou, that ȝe
be not bisi to ȝoure lijf, what ȝe schulen
ete; nether to ȝoure bodi, with what ȝe
schulen be clothid. Whether lijf is not
more than meete, and the bodie more
than cloth? Biholde ȝe the foulis of the
eire, for thei sowen not, nethir repen,
nethir gaderen in to bernes; and ȝoure
fadir of heuene fedith hem. Whether ȝe
ben not more worthi than thei? But who
of ȝou thenkynge mai putte to his
stature o cubit? And of clothing what ben
ȝe bisye? Biholde ȝe the lilies of the feeld,
how thei wexen. Thei trauelen not,
nether spynnen; and Y seie to ȝou Salomon in al his glorie was not keuered as
oon of these. And if God clothith thus
the hei of the feeld, that to day is, and to
morewe is cast in to an ouen, hou much
more ȝou of litel feith? Therfor nyle
ȝe be bisi, seiynge, What schulen we
ete? or, What schulen we drinke? or,
with what thing schulen we be keuered?
For hethene men seken alle these thingis;
and ȝoure fadir woot, that ȝe han nede
to alle these thingis. Therfor seke ȝe
first the kyngdom of God, and his
riȝtfulnesse, and alle these thingis shulen
be cast to ȝou. Therfor nyle ȝe be bisy
in to the morew, for the morew shal be
bisi to hym silf; for it suffisith to the dai
his owen malice.

Se that ye gaddre you not treasure vpon the erth,
where rust and mothes corrupte, and where theves
breake through and steale. But gaddre ye treasure
togeder in heven, where nether rust nor mothes
corrupte, and where theves neither break up nor
yet steale. For where soever youre treasure ys, there
will youre hertes be also. The light of the body is
thyne eye. Wherefore yf thyne eye besyngle, all thy
body shalbe full of light. But and if thyne eye be
wycked then all thy body shalbe full of derckenes.
Wherefore yf the light that is in the, be darckenes:
how greate is that darckenes. No man can serve
two masters. For ether he shall hate the one and
love the other: or els he shall lene to the one and
despise the other: ye can not serve God and
mammon. Therefore I saye vnto you, be not
carefull for your lyfe, what ye shall eate, or what
ye shall drincke, nor yet for youre body, what ye
shall put on. Ys not the lyfe more worth than
meate; and the body more of value than rayment?
Beholde the foules of the ayer: for they sowe not,
nether reepe nor yet cary in to the barnes: and yet
youre hevenly father fedeth them. Are ye not moche
better then they? Which of you (though he toke
thought therfore) coulde put one cubit vnto his
stature? And why care ye then for rayment?
Considre the lylies of the felde, how they growe.
They labour not nether spynne. And yet for all
that I saye vnto you, that euen Salomon in all his
royalte was not arayed lyke vnto one of these.
Wherefore yf God so clothe the grasse, which ys
to daye in the felde, and to morowe shalbe caste
into the fournace: shall he not moche more do the
same vnto you, o ye of lytle fayth?
Therefore take no thought sayinge: what shall we
eate, or what shall we drincke, or wherwith shall
we be clothed? After all these thynges seke the
gentyls. For youre hevenly father knoweth that
ye have neade of all these thynges. But rather
seke ye fyrst the Kyngdome of heven and the
rightwisnes thereof, and all these thynges shalbe
ministred unto you.
Care not then for the morow, but let the morow
care for it selfe: for the daye present hath ever
ynough of his awne trouble.

FOUR VERSIONS OF A WELL-KNOWN PAS

Lay not up for yourselves treasures on earth, where moth and rust doth corrupt, and where thieves break through and steal: But lay up for yourselves treasures in heaven, where neither moth nor rust doth corrupt, and where thieves do not break through nor steal: For where your treasure is, there will your heart be also. The light of the body is the eye: if therefore thine eye be single, thy whole body shall be full of light. But if thine eye be evil, thy whole body shall be full of darkness. If therefore the light that is in thee be darkness, how great is that darkness! No man can serve two masters: for either he will hate the one, and love the other; or else he will hold to the one, and despise the other. Ye cannot serve God and mammon. Therefore I say unto you, Take no thought for your life, what ye shall eat, or what ye shall drink; nor yet for your body, what ye shall put on. Is not the life more than meat, and the body than raiment? Behold the fowls of the air: for they sow not, neither do they reap, nor gather into barns; yet your heavenly Father feedeth them. Are ye not much better than they? Which of you by taking thought can add one cubit unto his stature? And why take ye thought for raiment? Consider the lilies of the field, how they grow; they toil not, neither do they spin: And yet I say unto you, That even Solomon in all his glory was not arrayed like one of these. Wherefore, if God so clothe the grass of the field, which to day is, and tomorrow is cast into the oven, shall he not much more clothe you, O ye of little faith? Therefore take no thought, saying, What shall we eat? or, What shall we drink? or, Wherewithal shall we be clothed? (For after all these things do the Gentiles seek:) for your heavenly Father knoweth that ye have need of all these things. But seek ye first the kingdom of God, and his righteousness; and all these things shall be added unto you. Take therefore no thought for the morrow: for the morrow shall take thought for the things of itself. Sufficient unto the day is the evil thereof.

Do not store up for yourselves treasure on earth, where it grows rusty and moth-eaten, and thieves break in to steal it. Store up treasure in heaven, where there is no moth and no rust to spoil it, no thieves to break in and steal. For where your wealth is, there will your heart be also.

The lamp of the body is the eye. If your eyes are sound, you will have light for your whole body; if the eyes are bad, your whole body will be in darkness. If then the only light you have is darkness, the darkness is doubly dark.

No servant can be slave to two masters; for either he will hate the first and love the second, or he will be devoted to the first and think nothing of the second. You cannot serve God and Money.

Therefore I bid you put away anxious thoughts about food and drink to keep you alive, and clothes to cover your body. Surely life is more than food, the body more than clothes. Look at the birds of the air; they do not sow and reap and store in barns, yet your heavenly Father feeds them. You are worth more than the birds! Is there a man of you who by anxious thought can add a foot to his height? And why be anxious about clothes? Consider how the lilies grow in the fields; they do not work, they do not spin; and yet, I tell you, even Solomon in all his splendour was not attired like one of these. But if that is how God clothes the grass in the fields, which is there today, and tomorrow is thrown on the stove, will he not all the more clothe you? How little faith you have! No, do not ask anxiously, 'What are we to eat? What are we to drink? What shall we wear?' All these are things for the heathen to run after, not for you, because your heavenly Father knows that you need them all. Set your mind on God's kingdom and his justice before everything else, and all the rest will come to you as well. So do not be anxious about tomorrow; tomorrow will look after itself. Each day has troubles enough of its own.

15

IN A THOUSAND TONGUES

In 1790 a little girl named Mary Jones lived in the Welsh village of Llanfihangel. Her parents were poor weavers, at a time when the poverty of Wales was a byword. Almost unaided, Mary had taught herself to read, and she took it into her head that she wanted a Bible. A Bible! Her parents could barely afford the simplest food and clothing. If Mary wanted a Bible, she must buy it for herself. So she began to save her pennies earned by running errands, helping the neighbouring women in their homes, and putting by each painfully earned coin for the book she yearned for. At the end of a year she had saved a shilling—about one⁄twentieth of the price of the cheapest Bible on sale. Then her father lost his job, her mother fell ill, and even the shilling had to be spent—on medicine. Un⁄daunted, Mary began again. For years she struggled and denied herself everything that most girls take for granted. At last she thought she had enough money for a Bible. But where could she buy one? There was no one in the village who owned a Bible—even the vicar had no Bible in Welsh. But he knew another clergy⁄man, in Bala, who had a spare copy, and he was willing to give Mary a letter of introduction to him. So Mary set out to walk to Bala, twenty⁄five miles into the next county. But what were twenty⁄five miles of hard walking after so many years of perseverance? With only verbal directions for a guide, the journey took her two days. When she reached Bala her first act—before eating, drinking, rest⁄ing, or washing off the grime of her journey—was to visit the Rev. Thomas Charles. She trembled with excitement as she told him

Hunger for the Word of God *is sym bolized by the story of Mary Jones and h determination to acquire a Bible in Welsh. contemporary drawing shows her as she set o to walk barefoot to Bala. The Bible s bought is now a treasured possession of t British and Foreign Bible Society. Wi touching pride she set the mark of ownersh upon it, in what was to her a foreign language 'Mary Jones His the True Onour of th Bible'.*

her story and what it was she wanted: would he sell her his Bible? Then came the crushing blow. Charles had promised his Bible to someone else and, in any event, the sum she had saved was far too small. Mary broke down. It seemed the end of everything.

Charles then relented and gave the girl his Bible. Mary went happily back to Llanfihangel; her quest was over. But the vicar of Bala had been so impressed by her visit that he could not get it out of his mind. Eventually he mentioned it at a meeting of the Religious Tract Society in London. 'We must find ways and means of printing the Bible for the poor people of Wales!' he cried. And almost as soon as the words were uttered another delegate, a Baptist minister named Hughes sprang to his feet and shouted: 'Why only for Wales? Why not for the whole country? Why not for the whole world?'

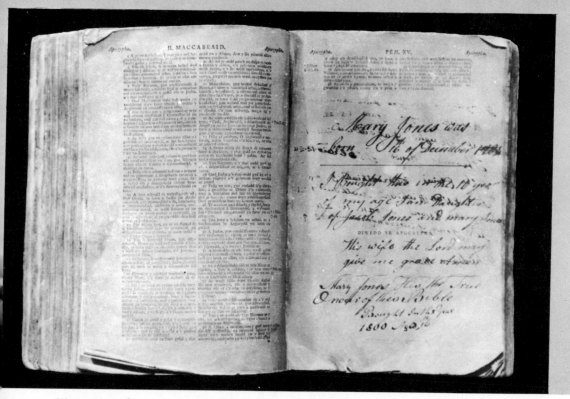

Two years later, in 1804, the British and Foreign Bible Society was founded.

The idea was not new. The first to hit upon it was Anemont de Coct, a French Protestant, who fled to Basle from the Counter-Reformation and spent his entire fortune on the printing of cheap Bibles. These were smuggled across the frontier and given away by pedlars. Then there was Hans Ungnad, Baron von Sonnegk, a former Captain-General in the Austrian army. He, at his own expense, had the Bible translated into Slovene and Croat and had copies distributed throughout the Balkans 'so that there may be gathered together Croats and Slovenes—yea, even Turks—into the Church of Christ'. These were the forerunners.

Around the beginning of the eighteenth century their effects began to appear. But another body had already been at work for more than one hundred years. This was the Society for Promoting Christian Knowledge, set up in 1698 with the object of distributing the Bible, establishing libraries of Christian literature, and educating the children of the poor. Today, the missionary activities of this body, usually referred to as the SPCK, are world-wide.

At first the work of such pioneers was restricted because the cost of books was prohibitive. It was not until a printer named Eler was moved to set up the whole Bible in type and then make brass plates of each page that the aim of producing cheap Bibles for large-scale distribution became practicable. These 'stereotype plates', as they were called, demanded a large initial outlay, but once they had been made they cut costs to a minimum. Between 1712 and 1722 Eler printed twenty-eight editions of the New Testament and sixteen editions of the complete Bible, amounting to 180,000 copies, and each cost a fraction of past prices.

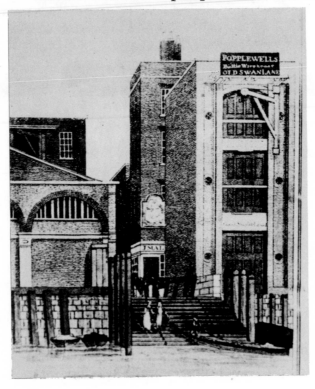

Next door to a bottle warehouse *amid the noise and dirt of a Thames-side wharf, the first meeting of the British and Foreign Bible Society took place in 1804. Today it is one of the biggest missionary organizations in the world.*

Remote missionary stations—like this Baptist mission on the lower Congo in 1884—needed endless new translations of the Bible. Frequently the missionaries themselves were the translators.

Despite this enormously increased output, there were still, at the beginning of the nineteenth century, large areas where not one Bible was to be found. And so Hughes's spontaneous reaction to the Rev. Thomas Charles's plea became a world slogan. 'The Bible for the whole world'—that was the objective. Bible societies were set up in Basle, Philadelphia, Berlin, Elberfeld, Dresden, Amsterdam, Oslo, Nuremberg, New York, Stuttgart, and elsewhere. The Stuttgart society alone printed more than forty million Bibles between 1812 and 1956. Thanks to the efforts of Elias Boudinot, president of the New Jersey Bible Society, no fewer than 128 local Bible societies united to form the American Bible Society in 1816 and this body is still active. In Eichsfeld a combined Roman Catholic-Protestant society was founded, though the Catholic side gradually dropped out, for these societies were not always regarded with favour by the Vatican. Indeed, Pope Pius IX denounced them in 1864 as 'one of the plagues of the age'. This, however, is no longer the attitude of the Roman Catholic hierarchy.

All the Bible societies were run on entirely non-profit-making lines. Funds were raised through the churches, by donations, legacies, charitable organizations, and in other ways and this enabled editions to be published which cost less than the price of two dozen eggs. If it is remembered that the Bible usually contains more than one thousand pages, it will be seen that this was a considerable feat.

255

To this day the Bible is sold in many countries from door to door by salesmen with all the energy and persistence of vacuum-cleaner salesmen. It is handed out in prisons and refugee camps, in infants' schools and in old people's homes. It is to be found in waiting-rooms and hotel bedrooms, in hospitals and condemned cells, in barracks and on shipboard. It has been calculated that 1,250,000,000 copies have been printed since 1804.

Bringing the Bible to the people means new translations as well as cheaper copies. Until it is translated into the native tongue of a people, it is meaningless to them. As missionaries began to penetrate into the 'uncivilized' regions of the world, it became necessary to have versions of the Bible in the local language. How else could the missionary convey the meaning of Christianity and put over its message?

ONE THOUSAND, ONE HUNDRED TRANSLATIONS

When Luther worked on the Bible there were fifteen translations in existence. By 1600 there were forty, and by 1700 fifty-two. Next year the Church of England founded the Society for the Propagation of the Gospel in Foreign Parts and suddenly the number of translations leapt up into the hundreds. There were the needs of the whole of the British Empire to be met, half the world in itself, and before long Japan, China, Korea, Palestine, and Madagascar were added to the list. The Society took on immense size and is nowadays the largest of all European missionary societies. It has 1,500 missionaries in its service.

The idea spread to the Continent. In 1732 the United Brotherhood, a German Protestant sect, sent missionaries to St Thomas in the Danish West Indies, and then others to South-West and South-East Africa, Surinam, and Samoa. In 1795, mainly on Low Church initiative, the London Missionary Society was founded, followed by a Dutch Society in 1797. In England the Church Missionary Society for Africa and the East was formed in 1799. After this a spate of societies sprang up all over Europe.

The Nepomuk dialect *of the Massachusetts Indians—into which this early translation was rende* *by John Eliot—evidently had no words for such concepts as 'God' or 'Testame.*

MAMUSSE
WUNNEETUPANATAMWE
UP-BIBLUM GOD
NANEESWE
NUKKONE TESTAMENT
KAH WONK
WUSKU TESTAMENT.

Ne quoſhkinnumuk naſhpe Wuttinneumoh *CHRIST*
i.oh aſoowefit

JOHN ELIOT·

CAMBRIDGE:

Printeuꝏp naſhpe *Samuel Green* kah *Marmaduke Johnſon.*

1 6 6 3.

THE
HOLY BIBLE,

Containing the OLD and NEW

TESTAMENTS:

Newly translated out of the

ORIGINAL TONGUES;

And with the former

TRANSLATIONS

Diligently compared and revised.

PHILADELPHIA:

PRINTED AND SOLD BY R. AITKEN, AT POPE'S
HEAD, THREE DOORS ABOVE THE COFFEE
HOUSE, IN MARKET STREET.
M.DCC.LXXXII.

அஞ்ஞாயிச்சுபடமகதெயசுஉெணக்ஞஆளஞ்திஅஞ்த
தசுஜ்ஜிஜெஉடம
முதலாமஅதிகாரமெ

Among the flood of translations in the early eighteenth century was this version in Tamil—a language of Ceylon and southern India—published in 1728.

As early as 1661 John Eliot prepared the first translation of the Bible into a totally unknown tongue—the Nepomuk dialect of the Massachusetts Indians—and completed the work in two years. About the same time Daniel Gravius of Holland did the same thing for the Sing-Kang dialect of Formosa. Job Ludolf published a Psalter in Ethiopian at the beginning of the eighteenth century. The Bible in Tamil appeared in 1728, in Sinhalese in 1739, and in Eskimo in 1744. Missionary after missionary, whether he had a gift for languages or not, forced himself to undertake the wearing task of translating into hitherto entirely undocumented languages, languages without dictionaries, often without books at all. One of the

he first English Bible *to be printed in America is the so-called Aitken Bible of 1782. The title-page*
rs the arms of the young state of Pennsylvania.

فصل اوّل

تسب نامهٔ عیسی مسیح پسر داود وپسر ابراهیم * و ابراهیم پدر اسحق و اسحق پدر یعقوب و یعقوب پدر یهودا و برادرانش * ویهودا پدر فارض و زارح بود ازثامر وفارض پدر حصرون وحصرون پدر ارام * و ارام پدر عمیناداب وعمیناداب پدر نحشون و نحشون پدر سلمون * وسلمون پدر بواعز است ازراحاب و بواعز پدر عوبد است ازراعوث وعوبد پدر ایشی * وایشی پدر داود ملک و داود ملک پدر سلیمان ازاوریا وسلیمان پدر رحبعام ورحبعام پدر ابیا وابیا پدر اسی * واسی پدر یهوشافاط ویهوشافاط پدر یورام و یورام پدر عوزیا * وعوزیا پدر یوثام ویوثام پدر احاز و احاز پدر حزقیا * وحزقیا پدر منسا و منسا پدر امون وامون پدر یوشیا * و یوشیا پدر یوکانیا و برادرانش درزمان

A village cobbler who rose to the Chair of Theology at Fort William College, Calcutta, William Carey was one of the great figures in Bible translation. He and his pupils were responsible for forty new versions in various Asian languages, in no more than twenty years. Among the most important of these were (above, l. to r.) versions in Persian, Chinese, and Sanskrit.

most extraordinary of these men was William Carey, who rose from being a village cobbler to a Baptist benefice and later to the Chair of Theology at Fort William College, Calcutta. Carey founded a school of translation which produced no fewer than forty different versions of the Bible within twenty years—versions in Persian, Chinese, Sanskrit, Hindi, Marwari, Punjabi, Kashmiri. . . . And elsewhere, often in primitive huts surrounded by jungle or desert, even less-known languages were being adapted to the Jewish and Christian ideas expressed in the Bible—Nsenga, Mpoto, Bachama, Omyene, Brij-Bhasa, Kachchhi, Panaieti, Ponerihouen—names that convey nothing but a vaguely exotic idea to the average person. Today more than 1,100 different translations testify to the zeal of the missionaries.

But what a task it was! One missionary had to cast his own type because none existed for the languages he was working in—Mam-pua, Mende, and Ibo. Another worked for nineteen years on a

Kaffir Bible. A third spent years translating the Bible into Ero-manga, only to be killed by tribesmen when he was about to have his work printed. His brother carried on and had reached the seventh chapter of the Acts—'And they stoned Stephen. . . . And he kneeled down, and cried with a loud voice, Lord, lay not this sin to their charge'—when he was struck by an arrow and killed.

Above all, there was the almost impossible task of translating all the rich polyphony of the Bible into primitive languages which had no more than a few hundred words. The missionaries had almost no linguistic tools for their work, and even the most exhaustive enquiries among the natives and study of their way of life and modes of expression could not prevent a good many of their trans-lations from being pitifully inadequate and feeble. One Negro tribe used to call its missionary 'the-white-man-with-the-book-who-torments-us-with-questions'. But he was only following Luther's advice and listening to 'the mother in her house, the children in the street, and the ordinary man in the market-place'.

Missionaries like these had to create words which would not only convey the Hebrew and Greek meaning but be readily understood by the local people with their vastly different outlook and way of life. Often they had to start from the very beginning and make a coherent enriched language out of the disjointed materials that came to hand. Naturally enough, mistakes—sometimes ludicrous—were frequent. One missionary felt pleased with the way his version of the Lord's Prayer had caught on with his Central African flock: it had become a much-loved feature of his services. Then a European who knew the language better than he did chanced to visit the settlement. He roared with laughter when he heard the congregation praying. Chastened, the missionary asked him what the joke was. 'My dear chap,' said the visitor, 'I suppose you think they are saying "Lead us not into temptation, but deliver us from evil." Well, they're not. What they are saying is:"Dear God, do not catch us when we sin."' Another unhappy translator rendered 'heavenly Father' as 'sky-blue Father'—an image which must have puzzled the minds of the people.

But, howlers apart, the chief difficulty lay in the sheer poverty of words. 'I feel as though I were trying to play the Choral Symphony on a mouth-organ,' one translator lamented. 'How can I express burning heat, thirst, and desert-land to the Eskimos, let alone lions, crocodiles, palm-trees, and pomegranates? How can I express the thoughts of a scholar like Paul or abstract ideas like redemption, grace, and salvation? I cannot even call Christ the "lamb of God", because there are no lambs here.' This missionary eventually found a way out by describing Christ as a seal-pup, which conveyed an idea of innocence and tenderness to the Eskimos.

Mistakes were not confined to the amateur translators. For years it was thought that when Moses descended from Sinai after he had talked with God, he had horns on his head (Exodus 34). Michel-angelo even incorporated this idea into his statue of Moses which stands in the chapel of St Peter ad Vincula in Rome. But this curious notion arose from reading the Hebrew word *karan* as *keren*; in fact, Moses's face when he came down from the mountain was not 'horned' but 'shining'. And this was not the only error to slip into the text as the years passed by and more and more translations and new editions were made.

CAMEL OR CABLE?

There appeared in the popular press in 1952 an article which was headlined *Fifty Thousand Mistakes Discovered in Bible*. But as long ago as 1701 John Mill had published a critical edition of the New Testament which alone showed 30,000 questionable readings.

Mill was one of the first textual critics. Textual criticism must not be confused with criticism of the text; it concerns itself not with the validity of what is written but the means used to say it, with the linguistic accuracy of the various editions and translations of the two Testaments. And to do this, it goes into the greatest detail. Mill compared ninety-eight versions of the text, picked out every word, every syllable, every letter which was not common to all. In each instance he considered whether the word, syllable, or letter represented a later addition or omission, an accident or a deliberate act, in the light of the age and reliability of the manuscript. If his research justified the word, he left it in its place; if not, he marked it with an asterisk and qualified it with a marginal note to explain its provenance. Most of Mill's discoveries, and those of later critics, were tiny divergences of style or grammar, insignificant quibbles such as the difference between 'await' and 'wait for', or 'he came' and 'he arrived'. It was trivia of this kind that the journalist found to the number of about 50,000. Only rarely did an error of sense emerge under the scrutiny of the textual critics, such as the 'horned' Moses or the camel which cannot go through the eye of a needle. In Matthew 19, 24, Mark 10, 25, and Luke 18, 25 Jesus is reported as saying: 'It is easier for a camel to go through the eye of a needle than for a rich man to enter the Kingdom of God.' This passage has aroused much dispute. 'Needle's eye', some authorities say, was a narrow gate in the city wall of Jerusalem, almost too narrow for a laden camel. But this is guesswork, because though such a name was used in medieval times for a small wicket gate, we do not know of its use any earlier than this. In a few less ancient manuscripts we find, instead of *kamelos*, a camel, the word *kamilos*, a ship's cable. This alteration of one letter, with whatever authority, makes it much less puzzling, and it was adopted by George Lamsa, an American translator, in 1957: 'It is easier for a ship's cable to pass through the eye of a needle . . .' We must remember that small, and for the most part, unimportant errors could easily creep into manuscript copies. The final verse of the New Testament has no fewer than ten variant readings.

But most mistakes of this kind, interesting though they are to the specialist, have little bearing on the main substance of the Bible. So far as the ordinary Bible-reader is concerned, such preoccupations are as remote from his day-to-day religious life as the study of Roman law is from his rights and duties as a citizen. Textual criticism has little to do with the Bible as a religious document; it can be, and often is, equally well adapted to books of a totally different nature.

The revisers of the Old Testament—*scholars of many denominations—met in the Jerusalem Cham* *of Westminster Abbey in June 1870. Their work took fourteen years.*

The work of such eminent critics as Mill, Ellicott, Hort, Tregelles, and Kirsopp Lake of England, and of Wettstein, Bengel, and Lachmann of Germany does nothing to shake the Bible's firm foundations; on the contrary, it guarantees the reliability of the text now used.

Between 1611, when the King James Authorized Version was published, and 1880, no fewer than seventy English translations were made of the Bible or of considerable parts of it. None of these ever achieved sufficient popularity to challenge the Authorized Version seriously and need not concern us here. But these many attempts served to show that as English, a living language, evolved so the great work of 1611 began to sound archaic and strange to modern ears. There was a feeling of uneasiness that the Authorized Version was not as good an expression of God's Word as the times demanded, and this uneasiness was increased by the work of the textual critics. Eventually, the Convocations of the Church of England agreed in February 1870 that a new version of the Bible in English must be made and drew up a set of rules to guide the men who were asked to undertake the work. It was a revision that was commissioned, not a new translation, but it was to comprise

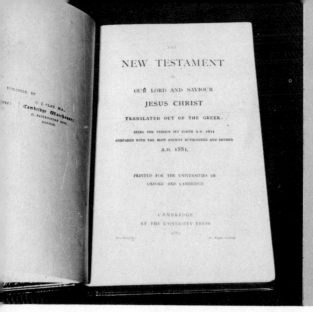

The Revised Version of the New Testament came out in 1881 (left). Proofs were sent to America, where a committee of scholars made further amendments, resulting in the Standard Version of 1901, which found greater favour with American readers (centre). Finally, after World War II, the Standard Version was itself revised and amended, and now appears in a wrapper of a dignified contemporary design.

both marginal renderings and such emendations as it might be found necessary to insert in the text. But the style of the Authorized Version was to be followed as closely as possible, and changes of language were to be confined to those which the most competent scholars judged necessary. The headings of chapters, pages, paragraphs, italics, and punctuation were also to be considered.

Two companies of scholars were appointed to make the revision —one for the Old Testament and the second for the New. They were not confined to Anglicans but included members of the Church of Scotland and the English and Scottish Free Churches. Even John Henry Newman, who had broken with the Church of England and become a Roman Catholic, was invited to join the New Testament Committee; he was, however, unable to do so. But a leading Unitarian, Dr G. Vance Smith, took part in the work.

The companies began their task in the Jerusalem Chamber at Westminster Abbey in June 1870. The New Testament company sat for six and a half hours on four consecutive days in ten months of the year for ten years. It finished its work in November 1880 and its Revised New Testament was published the following year. The revision of the Old Testament occupied 792 days, each of six hours. The work was not completed until June 1884 and the revised Old

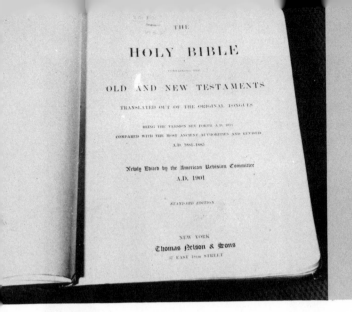
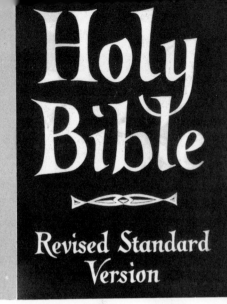

Testament came out in 1885. Finally, the Apocrypha was revised, and this took another ten years.

In two respects these immense efforts were successful. Many obscure passages were made clearer, and many inaccuracies in the Authorized Version were corrected. For this reason the new Revised Version was adopted by many schools, colleges, and universities, and also by numbers of readers who took their Bible studies conscientiously. But in general it failed to win popularity; something was missing. The ordinary churchgoer, even though he might be perplexed or even irritated by certain mannerisms and outdated language, stuck to the Authorized Version while he waited, with varying degrees of expectancy, for a better translation to be made.

Meanwhile, an American Committee had been working over the proofs of the Revised Version as these came from England and preparing them for transatlantic readers. The suggestions which the Committee sent back were included in an appendix to the Revised Version. When American publishers pirated the new Bible it was agreed that the American Committee should bring out the version it wished to see. This was done in 1901 and became known as the Standard Version. This was substantially amended after World War II.

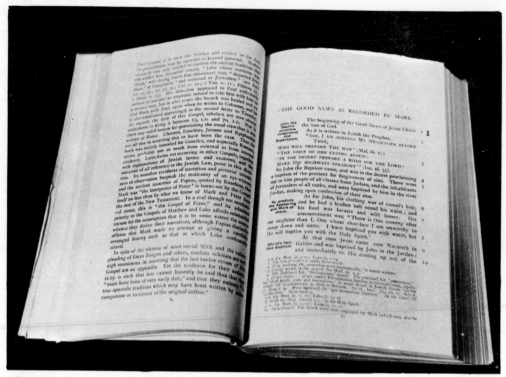

The New Testament in modern speech (*1903*) *has been one of the more successful of the modern versions.*

PAPER-BACK AND COMIC STRIP

But in Britain the question remained: why had the Revised Version failed to capture the ordinary Bible reader? Decade by decade trans-lators have tried to answer this question and produce improvements of their own. First, there was the *Twentieth Century New Testament* published in 1902. This was initiated by Mrs Mary Higgs, the wife of a Congregational Minister in Oldham, and Ernest Malan, a telegraph engineer in Hull, who brought together more than thirty clergymen and lay people to help them in their task. A year later saw the publication of *The New Testament in Modern Speech* by Dr R. F. Weymouth, a former headmaster of Mill Hill School. This has enjoyed considerable success and has gone through many editions. Its chief rival has been the work of Professor James

Moffatt, who brought out *The New Testament: A New Translation* in 1913, and *The Old Testament: A New Translation* in 1924. This version has achieved the distinction of having its own Concordance, published in 1949, and Moffatt's translation of the Gospels is now in wide circulation as a 'paper-back'.

After Moffatt there was a lull in British revisions of the Bible, not broken until 1941 when Professor S. H. Hooke rendered the New Testament into Basic English; eight years later he published the complete Bible in the same idiom. Basic English was the invention of Mr C. K. Ogden, and is a device which won, during the war years, the approval of Sir Winston Churchill, who saw in it a means of enabling people to communicate with each other in a common tongue. Ogden's Basic English reduces the language to a vocabulary of 850 words and this, it is argued, is capable of expressing the gist of anything to be communicated. Professor Hooke set out to rewrite the Bible with this vocabulary. He found in prac-

The Basic English Bible of 1941 had to use 150 words more than the basic 850. Note how it economizes on verbs by using 'give' and a noun: 'given baptism', 'gave teaching', 'gives orders', and so on.

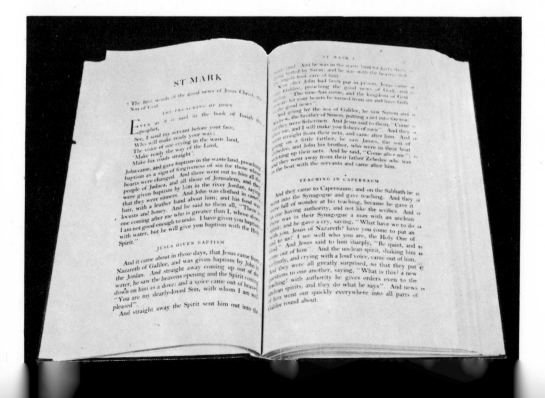

tice that he had to add 150 special 'Bible words', but even so the result is noteworthy. Unexpectedly, there is little that is stilted about this version, and unquestionably it can be 'understanded of the people'; even so, it has failed, in common with other attempts, to supplant the King James Bible it was challenging.

A parallel to *The Bible in Basic English* is *The New Testament: A New Translation in Plain English* which was published in 1952 by C. Kingsley Williams, Vice-Principal of Achimota College, Ghana, who used a vocabulary of 1,660 words. This year, 1952, was a vintage one, for it also saw the coming out of two notable new translations of parts of the New Testament. Dr E. V. Rieu, an accomplished scholar and distinguished translator, made a fresh rendering from the Greek of *The Four Gospels*. This was published by Penguins at 3s. 6d. and has been a runaway success: its sales are reported to have exceeded one million. That same year the Rev. J. B. Phillips, vicar of the Church of the Good Shepherd, Lee, in south-east London, also published his translations of the Gospels. Phillips had begun five years earlier by publishing the translation he had made for his Youth Club of the Epistles, which he re-titled, characteristically, *Letters to Young Churches*. He rendered the Acts of the Apostles into modern English in 1955 and called it *The Young Church in Action*. Phillips finished his work on the New Testament in 1957 with the *Book of Revelation*. Next year the complete work was put out as *The New Testament in Modern English*. This has been extraordinarily popular and its sales, all over the English-speaking world, are phenomenal. In the opinion of many people, scholars as well as ordinary readers, Phillips has made the best attempt yet to provide a challenger to the Authorized Version.

However this may be, the Churches were stirred to take action and officially produce a modern Bible of their own. On the initiative of the Church of Scotland a joint committee of the Anglican and Free Churches was set up in 1947 to prepare a new translation of the English Bible. The chairman has been the Bishop of Winchester (the Rt. Rev. Alwyn Williams) and the work has been directed by the Rev. Professor C. H. Dodd of Oxford, a Congregationalist. The men who are engaged on the task include Anglicans, Presbyterians, Methodists, Baptists, and a Quaker. One member is Dr E. V. Rieu, whose own translations of the Gospels was mentioned above. The labours have been immense, and it was not until March 1961 that the first part, the New Testament, was published.

On the day of publication one million copies of the *New English Bible* were in bookshops throughout the world, 250,000 of them in the United States. Orders were so heavy that a further 350,000 copies were being printed. From all sides congratulations poured in. The press treated the publication as a major event and accorded it considerable space. For the most part the critics were favourable. John Masefield, the Poet Laureate, acclaimed the *New English Bible* in *The Times*. He wrote: 'The work, greatly planned, has been manfully done, that which slept has been awakened.' Bishop Wand, the former Bishop of London, found that his 'appetite had been whetted for more'. The *Guardian* said that the new translation 'forces us to think again and again of the meaning behind the words—of the preaching behind the poetry'. To the *Daily Mail* the task had been 'brilliantly accomplished'. And so on. But here and there a sour note was heard, and even downright scepticism. It is too soon to judge how the issue is likely to be decided and whether the *New English Bible* will reduce the Authorized Version to a museum piece. But of one thing there is no doubt: the furore was evidence enough of the living power of the Bible still to quicken men's minds and interest.

Along with changes in the idiom of the Bible have come changes in its outward appearance; its livery has been brought up to date. The forbidding black-bound volumes beloved of our grandparents, and the arm-breaking family Bibles in stamped calf, have been replaced by less formal productions, attractively designed. Coloured bindings have been adopted, together with multi-coloured jackets and illustrations. The two-columned, *Bradshaw*-like page has given way to a continuous, readable text. One publisher has brought out the Bible in the form of a glossy magazine with a photographic cover, headlined text, and contemporary pictures.

Is this going too far? Not if you reflect that the Bible was written for the masses as well as for the élite, for the lowbrow as well as for the intellectual. Too many possible readers are frightened off by the gloomy black tome with a gold cross on the cover. Such a book is associated with uncomfortable clothes, uncushioned pews, and narrow minds. That is the 'image' conveyed by religion to many people, and the old-style Bible is part of it. Better to run the risk of vulgarity than to remain safe in genteel obscurity. The modernization of the Bible is nothing new. It has usually worn the dress of the period it ministered to, from the picture-Bibles of the Middle Ages to the parchment scrolls of ancient Jerusalem.

What really matters is the message that the Bible brings. Year after year scholars go on comparing, sifting, accepting, and rejecting so as to make that message as accurate as possible. This may seem odd at first sight. Surely by now every possible source must have been investigated and consulted? If the traditional sources were the only ones available, this would be true. But every decade new sources are being found and new yardsticks are being devised by which Biblical scholars must measure the achievements of the past. These new sources are provided by manuscripts—hundreds, even thousands of years old, fragile faded scraps of parchment or papyrus, found in dry caves or ancient monasteries. These have also a part to play in the history of the Bible and form perhaps the most exciting of that history's chapters. It is a story of adventure, hardship, and discovery, of forgers and detectives, and to it we shall now turn.

III

'What need we any further witness?'

16

COUNT TISCHENDORF

Scene: the desert of the Gaza strip. Time: a night in 1844. In the background, shadowy sandhills and a few sparse bushes. Silence—absolute, nerve-wracking silence, broken only by the occasional scream of a jackal. Enter a caravan of forty camels moving slowly northwards; it is headed by a white man and by an Arab with two pistols and a dagger stuck in his belt. Suddenly the noise of fighting is heard. A party of bedouins sweeps down on the caravan, bullets whistle through the air, the Arab draws his dagger, and the European cocks his rifle. They throw themselves to the ground and the bedouins hurtle past. The white man and his companion remount their horses and continue their journey.

This is not a scene from Rider Haggard, but an episode from the life-story of Constantine Tischendorf, a young theologian from Leipzig. He was at this time looking for manuscripts and ancient papyrus scrolls to take back to the quiet of his college rooms.

Tischendorf was made for this kind of work. Just as Paganini's abnormally large finger-span and exceptionally fine ear gave him a flying start over other masters of the violin, so Tischendorf was naturally gifted with all the attributes that go to make up the successful scroll-hunter. At the age of nineteen, when he went up to Leipzig University, he was already a superb classical scholar. Six years later he was appointed university lecturer. His speciality was the language of the New Testament, and at the age of twenty-seven he published a new edition of the Greek New Testament which was acclaimed as a masterpiece by experts. That same year Tischen-

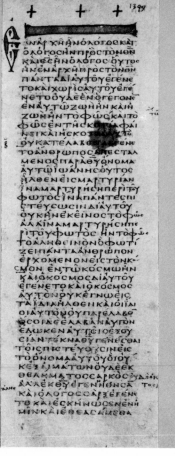

dorf wrote: 'My life-work will be to piece together the original New Testament.' Besides his academic knowledge—he was fluent in many of the dialects of antiquity as well as in Latin, Greek, and Hebrew—he was physically strong and gifted with abnormally good eyesight; he had also a talent for diplomacy, and was lucky into the bargain. Altogether, it is not surprising that he made more important discoveries single-handed than whole generations of scholars had done.

When Tischendorf began his life's work, the three oldest complete Bible manuscripts known to experts were the *Codex Vaticanus,* the *Codex Alexandrinus,* and the *Codex Ephraemi.* The first, belonging

276

The amazing Tischendorf: *he succeeded, where all others had failed, in deciphering the Codex Ephraemi.*

Among the oldest *complete Bible manuscripts known when Tischendorf began his work were: Codex Vaticanus (left, c.* AD *370) and Codex Alexandrinus (c.* AD *450).*

to the Vatican, was a three-columned volume in Greek which, for the Old Testament, followed the text of the Septuagint and was assumed to have been written about AD 350. The *Codex Alexandrinus*, also in Greek, had been given to James I of England by the Patriarch of Alexandria; it dates from the first half of the fifth century, and is now in the British Museum. The third codex, in the *Bibliothèque Nationale* in Paris, was more enigmatic than either of the other two. Written in Greek in the fifth century, it had been erased by a twelfth-century monk and re-used for the writings of Ephraim, an ancient Syrian divine. It was brought to Paris by Catherine de' Medici, but it was not until the end of the seventeenth century that

277

A vandal monk of the 12th century, wishing to copy a treatise by St Ephraim of Syria, cleaned off and used again a parc

it was discovered to contain two manuscripts. Scholars then set to work to decipher the earlier writing, but without success. Except for one or two lines, the erasures had been made too thoroughly.

Besides these complete manuscripts, several fragments were known to exist. Parts of the Old Testament in Greek and Latin had been acquired by Basle. In 1778 some valuable papyri had been salvaged by an antiquary from Egyptian peasants who were burning them. In 1839 Tattam, an English archaeologist, had managed to acquire

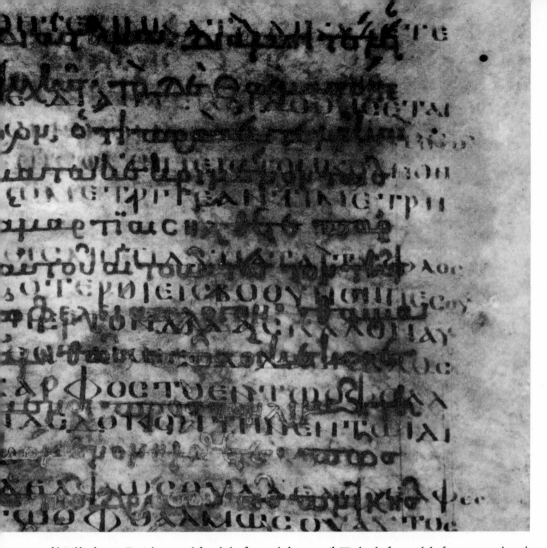

...g a very old Biblical text. Decipherment defeated the finest scholars—until Tischendorf succeeded after two years' work.

some fragments of the *Peshitto* from the monastery of St Maria Deipara in the desert of Lower Egypt.

Tischendorf's first step was to make what he could of the known manuscripts. At the age of twenty-six he borrowed enough money to take him to Paris where he asked permission to study the undeciphered *Codex Ephraemi*. Although the attempt seemed ridiculous —the world's finest scholars had admitted defeat—he was allowed to make the attempt. To the surprise of the authorities he was able to

ΙϹΟ ΤΗΙϹ ΚΛΟϹϢΟ
ΓΕΓΡΑΙΙΤΑΙ
ΟΤΟΠΟΛΥ
ΟΥ ΚΕΤΙΛΕΟΥ ΜΕ ϹΡΙ
ΚΑΙ Ο ΤΟ ΟΛΙΓΟΝ
ΟΥ ΚΗΛΛΤΤΟΝΗ ϹΕΝ
ΧΑΡΙϹ ΛϹ ΤϢ ΘϢ
ΤϢ ΔΟΝΤΙ ΤΗΝ ΑΥΤΗΝ
ϹΠΟΥΛΗΝ ΥΠΕΡ ΥΜϢΝ
ΕΝ ΤΗ ΚΑΡΛΙΑ ΤΙΤΟΥ
ΟΤΙ ΤΗΝ ΜΕΝ ΠΑΡΛΚΛΗϹΙΝ
ΕΛΕΞΑΤΟ
ϹΠΟΥΛΑΙΟΤΕΡΟ ϹΛΕ
ΥΠΑΡΧϢΝ
ΑΥΟΥΡΕΤΟϹ ΕΞΗΛΟΕΝ
ΠΡΟϹ ΥΜΑϹ
ϹΥΝΕΠΕΜΨΛΜΕΝ ΛΕ
ΜΕΤ ΑΥΤΟΥ ΤΟΝ ΛΛΕΛΦΟΝ
ΟΥ Ο ΕΠΛΙΝΟϹ
ΕΝ ΤϢ ΕΥΛΓΓΕΛΙϢ
ΛΙΛ ΠΛϹϢΝ ΤϢΝ ΕΚΚΛΗϹΙϢΝ

Tischendorf found it easy to read the Codex Claromontanus — a collection of the Epistles of St Paul written in Greek on parchment about AD 575. The lines are of irregular lengths, corresponding to the pauses in the sense, which also helps in the interpretation.

read it. Like the fairy-tale hero who answers the riddle and wins the hand of the princess, Tischendorf succeeded where all others had failed, and with no special apparatus—nothing but his naked eye.

He spent two years on the *Codex Ephraemi,* pausing only now and then to put in a little work by way of light relief on the *Codex Claromontanus*, a manuscript of St Paul's Epistles. He published the results of his work in 1852, but even before their publication he was recognized as the world's greatest palaeographer. Learned bodies vied with one another to put their libraries at his disposal. He visited the British Museum, the Bodleian, and the Cambridge University Library, the collections at Basle, Utrecht, Milan, Turin, Modena, and Naples. In his own field he was pre-eminent.

TREASURE IN ATTICS

In the spring of 1844 Tischendorf reached Cairo after a long and difficult journey. Cairo at that time was a small city where few Europeans lived. Tischendorf lost no time in searching out monasteries and was given a friendly reception everywhere he went. But when he enquired about libraries and manuscripts he found the monks unable to help, or even to grasp what he was talking about. Undaunted, he would ask them to show him over their monasteries; he would persuade them to open old, locked cupboards and chests, and would himself grub about in attics and among waste paper. It soon became clear to him that the worst hazard for the preservation of ancient documents was not the ravages of time but the ignorance and indifference of the monks.

In one establishment the key of the library was lost. After a lengthy search it was found, the door was opened, and the horrified scholar looked upon jumbled piles of books, manuscripts, torn and crumpled scraps of paper and parchment, all covered with a thick layer of dust. Obviously, no one had entered the room for decades, and priceless, irreplaceable treasures were rotting away for lack of a little care.

Much the same incident involving a missing library key was repeated during Tischendorf's travels in the Near East, some time after his visit to Sinai. This was at the monastery of Mar Saba, near the Dead Sea—a pleasant, well cared-for group of buildings with a garden, an ancient church, and a comparatively well organized library. Here, however, he could find nothing of value, and when he expressed surprise at such a scarcity of manuscripts in a monastery of such wide renown the monks recalled that there *was* another room full of books at the top of one of the towers, but unfortunately the key was lost. Tischendorf argued with the monks, he flattered them, he pleaded with them; he 'charmed them with smiles and soap'. And in the end his patience won its just reward: the key was found.

This second room was a treasure-house of much more valuable manuscripts, Greek, Russian, Syrian, and Arabic, mostly of the tenth and eleventh centuries, together with one Greek and two beautiful Ethiopian eighth-century Gospel MSS. There was also a heap of parchment scraps carelessly swept into a corner. Tischendorf begged permission to take one or two away as a souvenir, and quickly sorted out the most valuable. But then the monks recalled an old monastic rule that forbade the removal of any book or paper from the house, so Tischendorf had to leave empty-handed.

He gives the impression in his diaries that he sympathized to some extent with the monks' suspicions. Plainly, they were not without experience of clever merchants and unscrupulous treasure-seekers. Yet if a man has in his charge one of the world's cultural treasures and allows it to be damaged by neglect, has he not forfeited all right to it?

In Cairo, Tischendorf asked the Patriarch of the Coptic Church about a whole library of MSS which was said to have been sent to the city about twenty years earlier as a pledge for a loan. To add a touch of fantasy, this collection was reputed to have been walled into the room where it was stored. The Patriarch was doubt-ful. 'Can you even read Greek?' he enquired. Tischendorf laughed. The Patriarch sent for a book in Greek and asked him to read it, which Tischendorf did in his best classical Greek. The Patriarch, however, indignantly sent him away as an impostor, because the only Greek he understood himself was the modern variety.

Tischendorf's next move was to hire camels, drivers, guides, and interpreters, and investigate a few remote monasteries in the Libyan desert south-west of Cairo. Here it was the same story—piles of crumbling rubbish and nothing of any value apart from a few barely legible pieces which he later deciphered as seventh-century Coptic manuscripts. In one place he met with open hostility because Tat-tam, the archaeologist from England, had been there before him and taken the most valuable finds; too late, the monks had learned the value of what they had parted with for a song.

In the course of a few weeks Tischendorf combed the monasteries of Cairo and its environs, making notes and sketches. He found much that was interesting, but nothing world-shaking. The time had now come for the real objective of this trip—the monastery of Sinai.

The journey on camel-back took him for ten days through the furnace of the desert. At last the monastery of St Catherine rose before him, solidly built into the rock. This was probably the oldest of Coptic monasteries. It had survived the onslaughts of Islam by the simple expedient of building a mosque on the roof; this shielded all the buildings beneath it, for nothing connected with the True Faith could be desecrated. The monastery was enclosed by a massive wall in which at first sight there seemed to be no entrance, but presently Tischendorf noticed a small opening about thirty feet up in the wall. A monk lowered a sort of bo'sun's chair, and in this the traveller was drawn up into the hidden world.

This introduction was typical of the life of St Catherine's. The monastery was a maze of buildings—houses, shops, chapels, and courtyards. Tischendorf was welcomed by a crowd of grave, black-bearded monks who pressed him to join them in coffee and palm wine, and insisted on giving him a personal guide to help him in his search. The guide asked Tischendorf if he had ever been to the moon and his question made the traveller aware that the young man was without all his wits; but 'signor Pietro', as he was called, turned out to be charming, helpful, and a useful interpreter.

Another monk, Brother Gregorius, had a quiet and gentle dignity that seemed to testify to a lifetime of peace and holy meditation; but the good Father had previously been a doughty fighter, leader of a band of Mamelukes, warriors whose methods were not pretty.

Tischendorf presented his letters of introduction to the Prior. But before he was allowed to visit the library he had to be shown round the monastery. He was taken to the Church of the Transfiguration, with its beautiful Byzantine mosaic roof over the apse; the chapel of St Catherine with its three ponderous sarcophagi filled with relics of the saint; and the chapel of the Burning Bush, to enter which he had to remove his shoes as Moses had done: 'Put off thy shoes

A maze of buildings *surrounded by a high wall in which there was no opening—such was the*

from off thy feet, for the ground whereon thou standest is holy ground.' There were altogether twenty-two chapels, not counting the mosque on the roof which was used by the monastery servants. There was even a charnel-house, guarded at the door by a skeleton with a little black velvet cap on its head. This was Stephanos, who had been the monastery janitor 1,100 years before.

At last Tischendorf came to the library. The librarian, Kyrillos, was friendly and helpful, and did all he could to help the visitor, but he confessed himself ignorant about old documents. He knew there had been some—a copy of the four Gospels that had belonged to the Emperor Theodosius sprang to mind—but where these were

...monastery of St Catherine, where Tischendorf found his greatest prize, the Codex Sinaiticus.

it was impossible to say. Those manuscripts which were available were disappointing and Tischendorf began to lose heart. But he continued to take notes and to classify, convinced that if there was in fact anything of value in this library not one of the monks would be in the least interested.

He searched on doggedly, digging through piles of heavy folios where the worms had done their destructive work. He almost choked in clouds of dust as he sorted sheaves of half-decayed parchment. In a corner of a side room he found a capacious basket filled with manuscripts. And in this, with a shout of triumph, he came upon what he had been hoping to find. Here, carelessly thrown aside and

CΗCΤΗCΤΙΒΕΡΙΑΔ···
ΕΦΑΝΕΡΩCΕΝΔΕ
ΟΥΤΩCΗCΑΝΟΜΤ
CΙΜΩΝΠΕΤΡΟCΚΑΙ
ΘΩΜΑCΟΛΕΓΟΜΕ
ΝΟCΔΙΔΥΜΟCΚΑΙ
ΝΑΘΑΝΑΗΧΟΑΠΟ
ΚΑΝΑΤΗCΓΑΛΙΛΑΝ
ΑCΚΑΙΟΙΥΙΟΙΖΕΒ
ΔΑΙΟΥΚΑΙΑΛΛΟΙΚ
ΤΩΝΜΑΘΗΤΩΝΑΥ
ΤΟΥΔΥΟ:
ΛΕΓΕΙΑΥΤΟΙCCΙΜΩ
ΠΕΤΡΟCΥΠΑΓΩΑ
ΛΙΕΥΕΙΝΛΕΓΟΥCΙΝ
ΑΥΤΩΕΡΧΟΜΕΘΑΚ
ΗΜΕΙCCΥΝCΟΙΕΞΗ
ΘΟΝΟΥΝΚΑΙΕΝΕ
ΒΗCΑΝΕΙCΤΟΠΛΟΙ
ΟΝΚΑΙΕΝΕΚΙΝΗΤΗ
ΝΥΚΤΙΕΠΙΑCΑΝ
ΟΥΔΕΝΠΡΩΪΑCΔΕΗΔΗ
ΓΕΝΟΜΕΝΗCΕCΤΗ
ΕΠΙΤΟΝΑΙΓΙΑΛΟΝ
ΟΥΜΕΝΤΟΙΕΓΝΩ
CΑΝΟΙΜΑΘΗΤΑΙ·
ΤΙCΕCΤΙΝ·
ΛΕΓΕΙΟΥΝΑΥΤΟΙC
ΠΑΙΔΙΑΜΗΤΙΠΡΟC
ΦΑΓΙΟΝΕΧΕΤΕΑΠ
ΚΡΙΘΗCΑΝΑΥΤΩ·Υ
ΛΕΓΕΙΑΥΤΟΙCΒΑΛ
ΤΕΕΙCΤΑΔΕΞΙΑΜΕ
ΡΗΤΟΥΠΛΟΙΟΥΤΟ
ΔΙΚΤΥΟΝΚΑΙΕΥΡΗ
CΕΤΕΟΙΔΕΕΒΑΛΟΝΟΥΝ
ΚΑΙΟΥΚΕΤΙΑΥΤΟΙΑ
ΚΥCΑΙΙCΧΥΟΝΑΠ
ΤΟΥΠΛΗΘΟΥCΤΩΝ
ΙΧΘΥΩΝ·ΛΕΓΕΙΟΥ
ΟΜΑΘΗΤΗCΕΚΕΙ
ΝΟCΟΝΗΓΑΠΑΟΙC
ΤΩΠΕΤΡΩΟΚCΕCΤ
CΙΜΩΝΟΥΝΠΕΤ
ΑΚΟΥCΑCΟΤΙΟΚC
ΕCΤΙΝΤΟΝΕΠΕΝΔΥ
ΤΗΝΔΙΕΖΩCΑΤΟ
ΗΝΓΑΡΓΥΜΝΟCΙς

ΕΒΑΛΕΝΕΑΥΤ
ΤΗΝΘΑΛΑCCΑ
ΔΕΑΛΛΟΙΜΑΘ
ΤΩΑΛΛΩΠΛΟΙΑ
ΩΗΛΘΟΝΟΥΓ
CΑΝΜΑΚΡΑΝ
ΤΗCΓΗCΑΛΛΑC
ΠΟΠΗΧΩΝΔ
CΙΩΝCΥΡΟΝΤ
ΔΙΚΤΥΟΝΤΩΝ
ΩΝΩCΟΥΝΑ
ΒΗCΑΝΕΙCΤΗ
ΒΛΕΠΟΥCΙΝΑΝ
ΚΙΑΝΚΕΙΜΕΝ
ΚΑΙΟΨΑΡΙΟΝ
ΜΕΝΟΝ·ΚΑΙΑ
ΛΕΓΕΙΑΥΤΟΙC
ΝΕΓΚΑΤΑΙΑΠ
ΟΨΑΡΙΩΝΩΝ
ΑCΑΤΕΝΥΝ:
ΕΝΕΒΗΟΥΝCΙ
ΠΕΤΡΟCΚΑΙΕ
CΕΝΤΟΔΙΚΤΥ
ΕΙCΤΗΝΓΗΝ·
ΙΧΘΥΩΝΜΕΓ
ΕΚΑΤΟΝΠΕΝ
ΤΑΤΡΙΩΝ·ΚΑΙ
ΤΩΝΟΝΤΩΝ
ΚΕCΧΙCΘΗΤΟ
ΚΤΥΟΝ·ΛΕΓΕΙ
ΟΙCΔΕΥΤΕΑΡΙ
CΑΤΕΟΥΔΙCΔΕ
ΜΑΤΩΝΜΑΘ
ΕΞΕΤΑCΑΙΑΥΤ
ΤΙCΕΙΕΙΛΟΤΕC
ΟΚCΕCΤΙΝΕΡ
ΤΑΙΟΙCΚΑΙΛΑ
ΝΕΙΤΟΝΑΡΤΟ
ΔΙΔΩCΙΝΑΥΤ
ΤΟΟΨΑΡΙΟΝΟ
ΩCΤΟΥΤΟΔΕ
ΤΡΙΤΟΝΕΦΑΝ
ΘΟΙΣΤΟΙCΜ
ΤΑΙCΕΓΕΡΘΕΙC
ΝΕΚΡΩΝΟΤΕ
ΗΡΙCΤΗCΑΝΑ
ΤΩCΙΜΩΝΙΠ
ΟΙCCΙΜΩΝΑ

ΡΟΙΔΕΕΙΠΟΝΖΙΟΛΗCΤΗCΗΝΥΙΣΤΟCΕ
ΚΟΠΙΑCΑΙΙΕΝΙΣΑΙΟΥΔΑΕΗΘΑΑΒΟΛΙΕΝ
ΗΛΕΤΩCΙCΡΗΛΙΑΤΙΒΑΛΟΥΛΕΝ

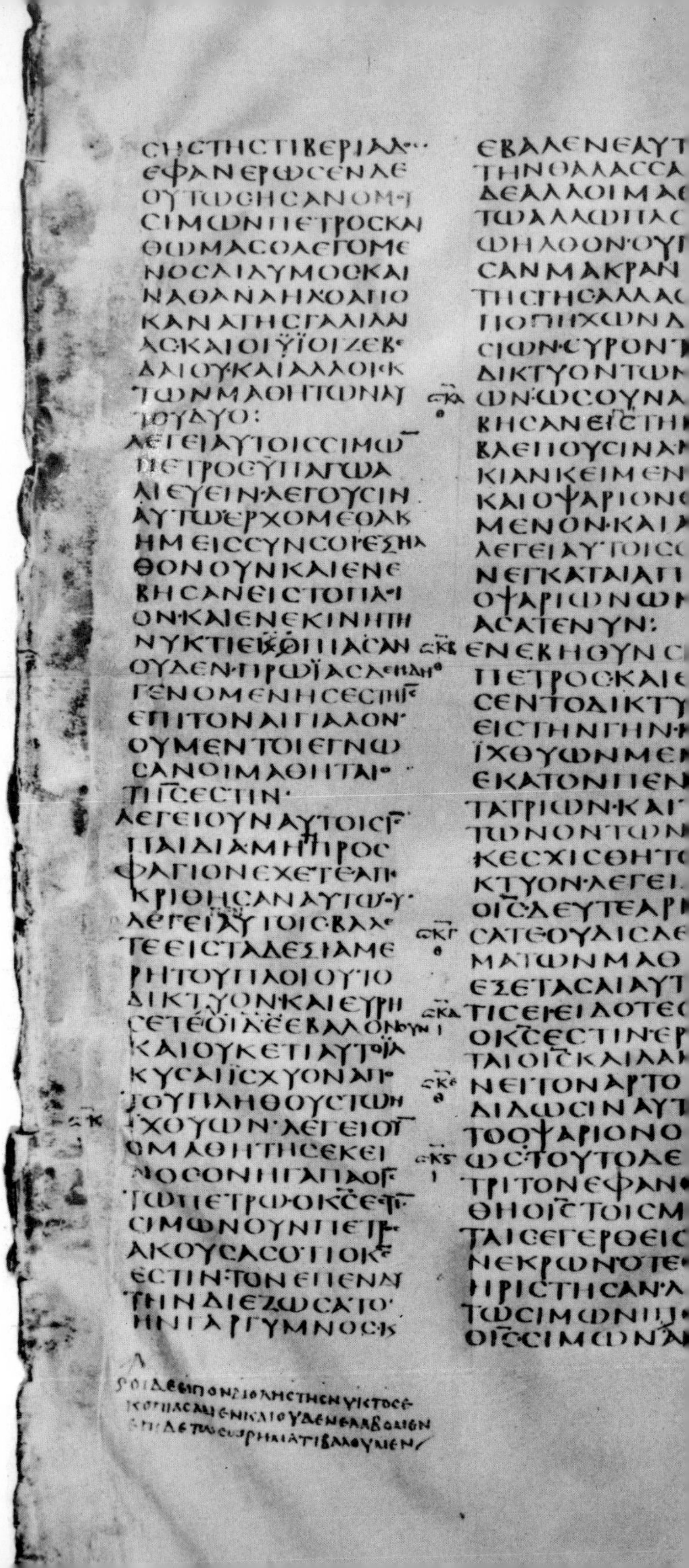

ΜΕΠΛΕΟΝΤΟΥΤ
ΛΕΓΕΙΑΥΤΩΝΑΙ
ΚΕCΥΟΙΔΑCΟΤΙ
ΦΙΛΩCΕΛΕΓΕΙΑΥ
ΤΩΒΟCΚΕΤΑΑΡΝΙ
ΑΜΟΥ ΠΑΛΙΝΛΕ
ΓΕΙΑΥΤΩCΙΜΩΝ
ΙΩΑΝΝΟΥΑΓΑΠΑ
ΜΕΛΕΓΕΙΑΥΤΩΝΑΙ
ΚΕCΥΟΙΔΑCΟΤΙ
ΦΙΛΩCΕΛΕΓΕΙΑΥ
ΤΩΠΟΙΜΑΙΝΕΤΑ
ΤΡΟΚΑΤΑΜΟΥ
ΓΕΙΑΥΤΩΤΟΤΡΙ
CΙΜΩΝΙΩΑΝΝ
ΦΙΛΕΙCΜΕΕΛΥΠΗ
ΘΗΔΕΟΠΕΤΡΟCΟ
ΤΙΕΙΠΕΝΑΥΤΩΤ
ΡΙΤΟΝΚΑΙΦΙΛ
ΜΕΚΑΙΛΕΓΕΙΑΥ
ΤΩΚΕΠΑΝΤΑCΥ
ΑCCΥΓΙΝΩCΚ
ΤΙΦΙΛΩCΕΚΑΙ
ΕΤΕΙΑΥΤΩΒΟCΚ
ΑΤΡΟΚΑΤΑΜΟΥ
ΜΗΝΑΜΗΝΛΕΓ
ΟΙΟΤΕΗCΝΕΩ
ΕΡΟCΕΖΩΝΝΥ
CCΕΑΥΤΟΝΚΑΙΠ
ΕΠΑΤΕΙCΟΠΟΥΗ
ΕΛΕCΟΤΑΝΛΕΓ
ΑCΗCΕΚΤΕΝΙCΤ
ΡΑCΟΥΚΑΙΑΛ
ΟΙΖΩCΟΥCΙΝCΕ
ΑΠΟΙΗCΟΥCΙΝ
CΙΟΕΟΥΘΕΛΕΙC
ΥΤΟΔΕΕΙΠΕΝ
ΑΙΝΩΝΠΟΙΩ
ΑΝΑΤΩΔΟΞΑCΕ
ΟΝΘΝΚΑΙΤΟΥΤ
ΠΩΝΛΕΓΕΙΑΥ
ΑΚΟΛΟΥΘΙΜ
ΠΙCΤΡΑΦΕΙCΔΕ
ΠΕΤΡΟCΒΛΕΠΙ
ΜΑΘΗΤΗΝΟΝΗΓ
ΠΟΙCΚΑΙΑΝΕΠ
ΝΕΝΤΩΔΕΙΠΝ
ΙΤΟCΤΗΘΟCΑΥ

ΤΟΥΚΑΙΛΕΓΕΙΑΥΤ
ΚΕΤΙCΕCΤΙΝΟΠΑ
ΡΑΔΙΔΟΥCCΕΤΟΥΤ
ΟΥΝΙΔΩΝΟΠΕΤΡ
ΕΙΠΕΝΤΩΙΥΟΥΤ
ΔΕΤΙΛΕΓΕΙΑΥΤΩ
ΟΙCΘΕΑΝΑΥΤΟΝ
ΛΩΜΕΝΙΝΕΩCΕΡ
ΧΟΜΑΙΤΙΠΡΟCCΕ
CΥΜΟΙΑΚΟΛΟΥΘΕΙ
ΕΞΗΛΘΕΝΟΥΝΟΥ
ΤΟCΟΛΟΓΟCΕΙCΤ
ΑΔΕΛΦΟΥCΟΤΙΟ
ΜΑΘΗΤΗCΕΚΕΙ
ΝΟCΟΥΚΑΠΟΘΝΗ
CΚΕΙΟΥΚΕΙΠΕΝΔ
ΑΥΤΩΟΙCΟΤΙΟΥΚΑ
ΠΟΘΝΗCΚΕΙΑΛΛ
ΑΝΑΥΤΟΝΘΕΛΩ
ΜΕΝΕΙΝΕΩCΕΡ
ΜΑΙΟΥΤΟCΕCΤΙΝ
ΜΑΘΗΤΗCΟΜΑΡΤ
ΡΩΝΠΕΡΙΤΟΥΤΩΝ
ΚΑΙΓΡΑΨΑCΤΑΥΤΑ
ΚΑΙΟΙΔΑΜΕΝΟΤΙ
ΑΛΗΘΗCΕCΤΙΝΗ
ΜΑΡΤΥΡΙΑΑΥΤΟΥ
ΕCΤΙΝΔΕΚΑΙΑΛΛΑ
ΠΟΛΛΑΛΕΠΟΙΗCΕΝ
ΟΙCΑΤΙΝΑΕΑΝΓΡΑ
ΦΗΤΑΙΚΑΘΕΝΟΥ
ΑΑΥΤΟΝΟΙΜΑΙΤΟΝ
ΚΟCΜΟΝΧΩΡΗCΕ
ΤΑΓΡΑΦΟΜΕΝΑΒΙ
ΚΛΙΑ

ΕΥΑΓΓΕΛΙΟΝ

ΚΑΤΑ

ΙΩΑΝΝΗΝ

destined for the bonfire, lay 129 parchment leaves covered with Greek characters: a Septuagint dating from about AD 350—one of the oldest of all Biblical manuscripts.

Now, of course, the monks' attitude changed completely. They had known all along that the manuscript was valuable, one of their greatest possessions; they could not possibly think of allowing Tischendorf to take it away. They bargained back and forth, and in the end Tischendorf succeeded in persuading them to let him take forty-three of the 129 sheets. The remainder, regretfully, he had to leave behind.

A WORD TO THE CZAR

In 1845 he was back in Leipzig, eagerly sifting, transcribing, and examining the writings he had collected on his travels. He presented the Sinai parchments to the library of Leipzig University, where they were given the name of *Codex Friderico-Augustanus* in honour of the reigning King of Saxony. In return the University accorded him the title of Professor. Only one thing marred his satisfaction—the knowledge that the other eighty-six pages of the book were still in Sinai for any other adventurer to acquire. Not that he had divulged where he had found his forty-three pages, but somebody might hit on the place by chance.

Nine years later Tischendorf made a second journey to Sinai. Nothing had changed. There were the same untidy buildings, the same deceptively meek-looking monks. Eagerly he asked after the eighty-six pages of parchment that he had left behind on his former visit. Of course they remembered his parchment! But of course! Only one thing worried them—where was the parchment now? They had all seen it only a few months ago ... or a year ... or two years. It must be there somewhere. Tischendorf was frantic. He begged Kyrillos the librarian to search his memory. In vain. Tischendorf began to fear that the monks had sold the Codex elsewhere. But could they be such expert liars? He found this difficult to believe. There was nothing he could do but give up and go home.

While he was in Egypt he took the opportunity of visiting other monasteries and these pilgrimages were not unrewarding. In less than three months he acquired sixteen palimpsests and a collection of various manuscripts in Greek, Coptic, Syrian, Arabic, and ancient Egyptian. Then he went back to Leipzig to study his finds, fulfil his academic duties, and publish the seventh edition of his Greek New Testament.

For the next five years Tischendorf lived in a torment of fear lest someone else should buy the lost parchment from the monastery of St Catherine. Every day he expected some publication or announcement to make the discovery known. But there was nothing. Was it possible that the monks had not betrayed him after all?

When he could bear the suspense no longer, he set out once again for Sinai. This time he was better prepared. He knew the respect the Copts had for the Russian royal family and so he spoke to the Russian ambassador in Dresden and hinted that he would be willing to give the fruits of his future researches to the Czar, if he could rely on the Czar's support and cooperation. The ambassador diplomatically gave the Czar's brother, the Archduke Constantine, to understand that Tischendorf should be cultivated. The Archduke spoke to the Dowager Empress, the Czar's mother. She whispered a word in the Czarina's ear. The Czarina mentioned it to the Czar—and the thing was done. The Czar, of course, thought it was all his own idea.

After that, everything went smoothly. Russia financed Tischendorf generously. At Sinai he was greeted, as usual, with lavish hospitality. Again he ferreted through drawers and cupboards, attics and cellars. Again he found nothing. Bitterly disappointed, he prepared to leave, and wandered round the monastery bidding farewell to his friends. On the very last day he was invited to join a young monk, the steward of the monastery, in a drink before his journey. As he sat, weary and thoroughly dispirited, in the monk's cell, the steward said, casually, 'By the way, I too have a Greek Testament here in my cell. You may care to look at it.' He rose and lifted down a bundle wrapped in red cloth from a shelf where the spare coffee-cups were kept for welcoming visitors to the monastery. The young steward cut the string and, to his guest's rapture, the missing leaves of parchment slid out on to the table. But instead of the expected eighty-six leaves there were far more.

Tischendorf broke out into a sweat of excitement and his heart pounded as he turned over the pages in front of him. These were certainly the missing two-thirds of the Septuagint that he had seen before but was not allowed to take away. But the rest? They were parts of the Old Testament and two early Christian works, the Epistle of Barnabas and the *Shepherd* of Hermas. What was of prime importance was that Tischendorf now held in his trembling hands a complete, perfect copy of the New Testament written in the same beautiful Greek script, and so dating from AD 350. It was one of the two oldest copies in the world; only the *Codex Vaticanus* could approach it. Altogether there were 346 leaves heaped on the table and each one was priceless. It transpired later that all this treasure-trove had been unearthed when the monks had been clearing out rubbish for burning in the bread ovens.

That night Tischendorf did not sleep. Instead, by the flickering light of a candle he copied, with the steward's permission, the Epistle of Barnabas, and when he had done he let leaf after leaf of the manuscripts slide through his fingers. He read a little here and a little there. This Codex he *had* to have. Here was new light on a mass of problems that hitherto had been utterly baffling.

Next day Tischendorf began to bargain with the monks. Money did not interest them. They were unimpressed by the Czar's authority. He begged them at least to allow him to take the manuscript to Cairo so that he could copy it; at St Catherine's there was not enough paper and ink. But he was told he must wait for the permission of the Archimandrite who had left for Cairo some days earlier.

Tischendorf was too impatient to wait. He hurried to Cairo and put his request to the Council of Archimandrites which was being held in the mother-house of the order. It seemed reasonable, and he was given permission to have the manuscript brought to Cairo and to take away eight pages every day to copy. Before the Fathers had announced the last syllable of their ruling, Tischendorf had sent an Arab servant to fetch the Codex. Within a fortnight he was at work, aided by two Cairo citizens, a doctor and a chemist, who knew Greek. There was a tremendous amount to do—110,000 lines of text to copy, with some 12,000 variants.

At the same time, Tischendorf went on negotiating for the sale of the manuscript. Luck was on his side. The Council of Archimandrites had been called to elect a new archbishop for the Sinai monasteries, and had reached a deadlock because the Patriarch of Jerusalem, who was the one man who could consecrate the new primate, disliked the man preferred by the others. The wily Tischendorf went to the Patriarch and suggested he could have the full support of Russia for any candidate he liked to propose if, on his part, he recommended that the Codex be sold to Russia. Tischendorf's proposal was unwittingly aided by a group of British scholars who wished to buy the Codex for England. For the country of heretics? Never! the Copts were shocked by the thought. They would rather *give* the manuscript to Russia than sell it to England.

Tischendorf's greatest find, *the Codex Sinaiticus, was bought by the British Museum from Russia in 1933 for £100,000. It was still a collection of loose vellum leaves, as Tischendorf had found it, but expert hands have now bound it into two volumes. Below: the leaves glued and taped together at the backs, without covers, as they were received at the Museum.*

All the better, Tischendorf considered. Russia would be even more pleased to acquire the Codex as a gift than as a purchase.

Meanwhile, Russia was putting pressure on Turkey to give some kind of a directive to the Patriarch of Jerusalem. But matters moved slowly. Whether through ill-will or mere indifference, the Turks allowed months to pass by without taking action. At last, the Russian ambassador to Constantinople brought matters to a head. He wrote to the monastery and promised that Russia would support them in the wrangle over the archbishop if they would lend the Codex to Russia. If the monks should wish to have it back, the ambassador promised, in the name of the Czar, that it would be returned immediately.

Eventually, the monks agreed to this proposal and Tischendorf bore off the Codex. He broke his journey to show the prize to the Austrian Emperor, Franz Joseph, and King Johann of Saxony. Soon he was in Russia where the Czar received him in his summer palace. After this, all question of the Codex being a loan seemed to fade from the mind. Nothing more was heard from St Catherine's: the monks seemed to have lost interest. And when in

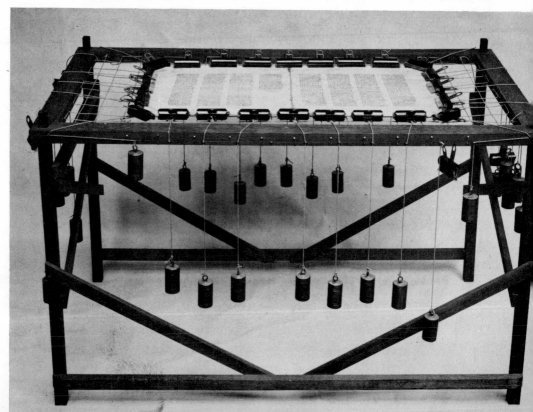

1933 Russia sold the manuscript to the British Museum for £100,000 she was assumed to be the real and only owner.

This was the end of the drama. At the age of forty-four Tischendorf had accomplished what he had set out to do. The discovery of this Codex, known as the *Codex Sinaiticus*, which Tischendorf published in 1862, is a milestone in the history of the Bible, for it is held to be amongst the best and most reliable sources of textual evidence. With the check it provides to previously known codices, it forms much of the foundation of later revisions of the text. It is one of the best guarantees of the reliability of the New Testament we read today, and every mid-twentieth-century reader of the Bible has reason to be grateful to the persevering professor from Leipzig.

And yet, in a sense, the discovery of the *Codex Sinaiticus* was only the prologue to the more complex drama which was to follow—a drama with more supporting characters, more wealth of incident, more subtlety of execution. It was only after Tischendorf had passed from the scene that the play really began of the quest for ancient Biblical documents.

Centuries of neglect *had curled and cockled the vellum leaves of the precious Codex, and gentle stretching in a frame was necessary to make them flat enough for binding. Right: the Codex Sinaiticus as it is today, bound in two volumes, in oak boards with morocco backs.*

BURIED TREASURE

Tischendorf had shown that there were still discoveries for the finding, walled up in ancient monasteries or mouldering in disused wastepaper baskets. Now a legion of scholars set about investigating the buried treasures of the East.

In 1868 a German missionary, the Rev. F. A. Klein, stumbled on a black stone, half buried in the sand, near Dibon, east of the river Jordan. He dismounted from his horse and examined the stone curiously. It was a piece of black basalt, about the same size as a tombstone, and had various writings engraved on its polished sur-face. Klein scratched away the sand with his penknife and found that the writing, thirty-four lines, was in the form of ancient Hebrew which appeared to be older than anything extant. While he was still studying his find he was surrounded by a band of local bedouins who made it clear that the stone was their property and that they did not intend to part with it. Klein asked them to name their price. They suggested a figure which was far beyond his means. So he made an exact sketch of the site, and set off for Germany to raise financial help.

But before he obtained the money he needed, the French scholar Clermont-Ganneau hurried to the spot and copied the inscription. The Hebrew writing turned out to be an account of the victory of the Israelites over King Mesha of Moab—the story told in Chapter 3 of Kings II. It was obvious that the stone must be 2,700 years old —easily the oldest 'document' in existence. The French government almost thrust the money to buy the stone into Clermont-Ganneau's hands, but it was too late. When he returned to the site he found the stone gone. The bedouins had smashed it into small pieces in the hope of getting more money for it. All that Clermont-Ganneau could do was to search for the fragments and then use these to reconstruct the black stone with the help of the copy he had made. This reconstruction is now in the Louvre.

The Moabite Stone, as it came to be called, has a two-fold importance. First, it is the oldest piece of Hebrew literature so far found. Secondly, it shows the origin of Hebrew script. The letters used were unlike anything hitherto seen. They were a mixture of Phoenician and ancient Hebrew, and were christened the Mesha Script.

Another inscription, discovered and photographed by Parker and Vincent in 1909, had the same kind of interest for experts, though its philological value outweighed its worth as a Biblical source. This inscription was an account of the building of an underground sewer from Gihon to the Siloah, but its age—it dated from 700 BC—and the script it used were enough to fascinate scholars.

One of the most interesting finds that now came to light was the treasure of the Cairo *geniza*.

In the ninth century AD a Coptic church had been built in Cairo and dedicated to St Michael. But when in 882 the central organization of the Copts had demanded a tax of 20,000 dinars to be paid by each church, the patriarch had decided to sell the building, along with others, to the Jews. St Michael's was converted into a synagogue, and next to it was built a *geniza* or lumber-room. Such a room was common; it provided a resting-place for worn-out scrolls before these were ceremonially interred in consecrated ground. The intention was to shield the name of the Lord from the eyes of the profane.

This particular *geniza* was walled up and almost forgotten. Its former function was occasionally remembered, and in 1864 Jacob Saphir obtained permission from the rabbi of the day to investigate the contents of the *geniza*. He found only a few pages of manuscript which seemed to him to be of little value. Later, Abraham Firko-

Discovered quite by chance *in 1880, this stone bears one of the earliest Hebrew inscriptions ever found. It records the building of an underground sewer by King Hezekiah, about 700 BC, as related in II Chron. 32.*

witsch, a celebrated antiquarian with the largest collection of Hebrew manuscripts in the world, also wormed his way through the dust and dirt but never revealed what he found.

In 1890 the synagogue and *geniza* were renovated and the rabbis uncovered various manuscripts which they realized were valuable. They sold these as souvenirs to tourists and conducted a brisk trade. Two of their customers were Scotswomen who showed their purchases to Solomon Schechter, at that time Professor of Talmudic Studies at Cambridge. With a thrill of excitement, Schechter recognized that they contained a page from an ancient Palestinian Talmud and another page from a second-century Hebrew edition of Ecclesiasticus. Until that time the earliest known version of Ecclesiasticus was the Septuagint; the Hebrew text was presumed to be lost.

Without any publicity, Schechter was given the means for an expedition to Cairo. He had *carte blanche* to buy everything of the slightest interest. The University furnished him with a letter to the

Jewish community of Cairo, and he was soon on friendly terms with the Chief Rabbi of the city, Raphael ben Simon, who personally took him to the *geniza*. And there Schechter was launched upon an extremely uncomfortable task. At every breath he took, a cloud of dust blew up and stung his eyes, nose, and throat. Each touch filled the air with dirt. The smell was vile. But Schechter persisted, and his reward was thirty large packing-cases filled with manuscripts which were gloatingly received by the Cambridge University Library.

It took ten years to catalogue the manuscripts even cursorily; the work of detailed examination is still going on. Amongst the dusty papers Schechter had salvaged were books of the Bible and the Apocrypha; pseudepigraphs in Masoretic script; *targums* in Aramaic; trilingual Biblical texts in Hebrew, Aramaic, and Arabic; Talmudic writings; dictionaries; textbooks of astrology; medicine, and mathematics; historical documents and poetry, philosophy and occultism; Jewish, Christian, and Mohammedan writings. . . . The whole collection fills 164 display cases in the University Library.

Much of this material is of interest only to historians, anthropologists, and philologists. But the manuscripts of Ecclesiasticus and the Masoretic writings help us to understand the development of Hebrew thought and writing. For the first time the evolution of punctuation could be seen, from its first hesitant beginnings to the perfected system. In short, the Cairo *geniza*, that forgotten graveyard of old documents, has proved an inexhaustible treasure-house for generations of scholars.

'APION TO EPIMACHUS, GREETINGS!'

While all this was going on, two more scholars, Grenfell and Hunt, both professors at Oxford, were making history elsewhere. They had found strange earthworks, some like small hills, others more like long sand-dunes, near some Arab encampments in the interior of Egypt. These were rubbish-heaps which had accumulated

From the treasure of the Geniza *comes this page of Aquila's translation of II Kings 23:15–19.*

ΘΙ ΕΙΝΟΙ ΚΑΙ
ΤΟΥ ...
ΑΥΘΙϹ ...
ΕΙΡΙ ...
ΜΑΘΟΙΡΥ ...
ΧΘΝ ...
ϹΕΜΑ ...
ΙΕΝΕϹ ...
ΟΥ ...

ΜΙΝΗ ...
ΚΑΙ ΕΝΙ ...
ΝΙ ΤΟΟΥ ΓΙΑϹΤΗ
ΚΑΙ ΕΜΙΑΝΕ
ΕΡΑΤΟΡΗ
ΑΡΟΕΑΛΛΗϹ
ΟΥΘΟΥ
ΛΘϹΘΝϹΥ

ϹΚ ΕΝ ...
ΟΘϹ ΘΥ ...
ΠΘΚ ...

ΤΑΝΤΙΛ ...
ΑΥΤΟΥ ΚΑΙ ΕΝ ...
ΡΙ ΕΩΘ ΧΝΟ ΕΙ ...
ΤΟΥ ΥΠΡΟϹ ΤΟΥ
ΟΘ ...

through the centuries and become part of the landscape. It was not until the second half of the nineteenth century, when cotton became an important industry in Egypt, that plantation-owners began to see in the sand-hills a source of superb manure and to use them for that purpose. And when they dug them up, they kept coming across small objects of various kinds—broken vases and slates, bits of pottery and metal, all the debris which had been thrown out down the ages. Many of the finds were swiftly consigned to modern rubbish-heaps, but a few of the Arabs took to hawking them to dealers, whence they found their way to Europe. Presently, scholars scented a new quarry, and tracked it down to Medinet el-Fajum, a town sixty miles west of Cairo. This fertile region had been inhabited from time immemorial and had been, in the days of the Pharoahs, a city with 100,000 inhabitants.

The first systematic excavations were begun in 1890 by archaeo-logists from the Berlin Museum, but it was not until five years later when Grenfell and Hunt took over that the real excitement began. Not that the finds were ever exciting in the sense that the magnificent treasures discovered in the royal vaults of Ur were exciting. What was found at Medinet el-Fajum were only the everyday things that ordinary people had used—tools, kitchen utensils, scraps of letters, and the like. But they combined to form a picture of life in the ancient world which was vivid and even sometimes moving. There was, for example, the letter written by Apion, an Egyptian soldier who had enlisted in the Roman army; here is an extract from one of his letters home found amidst the debris: 'Apion to Epimachus, his father and lord, greetings! First of all I hope you are in good health, and that everything goes well with you and my sister and her daughter and my brother. It is only thanks to the god Serapis, who saved me from a terrible storm at sea, that I am writing to you today. When I reached Misenum I got my pay—three gold pieces. I am very well. Please, father, write me a letter and tell me how you are and how my brother and sister are. Thanks to your training I stand a good chance of doing well in the service if the gods are with me. . . . I send you a little picture of myself. . . .' The letter could be that of any newly-enlisted private swaggering in his first uniform.

Even more moving is another letter, this time of the second century, from Antonius Longis of Karanus to his mother Neilus. Apparently Antonius was a Prodigal Son—a perfect illustration of Jesus's parable. He had left his mother and gone to the city where he passed rapidly from luxury to profligacy, and from profligacy to debt, despair, and beggary. He dared not face his mother with the clothes hanging off his back in rags. 'I am too ashamed to come home,' he wrote to her, 'because I am so shabby. I tell you that as I write to you I am almost naked. Please, please forgive me. I know that I have brought it all on myself, but I have been punished for everything.'

And then there was the letter from one of the earliest Christians to a co-religionist in El-Fajum. This is the earliest original letter in a Christian hand that we know of; it was written in Rome some time between AD 264 and 282 and it gives us an insight into the lives of early converts: 'You would do well, brother, to buy the linen. Then one of your company should go to Alexandria, sell the linen, and give the money either to Maximos the priest or to Primitinos, so that I can collect it when, by the grace of God, I reach Alexandria.'

Interesting though these glimpses of the everyday life of the past are, they are less important than the fragments of Biblical writing that Grenfell and Hunt dug up. Most of these did not come from Medinet el-Fajum but from the mounds at Oxyrhynchos, a tiny settlement on the edge of the Libyan desert; this had been the capital of a province in the time of the Pharaohs. Almost all the parch-ments found dated from the third century. There were bits of the Gospels, of the Acts, of Paul's Epistles, and of various apocryphal gospels. Moreover, there were sayings ascribed to Christ which were not in the canonical Gospels but may well be genuine. Alto-gether, out of this haul sixty-four papyri had to do with the New Testament, and more were discovered later. It was strenuous work.

Each handful of sand had to be sifted, examined, and felt for any object, however minute, that might be buried in it. If a sweating Arab digger decided that the back-breaking work was worth more than he was being paid in cash, and made up the difference by pocketing the odd parchment or two, we can feel for him.

Meanwhile, a compatriot of Grenfell and Hunt was also working in Egypt. His name was probably as much in the mouths of the intelligentsia at the end of the last century as those of Darwin, Huxley or Dickens. It was Flinders Petrie. In 1880, at the age of twenty-seven, he left England for Egypt and spent the next forty-six years there except for short intervals, digging for archaeological treasure. Petrie was the pioneer of systematic, layer-by-layer excavation, using scientific methods to examine and date the finds. He was also the first to realize the importance of trivial domestic rubbish—broken pottery, the seals of wine jars, and so on—in establishing chronology. By this revolutionary approach he was able to fill in most of the blanks in the history of ancient Egypt.

The Egyptian death-cult accounts for the wonderful state of preservation in which so many objects were found. It demanded that the bodies of the dead—especially those who had been rich and powerful—be preserved as long as possible in the form they had had when living. So each corpse was embalmed, wrapped in tar-saturated bandages, and enclosed in a lavishly decorated wooden coffin shaped like a man's body. Then the wooden coffin was placed in a stone one; sometimes there was even a third.

Of course, the poorer members of society could not afford to be buried on such a scale. Their coffins were made of a kind of papier-mâché moulded from any old papyri that came to hand. But, humble as these were originally, they proved perhaps more interesting, Biblically, than the magnificent sarcophagi of the wealthy. Flinders Petrie was the first man to destratify these papier mâché coffins and decipher what had been written on the papyrus. Mostly they were the remnants of old business letters or legal notices, such as a correspondence carried on in the first century by a lawyer's office

'The sayings of Jesus', *a few fragments of which were found by Grenfell and Hunt at Oxyrhynchos, are not among the canonical Gospels, but they have the ring of truth. One passage—most appropriately —runs, 'For there is nothing hidden which shall not be made manifest, nor buried which shall not be raised.'*

in Alexandria, but here and there fragments of Biblical writing turned up. Petrie found parts of Deuteronomy dating from the second century BC. So even Egyptian burials added to our knowledge of everyday life in Biblical times.

So did the discoveries at Elephantine in 1906–8. This was a town in the south of a long island in the middle of the Nile, opposite Aswan. It had been inhabited during the seventh century BC by a colony of Jews under Egyptian rule. They had permission to build

303

a temple and practise their religion. Naturally, they collected their sacred writings and these, dating mostly from the fourth century BC, were found under the ruins of the town. They were unearthed in such a compact pile that it was clear the excavators had stumbled on the temple library.

In 1906, Dr Rubensohn, an eminent Jewish scholar, had discovered the oldest Greek manuscript in the world on the Elephantine site—a marriage settlement dating from 311 BC. Next year he found numerous Aramaic papyri dating from the fifth century. These constituted one of the earliest sources of Jewish history.

Four years earlier William L. Nash had added yet another Biblical document to the growing collection. It was only a minute scrap of papyrus with twenty-four lines of Hebrew writing on it, but it was to acquire world fame. Nash bought it from some Egyptians who may have acquired it from one of the less trustworthy of the workmen employed by Grenfell and Hunt. Nash offered it to Cambridge University, and it was roughly identified as dating from the first or second century AD. The American scholar, William Foxwell Albright, was the first to recognize its true importance. In 1937 he headed an article in the *Journal of Biblical Studies*: 'A Biblical Fragment from the Time of the Maccabees: the Nash Papyrus,' and went on to prove conclusively that the page dated from the second century BC. Its twenty-four lines— an extract from the Ten Commandments—made up the oldest Biblical document that had then been discovered. It was not until the finding of the Dead Sea Scrolls in 1947 that anything of comparable age was known. There was only one other fragment that came anywhere near it, the Fuad Papyrus, so called because it is in the Fuad collection in Cairo. This contains four verses from the 31st chapter of Deuteronomy.

The oldest New Testament document was in an even worse condition than any of these. It was torn, crumpled, and all but worn away. It contained only seven lines, each with only a few words in it. And yet it transformed scholarly opinion. The reason for this was that it appeared to be a part of the Gospel of St John; on one side were a few sentences from Chapter 18, 31–33; on the other were parts of Chapter 18, verses 37 and 38—the story of the Passion. It appeared to have been written in AD 125. At least C. H. Roberts, Grenfell's successor at Oxford, thought so. But it had been assumed for years that the Gospel could not have been written before the second century, and most likely the second half of the second century. And, from this, it had been deduced that the Gospel could not possibly have been written by Jesus's disciple. Yet here it was—written proof that it was already in existence in 125. Like a reproach to the doubting, Jesus's words sprang off the faded page: 'To this end was I born, and for this cause came I into the world, that I should bear witness unto the truth. Every one that is of the truth heareth my voice.'

During the thirties two more discoveries were made. In 1930 it came to the ears of various scholars that dealers in Cairo were offering a number of Old Testament papyri in Greek for sale. All the great museums and universities were alerted and made offers, but the dealers, scenting a killing, put up their prices beyond the reach of any but a millionaire. A millionaire at once came forward, paid the dealers' prices without fuss, and handed over the documents to two scholars, F. G. Kenyon and H. A. Sanders, for detailed study. The millionaire was Chester Beatty, an American. Kenyon and Sanders found the haul to contain eleven codices, 190 pages in all, including parts of Numbers and Deuteronomy, Genesis, Ezekiel, Daniel, and Esther, some of which filled in gaps in the *Codex Sinaiticus*. There were also various portions of Paul's Epistles and of all four Gospels. The whole collection dated from the second and third centuries.

The experts were curious to know where these manuscripts had been found. Such a large collection must have been carefully preserved somewhere to survive so long: these were not just isolated fragments such as might have lain on a rubbish-heap. But the dealers were not talking. Even bribes could not open their mouths. At last Professor Carl Schmidt, of Berlin, took matters in hand, made enquiries in Sherlock Holmes fashion, and listened to everything the dealers said, either to him or among themselves. Anything which he could possibly construe as a clue he followed up and checked. Eventually he solved the mystery. The manuscripts had come from Aphroditopolis, not in the el-Fajum district as at first supposed, but on the other side of the Nile. Here Arab workers had found a clay pot containing papyri. Schmidt deduced that these must have been rejects from the library of the neighbouring monastery—documents that had been removed to make way for others, but were still too holy to be thrown away. Consequently they were placed in the pottery vessel and buried in a cave.

Five years later came news of another kind, this time in Tell ed-Duweir in Palestine. Tell ed-Duweir had been called Lachish in Biblical times. In the course of excavating the town, Starkey, a British archaeologist, came upon a room dug deep into the earth and half filled with the debris of a fire. He guessed it might be an old guardroom—it was near the foundations of the city-wall—and thrilled with expectation. This was the kind of place where something might have survived. . . .

Sure enough, he found eighteen fragments of clay tablets, each written on in Hebrew with a reed pen. These must have been some 2,500 years old, because they had obviously been buried before the great fire which was recorded as breaking out in Lachish in 588–7 BC. Mainly letters, they read vividly to this day. From the Commanding Officer of an outpost to the Commander of the Jewish forces in Lachish: 'I have followed your instructions, sir, and have waited for the signals from Lachish, for the signals from Aseka are invisible.' This soldier probably died in the war that followed; it wiped out most of the Jewish army.

Apart from their human interest, these letters are of value in the sphere of linguistics; they are the only group of documents of that period which are written in classical Hebrew. Moreover, they give an interesting sidelight on the Biblical story of Judah's downfall, as recorded in Jeremiah 34, verse 7.

These are a few of the riches dug up with spade and shovel or tracked down with the skill of a detective during the period following the discovery of the *Codex Sinaiticus*. Vivid, illuminating, fabulously valuable—they are all these. And yet they pale beside the next startling discovery to come to light—the Dead Sea Scrolls.

Last message from a beleaguered outpost: *a few words written on a clay tablet about 588 BC make a poignant link with dark days in Judah's history—days described by the prophet Jeremiah, 'when the king of Babylon's army fought against Jerusalem, and against all the cities of Judah that were left, against Lachish . . .'*

18

THE DEAD SEA SCROLLS

'THEY MIGHT BE OF INTEREST TO ME'

Why Mohammed adh-Dhib should have been climbing down a cliff-face to the west of the Dead Sea one spring morning in 1947 will never be known. He himself said he was going after a goat which had strayed, but this does not explain why he and his fellow herdsmen had made a wide detour from their route between Transjordan to Palestine. Would it be that they were trying to evade the customs? Were they enlivening the deadly routine of herdsmanship with a little smuggling? Whatever the reason, there they were, and there was fifteen-year-old Mohammed, unwittingly making his name famous.

His story was that he had thrown a stone which had disappeared into a cleft in the rock. When he had followed it he found several earthenware jars, out of one of which protruded a bundle of dirty parchment. He took the bundle and showed it to the leader of the bedouins who, much interested, entered the cave himself and counted forty jars, each containing the same old and rotten-smelling parchment. The Arabs took away some of the jars and consulted a sheikh in Bethlehem, who pronounced that they were Syrian scrolls and, as such, likely to fetch a good price. He suggested they should bargain with Khalil Iskander, a Syrian Orthodox dealer in Jerusalem. This could prove a nice little commercial sideline.

Iskander examined the manuscripts as well as he could, for they were too fragile with age for him to unroll. From the few characters he was able to decipher he inclined to the sheikh's opinion that the scrolls were Syrian. He consulted his friend, George Isaiah, another dealer in Jerusalem, who spoke to the Archbishop of the Syrian Orthodox community, Athanasius Yeshua Samuel. 'They might be of interest to me,' the Archbishop said cautiously. But when the scrolls were shown to him his tone changed. He recognized that they were written in Hebrew, not Syrian. Then he broke off a piece from the edge of one scroll and burned it; from the smell it gave off he knew it must be either parchment or leather. By now he was frantically eager to buy and past all pretence of caution. He made an offer. But it was not so easy. The bedouins had left the city some time ago and Iskander was only holding the manuscripts for them. He promised to watch out for their return and try to acquire their finds for a reasonable price as soon as they came back, probably in a few weeks' time. Meanwhile, Archbishop Samuel would just have to wait.

The Arabs returned at the beginning of July. At least, two of them did; the third, they explained, had sold his share of the parchments to a Moslem sheikh in Bethlehem. At this stage their price was £20 a scroll.

Feverishly Iskander communicated with Samuel. The two bedouins were sent to Isaiah, who took them to the monastery. Unfortunately the Archbishop was not in. The porter, somewhat aghast at the Arabs' disreputable appearance, dealt with them curtly. In a huff, they stayed away two weeks until all concerned began to think that the chance of a lifetime had slipped through their fingers. As soon as they reappeared, Samuel hastily snapped up the remaining five scrolls, two of which were actually pieces of the same scroll.

When the Archbishop came to examine his purchases, he found that two were Old Testament scrolls in Hebrew, one was in Aramaic, and one he could not identify at all. This last was later proved to be a sort of handbook of 'service regulations' for a pre-Christian Jewish sect. Samuel had no idea of the age of the scrolls nor exactly what they were. And the palaeographic experts he called in differed in their judgments. Stephen Hanna Stephen, the Syrian

The Manual of Discipline, *one of the first discovered Dead Sea Scrolls, gives some of the rules of the Essenes, a pre-Christian Jewish sect of ascetics who lived a communal life in strict accordance with the Law.*

Orthodox orientalist, believed the scrolls were worthless. The Dominican scholar, Father J. P. M. van der Ploeg, disagreed and told Iskander that one scroll at least was an extremely old and valuable Isaiah manuscript. Other Jewish and American scholars gave various opinions; on the whole, the consensus seemed to be that Archbishop Samuel had been misled and that his parchments were probably only fakes.

The months passed, and in February 1948 the parchments came into the hands of two young American scholars, Drs William Brownlee and John Trevor, of the American School of Oriental Research in Jerusalem. They found to their excitement that they were handling Biblical texts older than any hitherto known. To obtain confirmation of their findings, they photographed portions of the scrolls and sent the prints to the most famous of all palaeographers, Professor William F. Albright of Johns Hopkins University. Albright wrote back by return of post: 'This is the greatest discovery of modern times; these manuscripts date from the first century BC, or even earlier.' His opinion was conclusive. Brownlee and Trevor held a press conference in Jerusalem and gave precise details to all the journalists who swarmed to the spot, lured by the sensational news that Biblical manuscripts had been found which were nearer the events they described than any other—older than the *Codex Sinaiticus*, older than the *Codex Vaticanus*, and most probably older even than the Nash Papyrus.

Of course, there were sceptics. Professor G. R. Driver, of Oxford, asserted that the manuscripts could not date from a period earlier than the sixth or seventh century AD. Professors Hooke, Wechsler, and Zeitlin thought along the same lines and expressed their opinions forcibly. It was the beginning of the first Scroll War.

TREASURE IN THE 'WALL STREET JOURNAL'

While the scholarly world at large was at odds one with another, the investigators on the spot had other, and less polemical, problems of their own. Surely there must be more scrolls where these had come from? But where? The bedouins were not helpful; and to find the cave meant searching the entire area overlooking the Dead Sea, cave by cave and pothole by pothole. How was that to be done? Palestine was in the throes of war. The creation of the new state of Israel had led to bitter fighting between the Israelis and the Arabs— a shooting war of machine-guns and border raids, pitched battles and surprise attacks. So a carefully organized search for ancient manuscripts was out of the question. For a Jew to show himself on Arab soil meant instant death, and all Westerners were more or less identified with the Jews.

Archbishop Samuel fled with his scrolls to America, partly to seek refuge for himself, partly to find a bidder for the manuscripts.

Unexpectedly, there were few offers. It was not until someone had the brainwave of advertising in the *Wall Street Journal* that the right purchaser was found—General Yigael Yadin, the son of Professor E. L. Sukenik, who was state archivist to Israel. Incidentally, this must have been one of the oddest advertisements ever to appear in an Articles for Sale column: 'Biblical manuscripts for sale, dating from 200 BC at latest. Ideal gift for educational or religious institution.' It was good sales psychology. Yadin bought the scrolls for

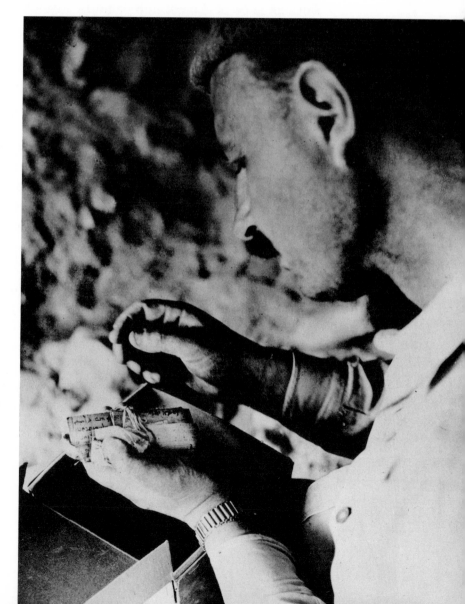

Still in its original cover, *one of the Dead Sea Scrolls is examined by General Yigael Yadin, scholar and chief of the Israeli General Staff. The Hebrew writing on the papyrus can be clearly seen.*

a quarter of a million dollars (nearly £90,000), or about 1,000 per cent profit for the Archbishop's funds, and took them back to Israel where they were personally received by Premier Moshe Sharett in the spring of 1955.

Meanwhile, a great deal had been happening since the first discovery made by Mohammed adh-Dhib in the cave at Qumran beside the Dead Sea. Professor Sukenik, General Yadin's father, had heard, as early as the autumn of 1947, that a merchant in Bethlehem had some ancient manuscripts for sale. This was before Sukenik knew of Archbishop Samuel's acquisitions. The archivist contrived to get through the fighting lines and reach Bethlehem, where he tracked down three scrolls at different dealers. These scrolls must have been those sold by the third bedouin to a Moslem sheikh. Sukenik became convinced that they must have come from one of the caves overlooking the Dead Sea.

By 1949 the war was nominally over, so that it was possible to mount a scientific expedition. Captain Philippe Lippens, a Belgian who was an official observer of the United Nations, began to prepare for one. He obtained the support of the American Institute in Jerusalem, interested the Commander of the British brigade of the Arab Legion, and won the backing of the head of the Papal Institute for Bible Studies. Matters moved quickly. Protected by the police and members of the Arab Legion, scholars and officers made several journeys to the Dead Sea, determined to search the cliffs yard by yard. Among these investigators were Father Roland de Vaux of the French Archaeological Institute, Colonel Ashton, and G. Lankester Harding, the head of the Transjordanian Ministry of Antiquities.

After a few false starts they found the cave which must have held the first scrolls. It was near the ruins of an old monastery at Qumran, about two miles from the edge of the Dead Sea. Their pulses quickening, the searchers entered the cave. It was empty. Somebody had been before them and swept the cave clear of everything of value. And yet this 'somebody' had not been completely efficient.

A few bits and pieces had been overlooked—scraps of pottery, fragments of parchment, leather, and linen. By the time all these had been carefully collected, shred by shred and splinter by splinter, and examined more closely, the experts realized that there was quite a lot left for them after all. They identified fragments of all five books of the Pentateuch, of Judges, Samuel, Isaiah, Ezekiel, and the Psalms. There were also bits of commentaries and the title-page of the scroll which had meant absolutely nothing to Archbishop Samuel—the 'service regulations'.

Unconsidered bits and pieces *from an already rifled cave yielded valuable fragments from many books of the Old Testament. Identifying them and piecing them together is a daunting scholastic jigsaw puzzle; these small patches were identified as part of the book of Isaiah.*

The scholars were not dissatisfied. But they argued that where there was one cave there must be others. So they continued their search, and came upon more caves, three, then four, then ten. In the end, the figure reached twenty-five, all in the neighbourhood of Qumran, where could still be seen the ruins of a pre-Christian monastery. But in every cave someone had been before them.

Again there was controversy. Why had the scrolls been hidden in the caves in the first place? Why had they been enclosed in clay pots? How old were the pots? If they were connected in some way with the monastery, what exactly was the connection?

Broken clay pots found in the Qumran caves, when pieced together, proved to be containers for the scrolls. This suggested that when the scrolls had been deposited in the caves, care had been taken that they should be properly preserved. But when had they been hidden, and why?

Blackmail prices, *up to £1 a square centimetre, were asked by the bedouins for torn fragments like these pieces of a scroll of Exodus. The scholars were powerless to do anything but pay up.*

While the experts were still puzzling over these questions, another problem came up. New manuscripts, or rather fragments of manu‑scripts, began to appear in the more questionable shops in Jerusa‑lem's bazaar‑quarter. They were evidently the fruits of the Arabs' raids on the Qumran caves, and ridiculous prices were being asked for them. To push the price up higher, each scroll was being divided into small pieces and the fragments sold, to different purchasers, at £1 a square centimetre.

So began a race between the scholars and the bedouins. If the scholars reached a cave too late or overlooked anything, it meant they would have to buy its contents later at blackmail prices. Time was money, in the truest sense of the words. The tension became severe; Father de Vaux and the others lived in a state of constant emergency, rushing off as soon as they heard that bedouins were at work in any particular place. Sometimes they arrived too late. Sometimes they were soon enough to drive off the Arabs before they had removed the loot. Sometimes they even captured a thief or two—but this led only to impasse and frustration. The bedouins knew how to hold their tongues, and if they were sent to prison the upshot might be that another manuscript might never come on the market. Government and scholars agreed that the best thing to do was to turn a blind eye to the more flagrant of the Arabs' activities in the hope that the end might justify the means. This was a ridiculous situation, because the contents of the caves belonged legally to the government, but what alternative was there? Black market or no black market, the Arabs had to be conciliated.

A JIGSAW PUZZLE OF THEOLOGY

In 1952 the French and American Institutes in Jerusalem undertook a detailed search of a five-mile strip of the Dead Sea coast. They combed two hundred caves, but found very little of interest. In fact, they were at the point of giving up when, not far from the ruins of Qumran, they stumbled on something quite unexpected—two rolled-up sheets of copper about a foot long, lying among scattered fragments of parchment and pottery. The metal was in the last stages of oxidization and crumbled as soon as it was touched, but writing could be seen on its ancient surface. This was the first known example of copper being used as a writing-material. The copper scrolls of Qumran are unique.

These scrolls were taken to Jerusalem, covered with a fine film of wax to preserve them, and sent to England. The first cursory exami-nations had shown that what was written on them was not Biblical passages but records of the Qumran monastery. Excavations were begun on the ruins of the buildings and more knowledge was gained of the Jewish sect which had occupied them, although they still remain shadowy figures.

It seems that in the middle of the second century BC certain of the Jews formed themselves into groups called 'chasidim' or 'holy ones'

—in its Greek form, Essenes. They tried to live completely spotless lives, abjuring all private property and sensual pleasure. Their monastery was governed according to strict rules aimed at stimulating love of God and their fellows, justice, and piety. In general, the Essenes were widely respected, and probably had as many as four thousand members through the years.

The excavations brought to light the foundations of a large building, with assembly halls, refectories, offices, living-quarters, and libraries. But where were the books or scrolls? Of these there was no trace, although there were pens and styluses enough—some of the inkwells even showed traces of ink that had long ago evaporated.

It was certain that the monks must have possessed books. That they wrote these themselves was more than likely from the evidence of the writing equipment found. Chemists proved that the traces of ink in the inkwells were the same as the ink used on the scrolls. Only one conclusion could be drawn. At a time of great danger, the monks must have cleared out all their library and hidden the documents where the enemy could not reach them. The only danger of this kind known was the period when the Jews rebelled against Rome and brought down on themselves a punishment which culminated in the destruction of Jerusalem and the extermination of all Jews within reach of the Roman army. The monks must have been massacred with the rest, but managed to conceal their treasures so well that these were not discovered until two thousand years later, and then only by chance.

New discoveries went on being made. In the autumn of 1952 more manuscripts appeared in shops in the Jerusalem bazaar. In the spring of 1955 archaeologists found more caves near Qumran which, like the others, became a target for the cave-robbers. The game began all over again—a race against time, the penalty for losing being the price of the fragments that the Arabs offered for sale. To this day, no one can tell the exact extent of the buried treasures or the number of those which are still in Arab hands.

When found, the scraps of parchment were collected together in the Palestine Museum in Jerusalem. There they were laid out on special benches, put together to form a coherent whole, and covered with glass. The process was like doing several jigsaw puzzles at the same time, with half the pieces missing and no means of knowing which of the existing pieces belonged to which puzzle. Sometimes the pieces were so small that they contained only one word or even

G. Lankester Harding, *head of the archaeological services of Arab Palestine and Transjordan, was the responsible 'man on the spot' in 1948, when the news of the Dead Sea Scrolls first broke.*

John Marco Allegro *of Manchester University, one of the international team of scholars who worked on the restoration and editing of the scrolls. Some of the fragments before him are smaller than a fingernail.*

only a few letters of a word. Sometimes they filled existing gaps; sometimes they seemed to come from new manuscripts altogether. Each new step necessitated a close study of the form of the letters, the composition of the ink, the chemical properties, colour, and strength of the parchment. Many a puzzled scholar has sat, and may for that matter still be sitting, for weeks over a tiny scrap of manuscript no larger than his fingernail, wondering where it belonged.

The 'Scrollery' *at the Palestine Archaeological Museum in Jerusalem. Here the precious fragments are assembled, cleaned and laid out on long trestle tables, for the patient, arduous work of fitting together an unknown number of jigsaw puzzles of which an unknown number of pieces may be missing.*

Then there was the problem of how to unroll the copper scrolls, rotten and decayed as these were. At every millimetre there was the risk of the whole thing crumbling away, and this often happened so that the scientist was left with a pile of disjointed bits and pieces to put together again.

But the biggest problem of all was, and is, money. The acquisition of the scrolls ate up thousands of pounds, even though the price had fallen by half to ten shillings the square centimetre. It was unthink‑able that even the smallest shred should be lost to posterity through lack of funds, but the academic bodies were beginning to reach the end of their resources. The Jordan government deserves praise for the way in which, despite its own restricted economy, it put more than £15,000 at the disposal of the foreign scholars on its soil. But even this rapidly disappeared, along with the loans which the institutes raised from other sources.

An easy way out would have been to seek funds from abroad, particularly from the USA, the world's treasury in matters of this kind, but Jordanian law forbade the export of its antiquities. In the end, G. Lankester Harding persuaded the government to agree to the sale of the manuscripts on condition that they were first fully investigated, photographed, and translated in Jordan. By this means, new supplies of money were put into the scholars' hands. Canada gave roughly £5,000, the Vatican £10,000, an English private donor £1,000, the University of Manchester £2,000, and the Bonn government, through the University of Heidelberg, £5,000. All this money was quietly absorbed by the wily bedouins of the Ta'amira tribe, who must have become fully convinced that smuggling—if it was smuggling that the first finders of the scrolls had been engaged in—pays.

Any doubts about the true age of the scrolls were swept away by the findings of Professor W. F. Libby of the Chicago Institute of Nuclear Studies. By means of the Carbon 14 Test, which will be described in the next chapter, Libby established beyond any doubt that the scrolls must have been written sometime between 167 BC and AD 233, and that the idea that they were either forgeries or medieval work could be dismissed. Since the scrolls, from the course of history, must have been hidden before AD 70, it follows that they were written either during or before the lifetime of Jesus. At least, this is the opinion of most of the leading experts today.

WAS JESUS AN ESSENE?

But if the age of the scrolls is more or less certain, their contents, and especially the interpretation of what is written there, is still a matter of controversy; and not only of controversy, but disillusionment and hysteria. Headlines such as 'The Dead Sea Scrolls have knocked the bottom out of Christianity', 'Was Jesus an Essene?' and 'Is Christianity Dead?' indicate the reaction of the vulgar and un-learned to the Dead Sea Scrolls. Some idea of the hypnotic influence they exercise over the academic and journalistic worlds can be seen from the 1,500 and more books and pamphlets on the subject that have been published during the last ten years.

Why all the fuss? Have two thousand years of Christian teaching really been cancelled out by a few pieces of old parchment? What exactly do the scrolls say?

323

The Isaiah manuscript, written in Aramaic on strips of leather, is about six yards long by a foot wide. It is generally agreed to date from 100 BC. Scholars waited in suspense while it was being deciphered and translated, for if it differed widely from the traditional text it would throw doubt on the whole of the Biblical canon as we know it today. If Isaiah had been mishandled through the ages, it could safely be assumed that this was also true of the other books of the Bible.

But when the translation was made known, it proved to tally almost exactly with the usual text. There were small variations, but none was startling. In Chapter 15, verse 9, the Authorized Version gives: 'For the waters of Dimon shall be full of blood: for I will bring more upon Dimon . . .' The scroll gives 'Dibon' instead of 'Dimon'. In Chapter 45, verse 2, the Authorized Version has: 'I will go before thee and make the crooked places straight,' whereas the scroll has 'you' instead of 'thee', and 'hills' instead of 'crooked places'. In Chapter 45, verse 8, the scroll gives 'rain down righteousness' instead of 'pour down righteousness'. But what do all these small points of difference add up to? Nothing more than another source of study for the textual critics. Men like H. M. Orlinski, for instance, may be fascinated by the difference between 'Dibon' and 'Dimon', but the ordinary Bible reader does not trouble himself about it. Isaiah is still the same book it always has been.

There is a second Isaiah scroll, bought by Professor Sukenik, but it is almost indecipherable. What can be made out, however, seems to agree perfectly with the other scroll.

A third scroll, about $1\frac{1}{2}$ yards long and not as old as the other two, contains an inter-linear commentary to Habbakuk. The text itself agrees with the established Habbakuk text, but the comments could give a clue to the exact date of the manuscript—that is, if the events and people mentioned could be identified. For example, underneath Chapter 1, verse 6—'For, lo! I raise up the Chaldaeans, that bitter and hasty nation . . .' the commentator has written, 'This means the Kittim, a swift and warlike people.' But who were the

A minor sect of the Jews at the time of the Roman Empire was the Essenes, ascetics who lived as hermits or in monasteries. Near their monastery at Qumran (above) are the caves where the Dead Sea scrolls were found.

Kittim? Nobody knows. Perhaps the Seleucids? or the Romans? But this is only guesswork. The whole commentary is written from the viewpoint of the Essene sect and interprets the words of the prophet according to the specific needs and outlook of the monastery. Broadly, it too is of little interest to anyone but the specialist.

Much the same is true of a fourth manuscript, an account of the 'Battle of the Sons of Light against the Sons of Darkness'. This was strictly an Essenian affair in which the 'Sons of Levi, Judah, and Benjamin' were instructed how to fight the 'Sons of Japhet, the Kittim, and the Kings of the North'. It gives all the details of the preparations for battle, the weapons to be used, and the battle-order, but wraps these up in a sort of liturgical cottonwool. 'When you go out to battle you must write on the first standard: God's

325

Community; on the second: God's Party; on the third: God's People. . . . Seven ranks of cavalry shall be on the right and the left of the troops; on both sides shall their ranks be, seven hundred cavalry on the one side and seven hundred cavalry on the other. Two hundred cavalry shall go out with every thousand infantry. The numbers shall be: 4,600 and 100 chariots for the infantry, 50 for each unit. . . .'

It is a curious document. The war never took place, and probably was never expected to take place on the plane of physical reality. It was a symbolic conflict in which all but the elect—that is, the members of the sect describing the battle—should perish. Once more, the manuscript is chiefly of interest to specialists.

Apart from these scrolls, there are various fragments; some, including twenty psalm-like hymns, bought by Professor Sukenik; some are parts of a bilingual Book of Daniel; and all are in an almost illegible condition. There is also the Lamech Scroll, so called because it was once thought to contain the Lamech Apocalypse. This resisted all efforts to unroll and decipher it for several years, but it was mastered in 1956 by Professor Bieberkraut of the Hebrew University, who found it contained a paraphrase of the first ten chapters of Genesis, including a touching description of Sarah's beauty. It has been given the name of *Genesis Apocryphon*.

Finally, there were the two copper scrolls. For years they remained an insoluble problem. The metal could not be unrolled because the slightest touch caused it to crumble to dust. The Palestine Museum sought, and obtained, opinions from various leading metallurgists, but they were all discouraging. Scientists of Johns Hopkins University, who had been making a special study of decayed metals, said outright that the flexibility of the copper could not be restored and that the only thing to do would be to cut up the scrolls into strips and then piece these together on a firm backing of some sort. Dr H. Wright Baker of the Manchester College of Technology undertook to do this delicate operation. He had a minute circular saw made, with a blade only 0.15 millimetre thick, and gradually stripped off layer after layer of the scroll, as an onion is peeled. Then, with another specially made instrument, he cleaned the metal and removed the dust and dirt of two thousand years. Finally, Dr Baker handed over the 'unrolled' scroll to John Marco Allegro, a specialist in Hebrew dialects, to study.

Allegro found that the scrolls contained a list of buried treasures which had belonged to Qumran. These the monks had hidden at the approach of a Roman army. Each hiding-place was most carefully described and identified. Allegro knew that if he published this list it would bring a swarm of treasure-hunters to the scene, so he divulged the details only to such scholars as Father de Vaux and G. L. Harding. And since the secret is still being kept, there is really little more to be said about the copper scrolls except that some of the hiding-places mentioned are no longer recognizable because

An almost insoluble problem was set by two scrolls of copper. Over the centuries the metal had become oxidized, and crumbled at a touch. But Professor H. Wright Baker of Manchester, using a very thin power saw, succeeded in slicing off layer after layer in narrow strips, which could then be cleaned and read.

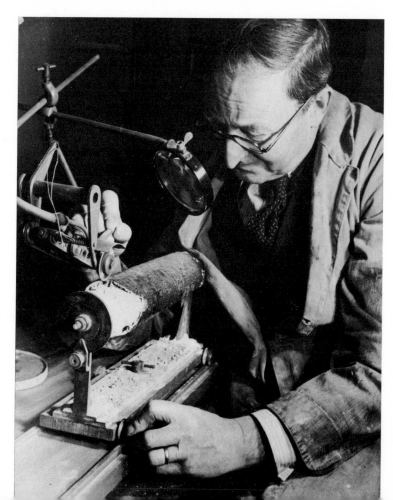

the landmarks used to identify them—trees, buildings, and so on—
have long since perished. In some instances, the scholars have
already been forestalled by treasure-hunters. Were these present-day
bedouins or Romans after the conquest of the Jews in the first
century? Who knows?

But these buried treasures, exciting as they are, have little to do
with the Bible as such. Certainly, they could not have stirred up
the storm of hysterical articles that appeared in the press, any more
than the Isaiah scrolls or the others. No. The cause of all the trouble
was the 'Handbook of Service Regulations' mentioned above—the
scroll which was among Archbishop Samuel's first purchases.
This is in two parts, originally joined together, and is about two
yards long. Although parts of the edges have been eaten away and
the beginning is missing, it is in good condition and comparatively
legible. It comprises a collection of rules and regulations for the
brothers of the Qumran community, liturgical writings, and
explanations of the doctrines practised by the Essenes. The surprising thing is that the picture which this document gives could
almost be that of an early Christian community.

THE CONFIRMATION OF FAITH

Although the Essenes called themselves 'the community of the
Many', they also spoke of 'twelve men . . . perfect in all things'. They
evidently practised baptism, though they conceived it as a repeated
act rather than a sacrament to take place once in a man's lifetime,
They demanded the confession of sins, repentance, and atonement.
They awaited the 'anointed of Aaron and Israel', a Messiah figure.
and they celebrated a form of Holy Communion, when they
believed the Messiah to be in some mystical way among them. Their
monks were sworn to poverty, humility, obedience, chastity, and
righteousness. All worldly goods belonged to the community as a
whole.

These striking parallels prompted a search of the other Dead Sea
Scrolls for similar ones. It began to seem as though Christianity was

merely a copy of an older faith, as though Jesus himself might have been an Essene and derived his teachings from the long-established doctrines of the sect. Much wishful thinking became mixed up with the affair. Where scholarly opinion was not completely misrepresented in the newspapers' thirst for bigger and better sensations, it tended to be led away from objectivity by theories—wonderful, stirring theories which could explain many things that have puzzled mankind.

And yet theories are not proof. The only proof that the scrolls give is of a pious sect which combined Jewish doctrines with tendencies towards asceticism. Its strongest resemblance to Christianity lies in the fact that it idealized 'the good life', just as Jesus and John the Baptist did. On this flimsy foundation is based the whole structure of theory and conjecture which seeks to discredit Christianity. It resolves itself into nothing more than that both the Essenes and Jesus based their ideas on the teachings of the Old Testament. Those parts of Christianity which are foreign to the Old Testament—the Incarnation, the Resurrection, and the Redemption, for example—were equally foreign to the Essenes. In short, Christianity and Essenism are as like, and as different, as the oak and the reed, both of which grow out of the same ground but are still two entirely different plants.

This is not the place to evaluate the polemics stimulated by the Dead Sea Scrolls. It is enough to say that knowledgeable opinion now holds that the sensationalism of the early articles was entirely unwarranted. Like most journalistic furores, this one has been something of a nine days' wonder and has now died down of its own accord. There is no need for the Christian to fear for his faith or his Bible: they are as safe as they always have been. And if newspapers must have something to sensationalize, they might consider the case of the Isaiah Scroll. The earliest known Biblical text, it has served to confirm in every way the scrupulous accuracy with which the Bible has been preserved through the ages. It is far more reassuring than ever the Essene manuscript was disturbing.

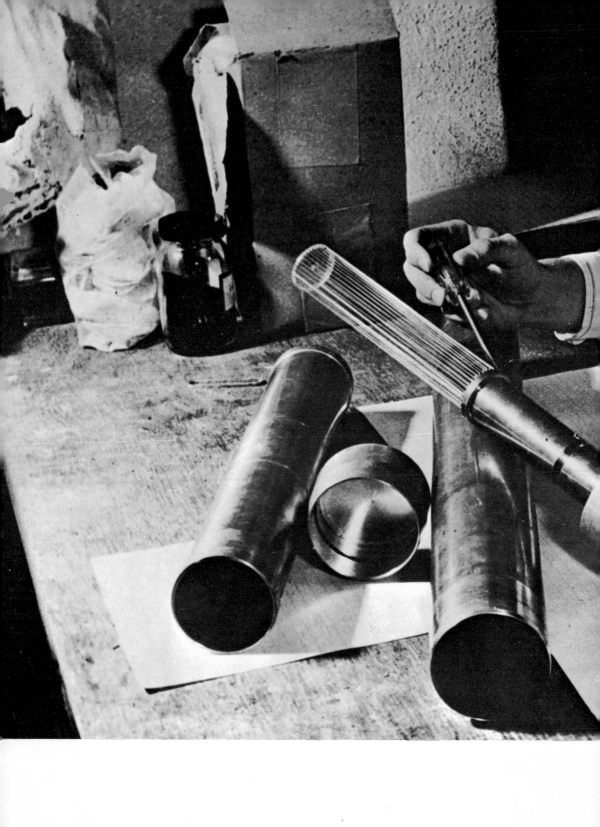

19

SCIENCE BEATS THE FORGERS

Like all commodities that cost big money, ancient manuscripts attracted their hucksters, profiteers, and forgers. Many people saw in the ready market for these articles a way of lining their own pockets. Khalil Iskander, who had bought the first Dead Sea Scrolls from the Ta'amira Arabs, was quick to realize that he was on to a good thing. There can be no doubt that he made the best of the opportunities offered him by the Arab-Israeli war and spurred the bedouins on to strip the caves before the scholars could reach them. Not that his name ever appeared when the manuscripts were later offered for sale; he was far too clever for that. He employed middle-men, retailers who acted as go-betweens. Iskander's appearance seemed harmless enough, that of a cobbler in the old quarter of Bethlehem who looked anything but the key figure in a vast operation.

It was not until 1949 that G. L. Harding's secretary, Yusef Saad, succeeded in having any direct communication with Iskander. Their first meeting was dramatic; the cobbler threw Saad out of his shop, and cursed him for being an interfering busybody. No doubt he saw in Saad a plain-clothes policeman and did not wish to have his premises raided. Saad was not discouraged by this brusque reception. He went back day after day, hinted that he had influence with prospective customers, referred casually to the risks involved in illicit manuscript-traffic, and finally won Iskander's confidence.

Saad understood the Oriental mind too well to make any direct offers or show the slightest impatience; the first move must come from the dealer. Sure enough, some weeks after Saad had left Bethlehem, he received a small parcel containing a minute scrap of parchment which proved to be part of a Dead Sea scroll. The ban was lifted. Iskander was willing to do business.

Saad had thought out a pretty little piece of fiction which was to put Iskander off the scent and take his mind away from all thoughts of governments, official bodies, and such dangerous topics. He explained that he was acting for a wealthy English professor who had a taste for old documents and was willing to see Iskander at a meeting-place of his own choosing. As soon as the Arab had named a time and a place, Saad collected £1,000 from Harding, got a young English archaeologist to act as the 'professor', and set off for Jericho. The assignation proved to be in a sort of eastern doss-house, like those described in Mayhew's survey of London's under-world in the nineteenth century. Menacing figures hovered in the background, dirt assaulted the eyes and nose, strange noises pene-trated the stealthy quiet from time to time. Saad later marvelled that he had come through the interview with his £1,000 still intact in his pocket.

They found Iskander in a back room, sitting behind a table, cautious, crafty, and prepared. He made no move until the bank-notes had been placed on the table. The bargaining began in the usual eastern style—threats, pleas, ribaldry, and despair—but no agreement was reached. It was not until the whole performance had been gone through again next day that a bargain was struck, and money and goods changed hands. The tension relaxed; suddenly everybody was in a good humour. 'By the way,' Iskander said, 'will you and the professor give my regards to Mr Harding?' Saad's opinion of himself as a secret agent dropped to zero.

But Iskander, though a shrewd businessman, dealt only in genuine goods. More dangerous were the men who, conscious that there was money to be made in old manuscripts, decided to provide a grateful public with a continuous supply of these, even if to do so they had to write the documents themselves. These forgers set the psychologist, or anyone who thinks he understands people, an odd problem. Forging manuscripts is not like forging banknotes; besides technical skill, the forger has to be a real scholar, equal to those who are going to examine his work, if he is to stand any chance of escaping detection. He must have a thorough knowledge of period, language, thought, and writing processes. In short, he must be a man who could easily make his mark in the legitimate academic world. Why should such a man trouble to forge manu- scripts, when forging banknotes would be just as profitable, if not more so?

With Abraham Firkowitsch, already mentioned in connection with the Cairo *geniza*, the motive for forgery was a sort of local patriotism. A well-known and respected collector of Hebrew manuscripts, he was also a member of a particular Jewish sect which came from the Crimea. To prove that his sect was part of the oldest Jewish heritage, he did not hesitate to fake 'ancient' papyri or to alter the dates on old tombstones and manuscripts to prove his argument.

His motives were worthier than those of another forger who became world-famous. Constantine Simonides was an acknow- ledged expert on palaeography. He was born in 1815 on a Greek island and brought up by his uncle, the prior of one of the monas- teries on Mount Athos. When his uncle died, Simonides went to Athens and sold a number of ancient papyri to the Greek govern- ment. Nobody questioned their authenticity. Encouraged by this success, he produced two more and these excited the academic world. The manuscripts were supposed to date from the thirteenth century. One of them described the invention of paper and the telescope; the other attributed to a contemporary the invention of the diving-bell and the first steamship. Coolly, Simonides dedicated his translation of these two documents to Mustoxydis, a Greek statesman and a leading scholar of his day, who promptly denounced

333

the whole affair as a scandalous imposture. Not in the least ruffled, Simonides countered the charge with another manuscript, supposed to date from the fifteenth century, in which the hero was described as inventing photography.

By this time, the experts were in an uproar. But it was not easy to expose Simonides. Parts of his 'finds' seemed to be genuine, and it was difficult to believe that so many eminent men could have been taken in by an insignificant Greek. The storm died away. Two years later, however, Simonides reappeared and contrived to obtain permission to excavate the Hippodrome in Athens. True to form, no sooner had he put spade to earth than he discovered a jar full of old parchments. But this time one of his helpers had seen him put the jar there beforehand. The game was up, Simonides returned to Mount Athos and contented himself for a while with selling genuine documents which restored his reputation a little. Then came his final undoing. He offered the so-called 'Uranios Palimpsest', an ancient Egyptian manuscript, to Professor Dindorf, who submitted it to a commission of scholars and finally to Tischendorf himself. The verdict was a blunt declaration that the document was a forgery. Simonides was placed under house-arrest but was soon released. Scholars have always been shy of scandal and publicity. Besides, who likes to admit he has been taken in?

The forger's revenge on Tischendorf was as crazy as all his previous acts. He alleged that the *Codex Sinaiticus* was also a fake, and that he himself had forged it on Mount Athos and had left it in the monastery of St Catherine. Tischendorf was easily able to refute the accusation of having been deceived. And yet if it had not been for the scandal which Simonides raised by his own folly, his fakes might never had been exposed. A love of publicity was his undoing.

Shapira, a Polish Jew living in Jerusalem, was a more complex character. He had been converted to Christianity early in life and married the niece of Fliedner, the founder of a Protestant nursing order. Shapira was widely respected as an expert on theology,

Constantine Simonides, *one of the most blatant forgers of all time, had the technical skill to deceive the scholars, but was betrayed by his love of publicity, and by the intrinsic absurdity of some of his 'discoveries'—such as a 13th-century MS describing the invention of steamships.*

archaeology, and palaeography, and as a knowledgeable and trustworthy antique-dealer. He sold many objects of unquestionable authenticity both to the British Museum and the Berlin Museum.

Then, soon after 1868, he offered for sale some pottery vessels which he said had been found among the ruins of Dibon in the region where the Moabite Stone had been discovered. The pots were covered with the same script as the Stone and were bought for a suitably high price by Prussia. But, by an unhappy coincidence, the French archaeologist, Clermont-Ganneau, was travelling in the Moabite area at about the same time and came across a local potter who boasted to him of his skill in making 'ancient' pots. Clermont-Ganneau found in the man's workshop a list of letters in Mesha script—the script used on the Moabite Stone. From these discoveries it was only a short step to the conclusion that the list and the commission to make the pots had come from Shapira. But the evidence was not strong enough to convict the dealer. He

335

denied any complicity and said that he was himself the victim of forgers.

Then in 1883 he produced a real sensation—a scroll found by bedouins in a cave near the Wadi Modjeb. This scroll—he explained its wonderful state of preservation by the fact that it had been embalmed like a mummy—contained parts of Deuteronomy, including a hitherto unknown speech by Moses, and dated from 896 BC. That made it roughly 3,000 years old; in other words, it must have been written shortly after Moses' death. Shapira's price was one million pounds, and the British Museum was prepared to pay it. Of course, they would have to examine it thoroughly—even the prosperous Britain of the late nineteenth century was not going to hand over one million pounds on a plate for the asking. Dr Norman Ginsburg, a recognized authority, reaffirmed the scroll's authenticity. But when the Museum came to ask Clermont-Ganneau's opinion, Shapira refused to let him see the whole manu-script and he had to base his verdict on two small portions in the Museum's possession. For a number of reasons, one of which was the fact that the writer of the manuscript, though dividing the columns with guiding lines as the ancients had done, had written straight across the lines, Clermont-Ganneau judged the document to be a fake. He also suggested it was written on comparatively modern parchment which had been chemically treated to give it the appearance of extreme age. Biblical experts in Berlin were equally sceptical, though they covered themselves by attributing the forgery to the bedouins rather than to Shapira himself. The out-come of all this doubt and suspicion was that the British Museum refused the scroll and a warrant was taken out for Shapira's arrest. He heard the news while he was staying in Rotterdam; he was found next day, shot dead, in his hotel bedroom.

To this day he remains a strange, incomprehensible figure. Did he forge his own fakes or did he merely give the instructions? Or was he the object of a cruel conspiracy? Since his death, many writers have tried to clear his name, and the mystery remains unsolved. As late as February 1957 a Shapira champion asserted he had found new proof that the scroll was genuine. Whether he was right or not we still do not know; the scroll was never cata/ logued and now the Museum is unable to trace it. If it could be found, experts would be able to judge its authenticity at once. How? By using the new scientific techniques which have transformed palaeography since Shapira's day.

SCIENCE AND FAITH

In the nineteenth century the palaeographer had only his theoretical knowledge, his experience, and his five senses to help him. A man like Tischendorf could never have become the expert he was if he had been short/sighted. But all this was changed as soon as infra/red photography was discovered. The human eye is aware of only a very small part of the electro/magnetic vibrations of a given fre/ quency. It can take in no more than the colours of the spectrum from red to heliotrope; anything which lies outside the scope of the spectrum is, so to speak, 'invisible'. But it is not invisible to the photographic plate, which can be 'corrected' to record what man is conscious of only as heat. By means of an infra/red filter, a photo/ graph can be taken of a warm stove in a completely dark room. Similarly, old or erased writing which is quite invisible to the human eye throws back a slightly different light which an infra/red plate can record with the greatest exactitude as legible letters. This, broadly speaking, is the way in which ancient manuscripts are now uncovered. It is a process which has been of incalculable service to palaeographers, criminologists, and intelligence officers in wartime.

But infra/red photography can give the expert no more than a text to work on. It does not furnish clues to a manuscript's age—one of the things which can decide, in the last resort, whether a docu/ ment is genuine or spurious.

Before 1946 the usual method of establishing the age of a docu/ ment was to compare it with another document of similar age—to draw some kind of rough conclusion from the forms of the letters, the content, and the style. And, of course, if historical events were mentioned, this sometimes gave conclusive proof. But this works only when there are other manuscripts for comparison. If the document is in a hitherto unknown script, or if it is supposed to date from a period from which no other manuscripts survive, the method is useless. Supposing that Shapira's scroll was genuine and really dated from 896 BC, what could it be compared with? The oldest manuscript we know of dates from at least six hundred years later.

In 1946 this hit-and-miss technique was superseded by the Carbon 14 Test, developed by Willard Libby of the Chicago Institute of Nuclear Studies. The new method has been of such importance to Biblical scholarship generally that it is worth a closer look.

The air is made up of 75 per cent nitrogen, 20 per cent oxygen, and various other gases such as argon, neon, krypton, and hydrogen. In addition, faint traces of carbon drift around in the mixture. Carbon, for which the chemical symbol is C, has an atomic weight of 12 or 13. It is absorbed by organisms in relatively large quantities. At the same time the earth is continually under fire from neutrons, atomic nuclei which bear down on the globe at the rate of nearly 50,000 miles a second. This radiation penetrates through everything which lives on the earth, although plants, animals, and men have become so accustomed to it that they are not even conscious of its presence. But if one of these particles combines with a nitrogen atom (atomic weight 14), a curious thing takes place—the nitrogen turns into radio-active carbon with an atomic weight of 14. This change makes no difference to organisms, which merely absorb the radio-active carbon as though it were unadulterated.

Now all radio-active· materials gradually decompose. By constantly giving out a part of their mass in the form of radio-active rays, they lose radio-activity until at a given moment they are only half as radio-active as they were originally, then only a quarter, and so on until they become completely inactive. The time that a radio-active material takes to lose half its radio-activity is known as its half-life and is used as a means of identification for various materials. Radio-active iodine 131 has a half-life of eight days, and radio-active uranium 235 has a half-life of over 700 million years. Carbon has a half-life of about 5,568 years.

All this is long-established. Scientists have known about the properties of radio-activity for many years. They have used the knowledge, among other ways, to measure radio-active rays with a geiger counter. But Libby was the first man to grasp the notion that these facts could be used to determine age.

He reasoned this way: every plant absorbs a certain calculable amount of carbon 14 during its lifetime, and what it loses is speedily replaced, so the carbon content remains static. But when the plant dies, further carbon supplies are cut off and the carbon then present gradually disappears until one-half has gone at the end of 5,568

Where science and history meet: Dr Willard F. Libby with his apparatus for the carbon 14 test. In place of the old methods, dating by measurement of radio-activity brings the margin of error down to 400 years or less.

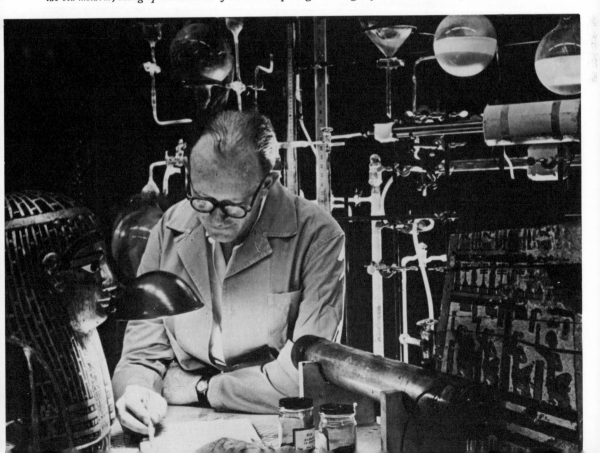

years. Thus, if the radio-active rays from an old oak can be shown to be half as strong as the rays from a newly-cut tree, then there is incontrovertible proof that the wood of the first tree is 5,568 years old. Similarly, by measuring the ray-strength of any organic substance its age can be calculated.

In practice the process is more difficult than it sounds. It means burning the material under examination so as to isolate the carbon to be measured. For a precise result, 65 grams of wood must be burned, or 200 grams of linen. This makes the method inapplicable to certain old manuscripts that have no marginal matter that can be sacrificed in this way. It is not much good knowing how old a document was if you have had to burn it to find out. But the technique works to perfection where there are wide margins to spare, or where, as with the Dead Sea Scrolls, the scroll is wrapped in linen. Some uncertainty remains—the scientific apparatus is accurate only to two hundred years plus or minus—but it is still a considerable advance on the hit-or-miss methods of earlier scholars who were sometimes at a loss whether to place a manuscript in the Middle Ages or pre-Christian times.

Infra-red photography and the Carbon 14 Test are only two of the new techniques which have transformed palaeography into an exact science. They will have to stand for all the exciting new discoveries and methods now at the disposal of the Bible expert. It is enough to say that science too has played its part in making the Bible speak.

We have come full circle. The great work that was begun 6,000 years ago in the East is still going on the world over. The spiritual message that was born in a society as close to nature as the open fields and woods it lived in is equally valid and powerful in the mechanized world of today. It has passed through all the stages of man's achievements and come out unscathed and full of life. And always will be, till the end of the world.

NOTES ON THE ILLUSTRATIONS

Title page: SS. Gregor and Gelasius, from the frontispiece of a hymnal, *c.* 975. University Library, Fulda.

8/9 Assyrian skin-covered coracle, similar to the modern *guffa*. From a relief (8th century BC) in Sennacherib's Palace, Nineveh. Courtesy, Trustees of the British Museum.

13 A fragment of Tablet XI, an Assyrian version of the Epic of Gilgamesh. Nineveh, *c.* 650 BC. Courtesy, Trustees of the British Museum.

15 Section of the flood stratum at Ur. Courtesy, Trustees of the British Museum.

17 The Flood Pit, Ur, taken at the time of the discovery. Courtesy, Trustees of the British Museum.

19 Menorah. Sandstone rock carving from Wadi Umm Sideira, Sinai.

23 Chefren. One of over a hundred polished diorite seated statues from his pyramid complex at Giza. Cairo Museum.
The Pyramids of Cheops, Chefren and Mycerinus. By courtesy of the Museum of Fine Arts, Boston.

24/5 Basalt relief of a warrior and a charioteer riding over the nude body of an enemy. Tell Halaf (Gozan), 9th century BC. National Museum, Aleppo.

26 Amun-ra. Silver and gold-plated statuette. XXIInd Dynasty (Late). Courtesy, Trustees of the British Museum.

27 Façade of moulded clay bricks from a Kassite temple at Uruk Kassite Period. Iraq Museum, Baghdad. Courtesy, Directorate General of Antiquities, Iraq.

29 Head of a limestone statue, one of a number of 'worshipper' figures which stood proxy in the temples. Abu Temple, Tell Asmar. Early Dynastic Period. Courtesy, Directorate General of Antiquities, Iraq.

30 Life-size bronze head of a king. Nineveh. Akkadian Period. Iraq Museum, Baghdad. Courtesy, Directorate General of Antiquities, Iraq.

31 Map of the world, drawn to illustrate the campaigns of Sargon of Agade, *c.* 2300 BC. Sippar, 6th century BC. Courtesy, Trustees of the British Museum.

32 Impression of an Akkadian seal showing the goddess Ishtar. By courtesy of the Oriental Institute, University of Chicago. Babylonian seals showing the god Marduk. Courtesy, Trustees of the British Museum.

33 The stele of Hammurabi. Susa, 18th century BC. Louvre.

35 Ziggurat of Aqarquf (Dur-Kurigalzu) made from baked bricks and strengthened with bitumen and twisted reeds. Kassite Period, 15th century BC. Courtesy, Directorate General of Antiquities, Iraq.

36/7 Ashurbanipal's wars against the Arabs. Part of an orthostat discovered by Rassam in 1854, carved from limestone. North Palace, Nineveh (668–633 BC). Courtesy, Trustees of the British Museum.

36 The god Ashur in his winged aurora, from a relief in King Ashurbanipal's Palace. Throne room, N.W. Palace, Nimrud. Courtesy, Trustees of the British Museum.

38 Inscription from the granite stele of Merenptah found in his mortuary temple at Thebes. XIXth Dynasty (1234–1222 BC). Cairo Museum.

40 Faience tile showing a bound prisoner, probably a Syrian. Thebes. By courtesy of the Museum of Fine Arts, Boston.

43 Moses leading the Israelites out of Egypt. Wall painting from the synagogue at Dura Europos, 3rd century AD. New Museum, Damascus. Courtesy, Directorate General of Antiquities, Damascus.

45 The Ark. Limestone carving from the synagogue at Capernaum. Custodia Terra Sancta, Jerusalem, Israel.

46 The twelve tribes. Wall painting from Dura Europos, 3rd century AD. New Museum, Damascus. By courtesy of Directorate General of Antiquities, Damascus.

49 Menorah on gilt glass. Courtesy, Biblioteca Apostolica Vaticana.

50 Wooden panel from the tomb of the official, Hesi-ra, showing him as a scribe. Sakkara, IIIrd Dynasty (c. 2780–2680 BC). Courtesy, Cairo Museum.

52 Limestone relief of a squatting scribe from the tomb of Khaemhet at Sheikh Abd el-Gurnah. XVIIIth Dynasty (14th century BC). Courtesy, Cairo Museum.

56 Limestone tablets from Kish. Uruk Period, c. 3500 BC. Courtesy, Department of Antiquities, Ashmolean Museum, Oxford.

57 Akkadian cuneiform tablets from Nuzi (Yorgan Tepe), c. 1400 BC. Courtesy, Trustees of the British Museum.

58 Bronze pens and inkwell, dating from Imperial Roman times. Courtesy, Trustees of the British Museum.

59 Egyptian papyrus scroll. Courtesy, Staatliche Museen zu Berlin.
Moses reading a scroll. Part of a wall painting from Dura Europos. 3rd century AD. New Museum, Damascus. Courtesy, Directorate General of Antiquities, Damascus.

61 Codex Nitrensis. Greek palimpsest over-written with Syriac. Gospel of St Luke. Courtesy, Trustees of the British Museum.

62 Detail from an ivory showing a king or prince seated on a sphinx throne and drinking from a bowl. Before him stands a woman who offers him a lotus flower. Megiddo, level VIIA, c. 1350–1150 BC. Courtesy, Palestine Archaeological Museum, Jerusalem.

64 Rock-drawing showing a plan of the fortified sheepfolds called kites. Safaite, 1st millennium AD. Courtesy, Palestine Archaeological Museum, Jerusalem.

69 Egyptian limestone relief commemorating Rameses III's victory over the Sea Peoples. Medinet Habu, north wall of the temple of Rameses III. XXth Dynasty (1197–1085 BC). By courtesy of the Oriental Institute, University of Chicago.

71 Temple of Solomon: wall painting from the synagogue at Dura Europos. New Museum, Damascus. Courtesy, Directorate General of Antiquities, Damascus.

73 King Bar-Rakab seated before his scribe. Zinjirli (Sam'al). Dolerite. Post-Hittite (8th century BC). Staatliche Museen zu Berlin.

75 Black Obelisk of Shalmanazar III, showing scenes of homage and tribute from foreign countries. Discovered at Nimrud in 1846. Assyrian, 858–824 BC. Courtesy, Trustees of the British Museum.

77 Clay tablet, one of the set making up the Babylonian Chronicle. Babylon. Neo-Babylonian Empire, 593 BC. Courtesy, Staatliche Museen zu Berlin.

79 Nash Papyrus. Hebrew. Egypt, 2nd or 1st century BC. Courtesy, University Library, Cambridge.

80 Life-size terracotta lion from the temple gate at Tell Harmel. 2nd millennium BC. Iraq Museum, Baghdad. Courtesy, Directorate General of Antiquities, Iraq.

82 Cylinder of Sennacherib. Nineveh, 702 BC. Courtesy, Trustees of the British Museum.

83 Scribes counting slain enemies. Limestone relief from the Palace of Sennacherib, Nineveh. 8th century BC. Courtesy, Trustees of the British Museum.

84/5 The Isaiah Scroll (IQ Isa), written on leather. Qumran, Cave I, c. 100 BC. By courtesy of the American School of Oriental Research.

87 Ruins of the Ishtar Gate quarter, Babylon. Cylinder of Cyrus II. Babylon, 536 BC. Courtesy, Trustees of the British Museum.

89 Seat of Moses, with Judaeo-Aramaic inscription Chorazin. Courtesy, Department of Antiquities, Jerusalem.

91 Handles of jugs bearing seal impressions. Lachish, 6th century BC. Courtesy, Trustees of the British Museum.

92 Part of the Pentateuch in Hebrew, with Masorah Magna and Parva in the margins. Written in an eastern hand on vellum. Early 10th century AD. Courtesy, Trustees of the British Museum.

93 Rabbi reading a Torah.

94 Head of Alexander the Great as Heracles/Zeus on a silver tetradrachm. Courtesy, Bibliothèque Nationale, Paris.

95 Fragments of a Greek Papyrus of the Book of Deuteronomy. 2nd century AD. Courtesy, John Rylands Library, Manchester.

97 Silver tetradrachm (equivalent to a shekel) of Bar-Kochba, leader of the Second Jewish Revolt (AD 132–135). The obverse shows a view of the Temple with shrine containing scroll of the law, and is inscribed 'Simeon'. Courtesy, Trustees of the British Museum.

98 The Ark of the Covenant, from a wall painting at Dura Europos. 3rd century AD. New Museum, Damascus. Courtesy, Directorate General of Antiquities, Iraq.

99 Bronze statue of Zeus. 3rd century BC. Courtesy, Trustees of the British Museum.

101 Bible with Masora Magna and Parva, part of Psalms, showing Menorah and altar tables. Parchment. Perpignan 1299. Courtesy, Bibliothèque Nationale, Paris.

102 Adoration of the Magi. Relief from tympanum in Neuilly-en-Donjon, Bourgogne. 12th century.

104 Gold *aurei* of (l. to r.) Augustus, Tiberius, Claudius, Nero, Titus. Courtesy, Trustees of the British Museum.

105 Engraved gem showing the Crucifixion. 4th century AD. Courtesy, Trustees of the British Museum.

107 St Paul disputing with the Greeks. Champlevé enamel. English (Winchester), c. 1160 AD. Courtesy, Victoria and Albert Museum; Crown Copyright.

109 The mocking of St Paul. 10th century. Courtesy, Stiftsbibliothek, St Gallen.

111 St John writing his Gospel. Illumination from the Maeil Brith MacDurnan Gospels. Irish, c. 800 AD. Courtesy, Archbishop of Canterbury and the Trustees of Lambeth Palace Library.

113 Four Gospels in Greek, bound in painted boards showing the four Evangelists. Small sloping uncials in dark-brown ink on parchment. 5th century AD. Acquired in Egypt, 1906. By courtesy of the Freer Gallery of Art, Washington.

115 Detail of a cupboard containing the Four Gospels, from a mosaic showing the martyrdom of St Laurence. Mausoleum of Galla Placidia, Ravenna. c. 450 AD.

117 Illumination showing St Matthew writing his Gospel. 9th century. Schatzkammer, Vienna.

119 'In Principio' from the beginning of St John's Gospel. Codex Aureus of Echternach. Latin, late 10th century.

120 Two fragments of papyrus of the Gospel of St John (chapter 18, 31-33, 37-38), acquired in Egypt by B. P. Grenfell in 1920 but not identified until 1935. 1st century AD. Courtesy, John Rylands Library, Manchester.

121 Illumination from the Commentary on the Apocalypse by St Beatus of Libana. 10th century. Courtesy, Courtauld Institute of Art, London.

123 Christ in Majesty. Detail from the gold cover of the Gospels made in Rheims for Charles the Bald. The cover was given to the monastery of St Emmeran by Arnulf of Carinthia. c. 870 AD. Courtesy, Munich Staatsbibliothek.

126 Martyrdom of St Edmund, from Queen Mary's Psalter. Courtesy, Trustees of the British Museum.

127 Martyrdom of St Kilian, from his *Life*.

129 Martyrdom of Bishop Polycarp. Coloured woodcut from the *Legenda Aurea*, Augsburg, 1494. Courtesy, Trustees of the British Museum.

130 Unknown Gospel: two leaves and fragment of third. Papyrus. Greek, AD 100-150. Courtesy, Trustees of the British Museum.

131 The Birth of the Virgin, from a version of the 'Infancy Gospels' in Latin rhyming couplets. 14th century. Courtesy, Trustees of the British Museum.

132 Jesus as a boy, from the 'Infancy Legends'. German, mid-14th century. Courtesy, Schaffhausen Stadt Bibliothek.

133 Wedding gift, gilded glass disk inscribed 'Dulcis anima vivas'. 4th century AD. Courtesy, Trustees of the British Museum.

135 St John on Patmos. French, late 15th century. Courtesy, Trustees of the British Museum.

136/7 The adventures of Thekla. Stone altar frontal from Tarragona Cathedral, Spain.

139 Illuminated Greek menology telling the story of Thekla. Greek, 12th century. Courtesy, Trustees of the British Museum.

140 Ivory showing St Peter dictating to St Mark while an angel watches. S. Italy, 11th century. Courtesy, Victoria and Albert Museum; Crown Copyright.

143 Stone altarpiece showing SS. Philip, Jude and Bartholomew. Catalan, c. AD 1120. Courtesy, Victoria and Albert Museum; Crown Copyright.

144 Fragment of Tatian's Diatessaron Papyrus, found at Dura Europos. 2nd century AD. Courtesy, Yale University.

145 The so-called Pax Gospel cover, in repoussé and filigree work inlaid with precious stones and enamel. 12th century. San Lorenzo, Chiavenna.

147 Part of the Epistle to the Hebrews. Greek papyrus, 3rd-4th century AD. Courtesy, Trustees of the British Museum.

149 Illumination from a 10th-century version of the Commentary on the Apocalypse by St Beatus of Libana. Courtesy, Courtauld Institute of Art, London.

150 St Ambrose (Bishop of Milan, AD 374-397) being called to Milan by the Holy Ghost. From an altar frontal, Church of S. Ambrogio, Milan.

151 St Cyprian before his conversion. 9th-century Byzantine illumination. Courtesy, Bibliothèque Nationale, Paris.

152 Part of a MS. Peshitto (Gen. 29, 25 to 30, 2) found at the St Mary Deipara Convent in the Nitrian Desert, Egypt. AD 464. Courtesy, Trustees of the British Museum.

154 St Athanasius, Patriarch of Alexandria. Mosaic from the Basilica di San Marco, Venice. 14th century.

155 Head of Constantine the Great from the Basilica of Maxentius. AD 312. Museo dei Conservatori, Rome.

243 James I of England. Portrait by an unknown artist. Courtesy, the Worshipful Company of Musicians, London.

245 Detail from the title page of the Psalter ('Great Bible' translation), 1639, with manuscript alteration made in 1661.

247 Tyndale's Bible, 1528. I Corinthians 13, 1–3. Courtesy, Corpus Christi College, Cambridge.
Authorized Version, 1611. I Corinthians, 13, 1–3. Courtesy, Corpus Christi College, Cambridge.

252 Mary Jones, engraving. Courtesy, British and Foreign Bible Society.

253 Mary Jones's Bible with her signature. Courtesy, British and Foreign Bible Society.

254 Swan Wharf, London. Engraving. Courtesy, British and Foreign Bible Society.

255 Station of the Baptist Missionary Society at Bayneston, Lower Congo. Engraving.

257 Title page of the Massachusetts Indian Bible, published in Cambridge, Massachusetts, by John Eliot in 1663. Courtesy, Trustees of the British Museum.

258 The Aitken Bible, 1782: the first edition of the English Bible avowedly printed in America.

259 The Bible in Tamil, 1714–28. The first page of Genesis. Courtesy, Trustees of the British Museum.

260 The Old Testament in Persian, 1878. First page of Genesis. Courtesy, Trustees of the British Museum.
William Carey (1761–1834). Courtesy, British and Foreign Bible Society.

261 The Old Testament in Chinese (1817), printed at Serampore with metallic, movable type. First page of Genesis. Courtesy, Trustees of the British Museum.
The Bible in Sanskrit translated by William Carey and printed at Serampore, 1811, in five volumes. Deuteronomy 2, from Vol. 1. Courtesy, Trustees of the British Museum.

265 The Revisers of the Old Testament, engraving. Courtesy, British and Foreign Bible Society.

266 Revised Version, 1881–85 (New Testament published in 1881, Old Testament in 1885, and the Apocrypha in 1895).

267 Standard Version, 'newly edited by the American Revision Committee, AD 1901'.
Dust-wrapper of Revised Standard Version, 1952.

268 *The New Testament in Modern Speech*, translated by Richard F. Weymouth in 1903 on the basis of the Resultant Greek Testament. Mark, Chapter 1. Courtesy, James Clarke & Co., London.

269 The New Testament in Basic English, 1941, supervised by S. H. Hooke of the University of London. Mark, Chapter 1. Courtesy, Cambridge University Press.

273 Fragments of the Dead Sea Scrolls under glass. Courtesy, Palestine Archaeological Museum, Jerusalem.

276 Codex Vaticanus 'B'. In the Vatican Library since at least 1481. 4th century. Courtesy, Biblioteca Apostolica Vaticana.
Codex Alexandrinus. Until 1621 it was in the library at Alexandria. 5th century. Courtesy, Trustees of the British Museum.

277 Count Constantine Tischendorf. Engraving.

278/9 Codex Ephraemi Syri or 'C'. Courtesy, Bibliothèque Nationale, Paris.

280 Codex Claromontanus c. AD 575. Courtesy, Bibliothèque Nationale, Paris.

284/5 St Catherine's Monastery, Sinai.

286/7 Codex Sinaiticus or Aleph (John 21, 1–25). 4th century. Courtesy, Trustees of the British Museum.

291 Codex Sinaiticus before binding. Courtesy, Trustees of the British Museum.

292 Frames on which each page of Codex Sinaiticus, after dampening, was stretched flat. This restoration work was undertaken by Mr D. Cockerell in 1935. Courtesy, Trustees of the British Museum.

293 The Codex Sinaiticus as it is today. Courtesy, Trustees of the British Museum.

294 The Moabite Stone, or the Stele of King Mesha. Basalt. *c.* 840–820 BC. Courtesy, the Louvre, Archives Photographiques.

297 Inscription in archaic Hebrew found in the Siloam tunnel, Jerusalem. *c.* 710 BC. Courtesy, Archaeological Museum, Istanbul.

299 Aquila's translation of II Kings 23, 15–19, found in the Cairo Geniza and now in the Taylor-Schechter Collection. Courtesy, University Library, Cambridge.

303 'Sayings of Jesus', now identified with the Gospel of Thomas. Found by Grenfell and Hunt at Oxyrhynchos in 1903. Courtesy, Trustees of the British Museum.

307 Lachish Letters, No. IV (front), found by Starkey in 1935–38. By courtesy of the Trustees of the late Sir Henry S. Wellcome.

308 A view of Qumran and the caves.

311 Title page of the Manual of Discipline. Parchment, Hebrew, source. Courtesy, Palestine Archaeological Museum, Jerusalem.

313 Professor Yigael Yadin examining a bundle of papyrus documents.

315 Fragments of the Book of Samuel, probably the oldest Biblical manuscript known. 3rd century BC.

316 Scroll jars in which the manuscripts were found, about 21–27 inches in height.

317 Fragments from a scroll of Exodus found in the Second Cave at Wadi Murabba'at, south of Qumran in Jordan. Parchment, Hebrew. Courtesy, Palestine Archaeological Museum, Jerusalem.

320 Mr G. Lankester Harding working on fragments of the Scrolls.

321 J. M. Allegro studying the Book of Nahum.

322 The 'Scrollery' in the Palestine Archaeological Museum. Courtesy, Palestine Archaeological Museum, Jerusalem.

325 A view of the Essene Monastery at Qumran, looking south. Courtesy, Palestine Archaeological Museum, Jerusalem.

327 Prof. H. Wright Baker cutting open a copper scroll.

330 'Atomic clock' containing a geiger counter used in the process of radio-carbon dating.

335 Constantine Simonides. Engraving.

339 Professor Willard F. Libby at Lamont Observatory, with apparatus for radio-carbon dating.

INDEX